Acknowledgements

The publisher would like to thank the following for permission to use photographs:

Abbot Hall, Marblehead, Massachusetts (reproduced by permission of the Board of Selectmen), p.50 (bottom); Courtesy Amon Carter Museum, Fort Worth, Texas, p.94; Amalgamated Engineering Union, p.82; Anglo-Chinese Educational Institute, p.136; Associated Press Ltd., pp.147 (bottom), 168 (top); BBC Hulton Picture Library, pp.39 (both), 49, 69, 79 (top), 80, 84 (top), 89 (bottom), 100, 110, 123, 130; UPI Bettmann Archives/BBC Hulton Picture Library, pp.67, 102 (both); British Film Institute, pp.92, 161; British Library, p.48; British Tourist Authority, pp.35, 66; Bundesarchiv, Koblenz, p.124; Camera Press, pp.137, 143 (bottom), 149, 150, 151 (bottom), 155 (top left), 160 (bottom) 165, 170 (top); Colorado Historical Society, Denver, Colorado, p.95; Colorific!, p.166; Dudley Public Libraries, p.79 (bottom); Edimedia, p.55; Mary Evans Picture Library, pp.11, 81 (right), 87 (top), 115; Fotomas, pp.14 (top and bottom), 20, 24 (bottom), 52, 59, 70, 134; Giraudon, pp.12, 15, 57, 58 (both), 60 (top), 62; Hutchison Library, pp.140, 146 (top); Imperial War Museum, pp.118 (top), 120 (top); India Office Library, pp.13 (top), 17, 19; Kobal Collection, p.158, John MacClancy Collection Ltd., p.118 (bottom); Mansell Collection, pp.13 (bottom), 21, 30, 31 (both), 37, 41, 60 (bottom), 65 (bottom), 74, 75, 81 (left), 83, 85, 106, 107, 110 (top); Metropolitan Museum, New York (Photo: Scala), p.96; Musée de Versailles, pp.56 (both); Museen der Stadt, Vienna, p.104; Museum of London, p.87 (bottom); National Cowboy Hall of Fame, Oklahoma, p.93; National Maritime Museum, pp.8, 10, 11 (bottom) 61; National Portrait Gallery, London, p.16; Courtesy of the Pennsylvania Academy of Fine Arts, p.97; The Photosource, pp.6, 86, 142, 143 (top); Popperfoto, pp.65 (top), 127, 129, 131, 135 (all), 141, 145, 146 (bottom), 151 (top), 155 (top right), bottom right and left), 160 (top), 162, 168 (bottom); Royal Library, Windsor Castle. Reproduced by Gracious Permission of Her Majesty the Queen, p.77; School of Soviet and Slavonic Studies, London University, p.155 (left); Trustees of the Science Museum, London (Photo: Ironbridge Gorge Museum), p.29; Frank Spooner, pp.45 (top), 147 (top), 152, 171; Sir John Soane's Museum, p.73; Jeffrey Tabberner, p.101; John Topham, p.45 (centre); Tressell Publications, Brighton, p.169; United Society for the Propagation of the Gospel, (Photo: John Webb) p.24 (top); United States Air Force Collection, p.156; United States Library of Congress, p.159; Valley Forge Historical Society, Pennsylvania, p.51; Victoria and Albert Museum, pp.18, 109, 11; Wilberforce House, Kingston upon Hull, p.7 Yale University Art Gallery, p.49 (top); Zeta, p.45 (bottom).

Illustrations are by John Ireland, Oxford Illustrators, and Bernard Robinson

Oxford University Press, Walton Street, Oxford OX2 6DP

Oxford New York Toronto
Delhi Bombay Calcutta Madras Karachi
Petaling Jaya Singapore Hong Kong Tokyo
Nairobi Dar es Salaam Cape Town
Melbourne Auckland

and associated companies in
Beirut Berlin Ibadan Nicosia

Oxford is a trade mark of Oxford University Press

© Oxford University Press 1987

ISBN 0 19 913313 1

Typesetting by MS Filmsetting Ltd, Frome, Somerset
Printed in Hong Kong

PRESENT

Reform and Revolution

Derek Heater

Oxford University Press   1987

Contents

Preface for teachers

This series of three books is intended for young people of average ability in the first three years of secondary school. Ideally it should serve as the core of a lower secondary course, around which more disparate teaching materials could be arranged.

In Books 1 and 2 the emphasis rests on British history and experience, with substantial sections on the wider world where appropriate. Book 1 makes a chronological survey of traditionally-popular subject matter, ranging from pre-Roman Britain to Europe at the time of the Black Death (c.55 BC to 1350). Book 2 surveys the period from the Peasants' Revolt to the Glorious Revolution (c.1381 to 1689). In both books plenty of room has been found within the chronological framework for in-depth treatment of key periods, personalities and problems. Care has also been taken to look beneath the headlines of history – to convey to the reader not only 'how people lived' but how they thought, what they believed and what they feared. Thus the reader is encouraged to experience the past on its own terms, while s/he is also offered more modern perspectives where these seem suitable. Book 3, while containing the same features, then provides a broader, more thematic coverage of Britain and the world from the 18th century to the present. It is felt that most teachers wish to concentrate on British and perhaps some American and European history in the eighteenth and nineteenth centuries; and so the reader will find this emphasis in the chapters dealing with these periods. Afro-Asian history is dealt with more fully in the twentieth century. A number of 32-page topic books, dealing with a variety of subjects, will supplement the series.

The approach of each book is to present information through a range of data, closely linked to simple but vividly-written text. This data takes the form of: documentary extracts (often modified to make them more accessible), pictorial source material, maps and occasional reconstruction drawings. The visual data is never merely cosmetic, and is usually accompanied by extended captions. The close integration of evidence and text trains the reader to appreciate a fundamental truth about the historical process – namely that the past has to be pieced together, rather like working on a jigsaw puzzle.

As the reader watches the jigsaw taking shape, it is explained that some of the pieces are more reliable or useful than others. S/he is also made aware that by no means *all* the pieces are available to historians. In this way he is shown the need for informed speculation. So this series presents history as a dynamic discipline, and it presents the past as a tantalizingly incomplete picture, which can be looked at in a number of different ways. Attention is paid throughout not just to those who made history, but also to those who first recorded it. The 'sources pages' at the start of each chapter, and the section on 'Historians and their sources' introduce the reader to some of the historian's 'raw materials'.

Each chapter is divided into easily-manageable sections, at the end of which the reader is invited to attempt follow-up exercises. These range from simple comprehension and observation to skills-developing extension work. The reader is encouraged not only to make judgements from the data presented, but also to express his/her own feelings and values, however acquired.

The aim of the series is to inspire young people to think actively about history, with a view to enhancing their understanding of the present. The approach taken will provide a good grounding for readers who might go on to take public, increasingly evidence-based, examinations in history. But perhaps more importantly, this approach can help to stimulate genuine enthusiasm for the subject, and thereby contribute a great deal to a wider education within the school curriculum.

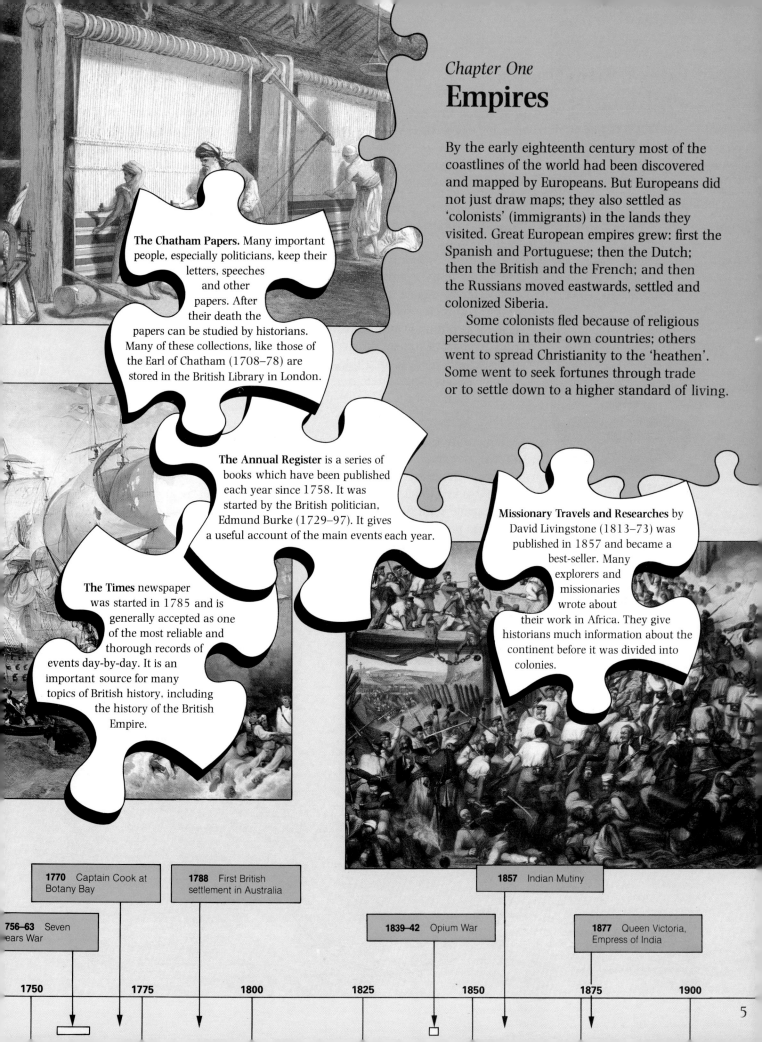

Chapter One
Empires

By the early eighteenth century most of the coastlines of the world had been discovered and mapped by Europeans. But Europeans did not just draw maps; they also settled as 'colonists' (immigrants) in the lands they visited. Great European empires grew: first the Spanish and Portuguese; then the Dutch; then the British and the French; and then the Russians moved eastwards, settled and colonized Siberia.

Some colonists fled because of religious persecution in their own countries; others went to spread Christianity to the 'heathen'. Some went to seek fortunes through trade or to settle down to a higher standard of living.

The Chatham Papers. Many important people, especially politicians, keep their letters, speeches and other papers. After their death the papers can be studied by historians. Many of these collections, like those of the Earl of Chatham (1708–78) are stored in the British Library in London.

The Annual Register is a series of books which have been published each year since 1758. It was started by the British politician, Edmund Burke (1729–97). It gives a useful account of the main events each year.

The Times newspaper was started in 1785 and is generally accepted as one of the most reliable and thorough records of events day-by-day. It is an important source for many topics of British history, including the history of the British Empire.

Missionary Travels and Researches by David Livingstone (1813–73) was published in 1857 and became a best-seller. Many explorers and missionaries wrote about their work in Africa. They give historians much information about the continent before it was divided into colonies.

1770 Captain Cook at Botany Bay

1788 First British settlement in Australia

1857 Indian Mutiny

756–63 Seven ears War

1839–42 Opium War

1877 Queen Victoria, Empress of India

| 1750 | 1775 | 1800 | 1825 | 1850 | 1875 | 1900 |

Colonies in the eighteenth century

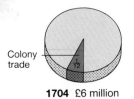

Colony trade

1704 £6 million

⅓+
Colony trade

1772 £16 million

These charts illustrate Burke's speech about the increase in British colony trade in the eighteenth century.

Trade

In a speech in the House of Commons in March 1775 the MP Edmund Burke explained how important colonies were for trade. He compared the value of British exports in 1704 and in 1772. He said:

> 'Our general trade has been greatly augmented [*increased*]..., but with this material [*important*] difference: that of the six millions [pounds] which in the beginning of the century constituted [*made up*] the whole mass [*total*] of our export commerce [*business*] the colony trade was but one twelfth part; it is now (as part of sixteen millions), considerably more than a third of the whole. This is the relative [*comparative*] ... importance of the colonies at these two periods.'

European trade with other parts of the world expanded in the eighteenth century. Between 1700 and 1770 British trade increased three times and French trade eight times. And Britain was importing more than any other country.

What was traded? What did the Europeans want to buy? Most of the imports were foods, drinks and fabrics which were not found, or would not grow, in the European climate.

European merchants made fortunes from this trade and many of the ports of Europe prospered: for example, London and Bristol, in Britain; Bordeaux and Brest, in France. But one of the items of trade is missing. And it was the one from which most profit was made. That item was people...

The slave-trade

Between 1526 and 1870, 10 million people were captured in West Africa, mainly by the British, and shipped across the Atlantic to work as slaves on plantations in the various colonies of North and South America and the West Indies. The effects of the slave-trade on the black people were horrific. Families and communities were broken up. Conditions on board ship were appalling. Hundreds were crammed side-by-side and head-to-toe for many weeks. Here is an extract from a description of a typical voyage by the captain of the slave-ship 'Hannibal' in 1693:

> 'We spent in our passage from St Thomas to Barbados two months eleven days ... in which there happen'd much sickness and mortality

	Across the Atlantic	From Asia	Total
Britain	5.6	2.2	7.8
France	5.2	1.4	6.6
Spain	4.9	–	4.9
Portugal	1.8	?	1.8 +
Holland	–	2.4	2.4

Imports in the 1770s, in millions of pounds.

This map shows the world according to Homan (outlined in blue) compared with the world as it really is (outlined in red). Homan's map was drawn in 1716. There are two important points to notice about it. One is that certain parts of the world were still unexplored, mainly in the Pacific Ocean – from Alaska and north-east Siberia to eastern Australia. Secondly, although the known coastlines are quite accurate in shape, they seem to have 'slipped'. The reason for this is that it was impossible until later in the century to measure lines of longitude at all accurately.

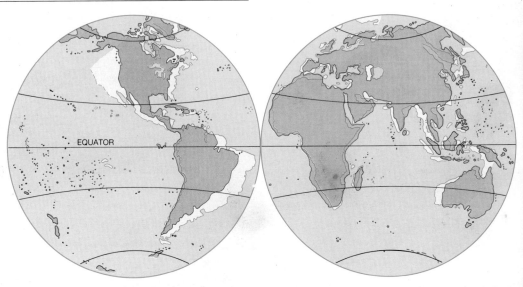

EQUATOR

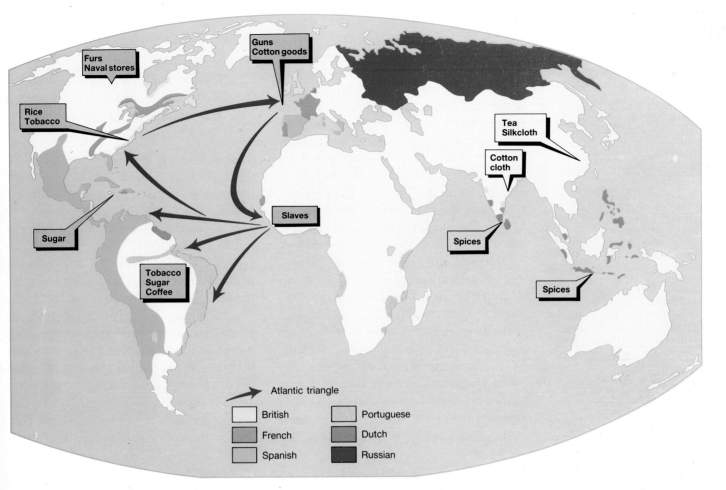

Atlantic triangle

British | Portuguese
French | Dutch
Spanish | Russian

Labels on map:
- Furs / Naval stores
- Rice / Tobacco
- Sugar
- Guns / Cotton goods
- Slaves
- Tobacco / Sugar / Coffee
- Tea / Silkcloth
- Cotton cloth
- Spices
- Spices

... 320 [negroes died] which was a great detriment [*loss*] to our voyage, ... whereby the loss in all amounted to near 6,560 pounds sterling.'

Those who survived were sold to plantation-owners, who branded them so that they could identify their slaves if they tried to escape. It was not until 1807 that the slave-trade was abolished in Britain. Even then slavery itself remained for many years in the West Indies and the Americas.

All this trading activity is important because it helps us to understand how the European empires developed. The merchants and then the governments of several European countries came to realize how profitable it was. They also realized it was important to control those parts of the world where the profits lay.

Empires in 1714. Notice that Spain had the largest empire and that very little land in Asia and Africa had been taken as colonies. The 'Atlantic triangle' shows how imported 'goods' (including slaves) were paid for by exports.

This photograph shows a model of a slave ship. They were used to transport slaves across the Atlantic. Each slave had a space about five feet by two feet. They were unshackled once a day for exercise and fed twice a day. On a good trip one in twenty died; on a bad one, about a third. A campaign to abolish the trade was led in Britain by William Wilberforce. This is the model he had made to show the House of Commons just how inhumane the trade was. Slaves were not freed in the British Empire until 1833. And other countries continued to sell slaves to north and south America well into the nineteenth century.

The wealth of India

With Spain in control of South America, the traders of Portugal, Holland and England had gone East, to the Spice Islands of the East Indies, and to India – a great civilized and wealthy land. For nearly two hundred years, from the early sixteenth century, much of India was ruled by Muslim Emperors called the Moguls. It was one of these Emperors, Shah Jeham, who built the Taj Mahal, the splendid tomb for his favourite wife, Mumtaz. It is one of the seven wonders of the world.

During the period of the Mogul Empire, several European countries set up trading stations round the coast of India. Sugar, pepper, indigo dye, cotton and calico (cotton cloth) were exported (see map page 7). ('Calico' comes from Calicut, a town on the west coast of India.)

In 1600 the East India Company was formed to handle English trade with India. For men who were willing to work hard India could lead to great fortunes. The following is an extract from a letter written in 1695; it is very revealing:

> 'I am extremely anxious to go as chaplain on the East India fleet. The stipend [*salary*] is small, only £40, but there are many advantages. The last brought home £3,000.'

That was a lot of money in those days! (To give you some idea, a family with three children would have spent only about 50p a week on food, clothes and rent!)

One of the most famous to make a fortune in India was 'Diamond' Pitt, the grandfather of William Pitt who became Prime Minister and Earl of Chatham. By the mid-eighteenth century the East India Company was firmly established in Calcutta, Madras and Bombay (see map page 12). The Company had its own warehouses, ships (called 'Indiamen', see picture below), administrators, and even its own army.

Sixty-four years after the British East India Company was founded, the French

From the seventeenth century the British East India Company built up a great fleet of merchant ships called 'Indiamen'. There were even complaints that they used up so much timber that they were destroying Britain's woodlands! This picture, painted in the early nineteenth century shows a fleet of Indiamen in the South China Sea.

founded their own (it was called the 'Compagnie des Indes'). The French also traded in Bengal, but their main settlement was at Pondicherry, not far from Madras (see map page 12). From 1741 to 1754 the French Governor in Pondicherry was Joseph Dupleix. He did not restrict himself to trading: he planned to make southern India a French colony. The British East India Company was worried that their trade would be seriously affected if he succeeded. In 1744 fighting between the British and French forces broke out. By this time the Mogul Empire was very weak.

The British and French in North America

While British and French merchants competed for trade in India, British and French settlers competed for land in North America (see map). The French first settled along the banks of the River St Lawrence, then explored the Great Lakes. From there they moved south along the eastern bank of the River Mississippi. The settlement which has become the great modern city of Detroit was founded in 1701. By 1718 the French had reached the Gulf of Mexico where they founded New Orleans, much later famous as the birthplace of jazz.

But the towns were not important. What really interested the French settlers was the fur of the bear, the seal and the beaver. The fur trade for clothes was very profitable. This huge area of North America, which was claimed by France, was in fact only sparsely occupied by trappers, who roamed over very great distances. There were fewer than 100,000 settlers, which is not a lot when you compare this with the population of France at the time – 20 million!

Despite the hardships and difficulties, some British people went to the northern part of America, now known as Canada. Why? There were profits to be made there in the fur trade. They settled round Hudson's Bay. A report from the Hudson's Bay Company in 1753 shows the great

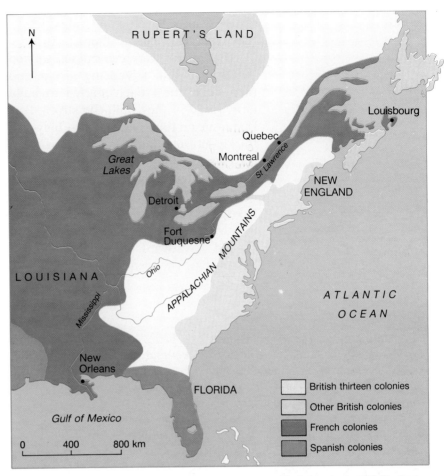

North America in 1756. The land was only thinly settled by colonists so the boundaries were in fact very vague. Rupert's Land was where the Hudson's Bay Company traded. The French also called Quebec 'New France'. Louisiana was named after King Louis XV of France.

problem of transport: 'The Indians cannot carry large quantities ... because their canoes, deeply loaden, are not able to withstand the waves and storms they may meet with upon the Lakes'. Another explains that: 'A good hunter among the Indians can kill 600 beavers in a season, and can carry down [transport] but 100'.

Most British colonists settled in a coastal strip between the Atlantic Ocean and the Appalachian Mountains (see map). By 1733 these settlements had been organized into thirteen colonies. These colonies were more densely occupied than the French areas. By the middle of the eighteenth century the population of the thirteen colonies was as much as one quarter of that of Britain (1½ million compared with 6 million).

Despite the great expanses of land available, the British and French came into conflict:

1 To the north there were quarrels between the fur trappers and traders.

2 To the south of the Great Lakes the British wanted to settle on land which the French claimed was theirs.

The French were determined to stop the British from advancing. To defend their lands the French started to build forts. In 1754 they built the strong Fort Duquesne on the River Ohio. In hilly and thickly-forested land the best way of travelling is along rivers. The River Ohio was very important to the French as a link between their settlements on the Great Lakes and on the Mississippi. It was also the obvious route for the British to use to expand westward. The British felt hemmed in. The scene was set for war.

This painting shows *The death of Captain Cook.* James Cook was a Yorkshireman who entered the Royal Navy without any formal education. However, he became the navy's most skilled map-maker. He made the detailed maps of the St Lawrence River which made Wolfe's defeat of the French possible (see page 14). His three voyages of exploration in the Pacific were extremely successful. He went further north (as far as Alaska) and further south (towards the Antarctic) than anyone had done before. He and his crew collected a huge amount of information. The exploration of the east coast of Australia eventually led to the first British settlers going to Botany Bay in 1788 – as imprisoned convicts! Cook was clubbed and stabbed to death in an unnecessary quarrel with the inhabitants of Hawaii.

Captain Cook

Were there rich parts of the world Europeans had not yet discovered? By the early eighteenth century most of the coastlines of the world were known, but the vast Pacific Ocean remained largely unexplored (see map page 6). There were stories of a wonderfully rich southern continent. The western coast of Australia had been discovered by the Dutch in the seventeenth century. But no one knew the size of Australia – this 'terra australis' (Latin for 'Southern land').

However, it was an interest in science rather than a search for riches which led people to explore the southern Pacific. In 1768 Captain Cook set sail in the *Endeavour*, fitted out as a sort of floating laboratory. He was employed by the Royal Society of London to explore and chart the islands of the Pacific Ocean and to 'observe the Nature of the Soil and the Products thereof, the Beasts and fowls that inhabit or frequent it ... You are likewise to observe the Genius [*laws and customs*], Temper, Disposition and Number of the Natives.'

In all, Cook made three voyages of exploration from 1768 to 1779. He landed on the east coast of Australia in 1770 at Botany Bay, near, what is today, Sydney. □

1 Make a list of ten items of food and drink which Britain imports today from countries not in Europe. Name the countries they come from and underline those which were British colonies in the eighteenth century.

2 Write an imaginary conversation on the question of slavery between a plantation-owner in North Carolina and a clergyman opposed to the slave-trade.

3 Imagine you are planning to visit the most important and interesting British colonies in 1750. Draw up plans for your journeys explaining where you will go and what you will be looking for in the various places you visit. Do not forget to use the maps.

4 Compare the quotation on pages 6–7 and the model of the slave ship on page 7. What different kinds of information can you gain from these two pieces of evidence?

England versus France

This engraving shows French infantry firing. The sergeant is using a halberd to make sure that their aim is straight. Notice also the bayonets on the ends of the muskets. This method of fighting required courage and discipline, especially because the range of the musket was quite short and it took a long time to re-load. The best infantry were those who stood in line while the enemy charged and shot at them, held their fire until the enemy were very close, then fired all together when given the command. At the Battle of the Heights of Abraham in Canada, for instance, in 1759, General Wolfe gave the order not to fire until the French were forty yards from the points of the British bayonets!

Armies and navies

From 1740 to 1815 Britain and France fought in four wars against each other:

1740–48 The War of the Austrian Succession
1756–63 The Seven Years War
1776–83 The War of American Independence
1792–1815 The French Revolutionary and Napoleonic Wars

Much of the fighting involved other European countries as well and many of the battles were fought in Europe. One of the main reasons for the two countries, Britain and France, quarrelling so much was their rivalry for trade and colonies.

The soldiers of many European armies in the eighteenth century were well trained. And discipline was harsh. Many soldiers were foreigners; they were people who would fight for any country who would pay them. They were called 'mercenaries'. In the middle of the eighteenth century there were 50,000 mercenaries in the French army. Most soldiers were infantrymen. They fought on foot and their main weapons were the musket and the

Fighting at sea was very difficult for two main reasons. First, the ships were moved by sails and therefore depended on the wind. Second, the cannon were mounted in rows along the sides of the ship and so could not fire *forwards* in the direction in which the ship was sailing. The heaviest gun-fire was achieved by arranging a fleet in a line and all firing their cannon together in what were called 'broadsides'. If both fleets were drawn up in a line, they just exchanged broadsides! This painting is of the Battle of the Glorious First of June, fought in the Western Atlantic in 1794. The centre of the picture shows the English and French flagships firing at each other.

bayonet. Others belonged to the cavalry: soldiers who fought on horseback and whose main weapon was the sabre. By the eighteenth century cannon had become more efficient and so artillery (large guns) became more important than before.

Whereas all European countries had armies, only a few had large navies. The British navy was the biggest. In 1783 Britain had 174 'ships of the line' and 294 smaller ships. (A ship of the line was a large warship with between 60 and 100 guns.) This was the strongest navy any country had ever had. The French navy was about half the size of the British navy. Life on board ship was hard and discipline sometimes harsher than in the army. Sailors were punished by flogging.

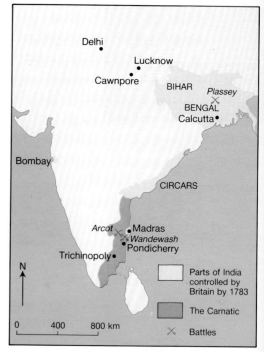

Battles in India. Delhi was the capital of the Mogul Emperors.

Fighting in India, 1744–63

During the 1740s the French Governor, Dupleix, gradually increased French influence and control in southern India. He did this partly by fighting; and partly by arranging that his Indian supporters became the local rulers. In 1749 he made one of his supporters the Nabob (ruler) of the Carnatic (see map). Dupleix then surrounded the rival ruler in a town called Trichinopoly. A twenty-six year-old ex-East India Company clerk volunteered to attack the French. His name was Robert Clive. He collected every soldier he could – 200 European soldiers and 600 sepoys (see page 20). In 1751 he captured Arcot, the capital of the Carnatic, and beat off attacks by a much larger French army. He then went to Trichinopoly and rescued the original Nabob.

A number of results followed from Clive's successes:

1 Clive became famous and rich.
2 The British gained control of the Carnatic through the now friendly and grateful Nabob.
3 Dupleix was summoned back to France in disgrace.

Clive returned to England in 1754 ill. He suffered from fits of depression and ill-health whenever he was not involved in something exciting.

This is a drawing of Dupleix. He spent over twenty years in India. In 1741 he was appointed Governor of Pondicherry. His job was to look after French trade. But he planned to drive the British from India and create a great French Empire. So he organized strict military training for Indian soldiers and plotted with Indian rulers. Neither the French Government nor the Compagnie des Indes wished to become involved in fighting in India: so in 1754 Dupleix was summoned back to France.

In 1756 war broke out officially between Britain and France. It was to last for seven years and by the end of it Britain had taken much of the French Empire.

Just before the Seven Years War started, the Nabob of Bengal tried to turn the British out of his land. The East India Company was making too much money by cheating his people and he was worried that the kind of trouble which had happened in the Carnatic might also happen in Bengal. He captured the fort which the British had built without his permission at Calcutta (see map).

Many of the British inhabitants of the town managed to escape by sea. The remainder (145 men and a woman) surrendered with the promise that they would be safe. The Nabob gave orders that they should be locked in the fort prison. What he did not know was that it was a small room with only two tiny, barred windows. The date was 20 June, the hottest and most humid time of year. The scene next morning was vividly described by the British historian, Lord Macaulay:

Robert Clive was born in 1725 and was an unruly boy. He joined the East India Company but hated his work as a clerk. He was more suited to a life of action. His victories in India so delighted William Pitt that he described him as a 'Heaven-born General'. For, when he brilliantly took Arcot in 1751, he had had no previous experience as a military commander. He became famous, rich, and was made a Lord. He lived in England, 1760-65. Then he returned to India for just over a year to try to organize the way the East India Company was governing Bengal. His huge fortune aroused suspicion in Britain, In 1773 the House of Commons investigated what he had done in India. But they dropped the proceedings after he angrily burst out: 'By God, Mr Chairman, at this moment I stand amazed at my own moderation'. He committed suicide in 1774. The painting shows Clive in 1765 receiving from the Mogul Emperor the right of the East India Company to control Bengal.

'... it was some time before the soldiers could make a lane for the survivors, by piling up on each side the heaps of corpses on which the burning climate had already begun to do its loathsome work. When at length a passage was made, twenty three ghastly figures, such as their own mothers would not have known, staggered one-by-one out of the charnel-house.'

The rest had died of suffocation during the night.

When the Governor of Madras heard about this tragedy of the 'Black Hole of Calcutta' he decided that an army must be sent to punish the Nabob and to recover Calcutta for the British. The commander of the expedition, Clive, was ready; he had returned from his holiday in England. He set sail with 3,000 well-trained men. He captured Calcutta. He then marched north to face the Nabob's army of 50,000 men at Plassey. Clive's troops scattered the Nabob's army. Clive had captured Bengal. His losses on the battlefield of Plassey on 23 June 1757 were just 22 of his men killed (see map).

Three years later a British army defeated the French at Wandewash near Madras. French influence and power in India were now at an end.

The black hole of Calcutta was a key factor in making the British angry with the Indians. This imaginary picture shows how people were reminded of it in the nineteenth century. No one until quite recently asked: 'How did it really happen?', or 'By what right were the British ruling India?'.

Fighting in Canada, 1754–60

We left the story of the quarrel between the British and French in North America with the French building the great Fort Duquesne (see map page 9). It was finished by the summer of 1754. The British colonists in Virginia were particularly worried by this. A small force under the command of a young man named George Washington was sent to attack the fort. The expedition was easily beaten back by the French. In 1755 a stronger British army was sent. It was ambushed by a large force of French and Indians. Nearly two-thirds of the British, including their commander General Braddock, were killed. The massacre was horrific. One survivor later wrote:

'I cannot describe the horrors of the scene; no pen could do it. The yell of the Indians is fresh on my ear, and the terrific sound will haunt me till the hour of my dissolution (*death*).'

When war was declared between Britain and France in 1756, it went badly for Britain at first. The French Governor of Quebec, Montcalm, started to advance southwards towards the British colonies of New England.

But by 1759 the British were better organized. Pitt was now the British Prime Minister and taking personal control. The French fleets were blockaded in the

harbours of Toulon and Brest, and when they tried to break out, were pursued and defeated. This meant the French could not send reinforcements across the Atlantic to Canada. Pitt ordered attacks on the French colonies in North America from several directions. The most important and famous was the expedition sent up the River St Lawrence. It is worth telling the story in some detail.

Pitt chose his commanders carefully. In charge of the army was Major-General James Wolfe; in charge of the navy was Vice-Admiral Sir Charles Saunders. Both were courageous and daring commanders. They assembled their forces at Louisbourg, a fort and harbour captured from

This is an engraving of the capture of Quebec. You also have on these two pages a map and a description of the event. What different kinds of information do you obtain from these different ways of presenting what happened?

James Wolfe was born in Kent in 1727. He never really considered any career other than the army and was passionately loyal to his country. He grew up to be a gangling red-headed six-footer, though he suffered from chronic ill-health: he had a kidney stone and acute rheumatism, and suffered from sea-sickness. Yet despite being so delicate he won rapid promotion, becoming a lieutenant-colonel by the age of 23. Until Pitt appointed him to attack Quebec, few British generals were having much success. But the appointment made the Duke of Newcastle very angry, mainly because Wolfe was not from an aristocratic family. Newcastle went to the King and said, 'The man is mad!' George II replied, 'Mad is he? Then I hope he will bite some others of my generals!' Wolfe was also, of course, very young: he was only 32 when he died. He was honoured by a monument to his memory in Westminster Abbey.

the French only the previous year, 1758 (see map, page 9). Wolfe described the force in a letter to his Uncle Walter:

'The fleet consists of twenty-two sail-of-the-line and many frigates, the army of 9,000 men – in England it is called 12,000. We have ten battalions, three companies of grenadiers, some marines (if the Admiral can spare them) and six new raised companies of North American Rangers – not complete and the worst soldiers in the universe; a great train of artillery, plenty of provisions, tools and implements of all sorts.'

You can see what he meant. Although he was well equipped, he did not have the number of troops he was promised. And they were not good enough for the job. His task was formidable – to capture Quebec, strongly defended by the French commander Marquis de Montcalm.

During the winter the St Lawrence was blocked by ice. They had to wait for summer. On 6 June 1759 they set sail. They made first for the island of Orleans in the river opposite Quebec (see map). From this island Wolfe scanned the northern bank of the river to find the easiest way of attacking Quebec.

There was no easy way. There were 106 cannon projecting from the walls of Quebec itself. In front and to the west of the town were steep cliffs, called the 'Heights of Abraham'. Down-river the French had built strong defence-works. Behind these Montcalm had concentrated 14,000 men. At first Wolfe launched attacks below these defence-works to try to bypass them. But Montcalm's troops beat off the British soldiers.

Time was running short. If Quebec were not taken by the autumn, the British ships would be frozen in the iced-up river. Wolfe made a desperate and bold decision. He moved his troops up river. In the early hours of the morning of 13 September Wolfe led a band of men in boats to a little cove under the Heights of Abraham. A midshipman, who was with them later told how Wolfe quietly recited Gray's poem, 'Elegy in a Country Churchyard'.

Montcalm came from a proud, aristocratic family. He had a sharp mind and a lively manner. He was also very brave: in one battle he received five sabre wounds! In April 1756 he left France to take command of the French forces in Canada. There he quarrelled with the Governor-General who really knew nothing about army matters, yet was his superior in command. Montcalm made the following entry in his diary after he and the Governor-General had inspected the army: 'As he had never seen a military camp or defence works everything appeared novel and amusing. He asked the most extraordinary questions.'

He proved himself to be a very able commander from 1757 to 1759. When the British broke the ranks of the French army at the Battle of the Heights of Abraham, Montcalm tried to rally some of his men and was fatally wounded. The picture shows Montcalm dying.

The siege of Quebec.

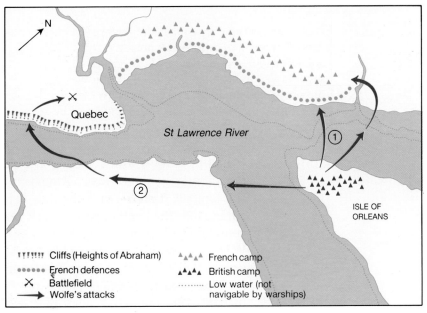

Legend	
⌇⌇⌇⌇⌇ Cliffs (Heights of Abraham)	▲▲▲▲ French camp
•••••• French defences	▲▲▲▲ British camp
× Battlefield	······ Low water (not
→ Wolfe's attacks	navigable by warships)

guarding the heights were taken by surprise. Soon after dawn a force of 4,500 British troops clambered up the cliffs and even cannon were hauled up. Montcalm was horrified when the news reached him. He marched a force round from the other side of Quebec. At 10 a.m. he attacked. The British held their fire, then they let loose a withering stream of musket-shot. The French broke ranks and fled. But in the battle both Wolfe and Montcalm were killed.

The British took Quebec. The following year they took Montreal. The French were completely defeated. Britain now had Canada. Wolfe was a hero. Or was he? Was he really so brilliant? He seemed to waste a lot of time in the summer. Wasn't he foolish, though extraordinarily lucky, to risk climbing the Heights of Abraham? Perhaps his success was mostly due to Admiral Saunders' control of the river with the navy.

The Treaty of Paris

In 1763 a peace treaty was signed bringing the Seven Years War to an end. Britain now had the most powerful empire in the world:

1 She gained some extra West Indian islands where there had also been a lot of fighting. They were important for producing sugar.

2 She gained control of north-east India. The French were allowed to keep three trading posts in India but were forbidden to fortify them.

3 The French were driven from North America. Britain gained Quebec and the land to the west of the Appalachian mountains. And the French sold Louisiana to Spain. ☐

William Pitt is sometimes called 'the Elder Pitt' to distinguish him from 'the Younger Pitt', his son, who was also a very famous politician. They were two of the greatest Prime Ministers Britain has ever had.

The Elder Pitt was born in 1708 and became an MP in 1735. He spent the rest of his life in politics, going to the House of Lords in 1766 as the Earl of Chatham. He was a cold, haughty person with a fearful temper and very difficult to work with. When he became Prime Minister at the beginning of the Seven Years War he said, 'I know that I can save the country and that I alone can.' He made great passionate speeches in parliament and dedicated himself to winning the Seven Years War. It was because of him that Britain built up the greatest eighteenth-century empire and became a wealthy country. And yet he was often too ill to do his work properly. He suffered agonies from gout and from mental instability. One historian has said that 'Pitt was ill, physically and mentally, every year of his life'. He was nursed through his bouts of mental illness by his devoted wife. He died in 1778.

It had to be in a low voice for fear the French sentries might hear. The poem is still famous: it starts with the line, 'The curfew tolls the knell of parting day' and contains the line particularly relevant to Wolfe; 'The paths of glory lead but to the grave'. Wolfe leaped on shore at 4.0 a.m.

Wolfe and his soldiers clambered up the cliff. The small contingent of French

1 Draw up a list of ways in which armies are different today from the middle of the eighteenth century.
2 Imagine you are a soldier who has served in Clive's army since 1750. Write a letter home after the battle of Plassey saying what you think about Clive.

British India to 1877

Why was India important?

For 190 years after the Battle of Plassey, from 1757 to 1947, Britain was the most important European country in India. India also became by far the most important part of the British Empire. From 1877 the monarchs of Britain also had the title 'Empress' or 'Emperor' of India. India came to be called 'the most truly bright and precious jewel in the Crown'.

Why were the British interested in India? It was for economic reasons. They could make money. At first only a few people made any money. Official parliamentary reports showed that from 1757 to 1766 alone the East India Company paid out nearly £6 million to its employees in 'presents' and 'compensations' [bribes]. Dishonesty was everywhere. Even the directors of the Company admitted to 'the corruption and rapacity [*obtaining money by threats*] of our servants' and that 'the vast fortunes ... had been obtained by a series of the most tyrannic and oppressive conduct that was ever known in any country'.

But by the middle of the nineteenth century the profits being made by the British in India were being spread more widely. Britain was becoming a wealthy country through trade. India was important for trade and in the nineteenth century trade between Britain and India increased enormously. The transport of goods between the two countries was made easier in the following ways:

1   Railways were built to make travel inside India much faster.

2   Fast sailing ships called 'clippers' were built.

3   The Suez Canal was opened in 1869. This greatly reduced the length of the journey because ships no longer had to travel round the south of Africa. India's trade increased by seven times between 1869 and 1929.

Britain was also becoming a great industrial country. So her factories needed raw materials and the factory-owners needed to sell what they made. India was very important because she provided raw materials as well as buying the manufactured goods. Cotton is a good example.

The spread of British control

One hundred years after the Battle of Plassey (in 1757), a great 'Mutiny' broke out in the Indian army. (A mutiny is when soldiers refuse to obey the orders of their officers.) During the hundred years between these events Britain gradually took over more and more Indian land. By 1857 Britain controlled about half of India (page 23). These conquests were partly the result of wars inside India, and partly the result of more wars between Britain and France:

1   Inside India there was much rivalry and fighting between different Indian rulers. Sometimes the British interfered and captured land for themselves at the same time. They also took the land of Indian princes who fought for the French against them.

2   Britain and France were at war with each other again during the time of the French Revolution and the rule of Napoleon. Holland was taken over by France. So Britain considered Holland an enemy too and attacked and took control of some Dutch colonies. Particularly important for India were the

y the late eighteenth century alcutta was the wealthy centre of e East India Company trade. This cture, painted in 1824, shows the and Government House.

Cape of Good Hope (on the route from Britain to India) and Ceylon (what is today Sri Lanka).

British government of India

We left the story of India with the British defeat of the French in the Seven Years War (see page 13). We also saw that Clive returned to India in 1765. We pick up the story from there.

Clive was sent by the directors of the East India Company to improve the way the Company was run in India. What he did in particular was to reduce the opportunities for individuals to make huge fortunes by corruption and private trading. These were important reforms (changes). But, naturally, they made him unpopular with the people they affected. When he returned to England he was himself accused of corruption. Although he was not found guilty, the worry plunged him into one of his moods of depression and he committed suicide.

In the seventeenth and eighteenth centuries and again from the late nineteenth century India produced much cotton cloth. But for most of the nineteenth century Indian cotton plantations were developed for the export of cotton to overseas factories instead.

In the eighteenth century Britain imported cotton cloth and clothes from India. As a result of the Industrial Revolution (see Chapter 2) factories were built in Lancashire to make cotton clothes. And so the Indians were forced to grow cotton to sell cheaply to the Lancashire factories. And they were also made to buy British cotton clothes instead of their own. In 1835 a British MP made a speech in the House of Commons in which he said, 'Some years ago the East India Company annually received of the produce of the looms of India to the amount of from six million pieces of cloth. The demand . . . has now nearly ceased altogether. . . . Terrible are the accounts of the wretchedness of the poor Indian weavers, reduced to absolute starvation. And what was the sole cause? The presence of the cheaper English manufacture. . . . The Dacca muslins, celebrated over the whole world for their beauty and fineness, are almost annihilated from the same cause.'

The picture shows Indian weavers at work.

One of the real problems was that the East India Company was trying to act as a government. There were bound to be difficulties. Very gradually and reluctantly the Government in London took on some share in the government of the British parts of India. In 1773 the first Governor-General was appointed by the Company and a Council was appointed by the British Government. The Governor-General was a man called Warren Hastings. He was very good. But one of the Council hated him and had Hastings recalled to London. He had to stand trial on several charges. The trial lasted from 1788 to 1795! Hastings was found not guilty.

It was a ridiculous situation. So it was arranged that the trading and governing work of the Company should be completely separated. From now on it would be the British Government who appointed the Governor-General.

The origins of the Indian Mutiny

Two Governors-General in particular decided to use their power in India to bring about changes. Those were Bentinck (1828–35) and Dalhousie (1848–56). The East India Company had been interested only in trade. Now the British were bringing about changes that affected the Indian way of life. The British thought that these were improvements; but some Indians objected to this interference.

It was Bentinck who developed tea plantations in India. He also introduced English-style schools and encouraged the use of the English language. The way in which the British and Indians disagreed about changes is well shown by the abolition of 'suttee'. In many parts of India, when a man died, his body was burned on a great fire called a funeral pyre. Tradition also demanded that his widow should be burned to death on this pyre. It was this burning of widows that was called suttee. A modern historian has described how in Bengal a widow 'was usually tied to the corpse, often already putrid; men stood by with poles to push her back in case the bonds should burn through and the victim, scorched and maimed, should struggle free.' Bentinck declared suttee illegal in 1829 because it was so horrible; many Indians continued what they thought was a proper tradition. They believed the wife should die so she could keep serving her husband after death.

Bentinck's changes were disliked by many ordinary Indians. But it was the rulers and the soldiers who disliked Dalhousie's changes. It was the tradition in India that if a ruler did not have an heir, he could adopt someone to succeed him. Dalhousie ignored this and when Indian rulers died without an heir he took control of their states for Britain. While he was Governor-General he took over seven states in this way, including the large and wealthy Punjab. Naturally the Indian princes were very angry.

In 1856 something happened which was to bring things to a head. Indian soldiers were called 'sepoys'. Most were recruited in Bengal and Oudh in the north of India. Some were Hindu by religion, others Muslim. Hinduism teaches that the cow is a sacred animal and Islam (the Muslim religion) teaches that the pig is an unclean animal. So a Hindu could not eat the flesh of a cow; and a Muslim could not eat the flesh of a pig. In 1856 the sepoys were issued with new rifles. In order to load them the soldier had to bite the end of the cartridge. The cartridges were greased with animal fat. The sepoys refused to bite them – the Hindus for fear that the fat was from cows, the Muslims for fear that it was from pigs. This problem started a mutiny which affected large parts of northern India.

Indian industry, agriculture and trade grew while Lord Dalhousie was Governor-General. He encouraged the coal and iron industries and irrigation schemes. But in particular he started important improvements in communications. He improved the postal services, developed the use of steamboats on rivers, and had railways built. By 1857, 200 miles of railway were in use. Because India is such a large country, railways became extremely important. Train journeys became very popular with the Indian people. Eventually, conditions on the trains became incredible: many people travelled outside, hanging on to doors or sitting on the roof! The photograph shows 'Agony Point' in Bengal. The gradient was so steep that sand had to be spread on the lines to prevent the wheels from slipping.

Above, Sepoys. Nearly five-sixths of the East India Company's soldiers were Indians. All the officers and a few soldiers were British. Sepoys were recruited from some parts of India more than others. Sikhs from the Punjab were particularly good soldiers. Many, like those above, came from Bengal. After the Mutiny the proportion of sepoys in the Indian army was reduced. *Below*, the storming of Delhi during the Mutiny.

The Indian Mutiny

The Mutiny did not affect the whole of India. In fact, many Indian soldiers remained on duty, particularly the Sikhs (recruited from the Punjab) and the Gurkhas (from Nepal).

However, in some areas where uprisings did take place, many people took part – peasants and princes, as well as sepoys. As a result many Indians today look back on these events as an attempted war of independence against the British rulers.

The main events of the Mutiny took place in Cawnpore, Lucknow and Delhi (see map page 12):

1 At Cawnpore the British civilians and a small garrison of British troops were besieged by a large force of Indians under the command of a prince named Nana Sahib. The situation looked hopeless for the British. So they negotiated. In return for a promise by the Indians that the British would not be attacked, the British agreed to leave. But as they opened the gates and moved out, all the British people were captured. The men were killed; the women and children taken back into the town. But a British relief force was already marching to Cawnpore. As it approached, the Indians killed the surviving British women and children. The relief force succeeded in recapturing the town, whereupon they killed many Indians without mercy.

2 The British were also besieged in Lucknow. But when relief forces marched there, they were not strong enough to break out again. So another relief force had to be sent.

3 At the start of the Mutiny sepoys captured Delhi and proclaimed the descendant of the Moguls as Emperor. Delhi was important because it was the capital of the old Mogul Empire. A force of over 30,000 Indians defended Delhi against an army of 5,000 brought together by the British to try to recapture the city. In September reinforcements of Sikh troops arrived, and the British recaptured Delhi in bloody fighting.

For all intents and purposes the Mutiny was now at an end, though sporadic fighting continued into 1858. And the British revenge was fearsome, as described in the very detailed history of the Mutiny written soon after:

'Volunteer hanging parties went into the districts, and amateur executioners were not wanting to the occasion [*not in short supply*]. One gentleman boasted of the number he had finished off quite ''in an artistic manner'' with mango-trees for gibbets and elephants for drops'.

After the Mutiny

The Mutiny shocked the British Government. They decided that they must treat the country rather better. The East India Company was abolished in 1858 and a new system of government was set up. At the head was the Viceroy, who represented the Queen. In Britain a minister was appointed, called the Secretary of State for India, to look after Indian matters. The British stopped Dalhousie's policy of taking over Indian states when a prince died without an heir. Some Indians were given jobs in the civil service.

However, the British remained very much in control. All the senior jobs in the civil service and all the top ranks in the army were reserved for the British. The British governed India and this system came to be called the 'Raj' – an Indian word meaning 'rule'. Many British families settled for much of their lives in India: army officers, civil servants, police officers, railway officials, businessmen. Many lived lives of some luxury, with Indian servants to do the hard work. When they returned to England for leave they made sure that their cabins on board ship were on the cooler, northern side away from the blazing sun. So they booked 'port out, starboard home', abbreviated to 'POSH'! Also Indian words were learned by the English and have become part of the English language, for example: 'polo'; 'bungalow'; 'curry'; juggernaut'.

"NEW CROWNS FOR OLD ONES!"

There was much comment at this time about Victoria becoming Empress of India. This cartoon, which appeared in the magazine, *Punch*, shows the Prime Minister, Benjamin Disraeli, in eastern dress giving Victoria the imperial crown. Many people objected to the title of Empress. Pamphlets were published, one of which was entitled, 'How Little Ben, the innkeeper, changed the Sign of the Queen's Inn to the Empress Hotel Limited and what was the Result'. On the other hand, Victoria was delighted. Exactly fifty years later a biography of Disraeli was published, written by a Frenchman. In this book the author described how:

'the new Empress gave a dinner, at which she appeared, contrary to all her customs, covered with Oriental jewels presented to her by the Indian princes. At the end of the repast [*meal*], Disraeli rose, in conscious violation of etiquette, and proposed the health of the Empress of India . . ., and the Queen, far from being scandalized, responded with a smiling bow that was almost a curtsey.'

The British Government of India was made even grander in the 1870s. On 1 January 1877 Queen Victoria became officially 'Empress of India'. She had rather liked the idea of having this title for some years. It was her favourite prime minister, Benjamin Disraeli, who passed the law through parliament. Until India became independent (in 1947) British coins had the following abbreviation on them: 'Ind. Imp.'. This stood for the Latin words 'Indiae Imperatrix' (or Imperator), Empress (or Emperor) of India. □

1 Make a list of all the ways in which the former British control of India is obvious in Britain today. (Think about words, food and drink, people for example.)
2 Imagine you are a member of the Viceroy's staff in Delhi. Write a letter to a relation in England explaining why you think that the British Raj is a benefit for India.
3 Imagine you are a sepoy in 1856. Write out a speech to the other soldiers in your barracks persuading them to mutiny.

Empires a century ago

Changes, 1815–1880

Most of the changes in the ownership of colonies from 1756 to 1815 were the results of wars between Britain and France:

1　Britain gained control of Canada and much of India in the Seven Years War.

2　France helped the Americans to free themselves from Britain in their War of Independence.

3　Britain gained Ceylon and South Africa from France's ally Holland in the Napoleonic War.

The Napoleonic War ended in 1815. About seventy years later several European countries started to divide up Africa into colonies. It is interesting to compare maps of empires in 1815 and 1880. Several changes are obvious (see maps):

1　By far the biggest is that the Spanish and Portuguese colonies in central and south America have become independent;

2　Britain has gained control of India;

3　Much more of Australia and Canada have been settled by Europeans;

4　Russia has gained more land in Asia;

5　France has colonies in North Africa and South East Asia.

Because the Spanish and Portuguese lost so much land, Europeans governed less land altogether in 1880 than they had in 1815. In fact, apart from the great British interest in India, most European governments at this time were not really interested in colonies. What were the advantages in having colonies? There did not seem to be many. For example, British trade with her former North American colonies had not been affected very much by their emergence as the USA. Indeed, many people thought that colonies were more trouble than they were worth – costing money to keep and defend rather than making a profit for the mother-country. The British politician, Disraeli, expressed this view in 1852. He said, 'The

Empires in 1815.

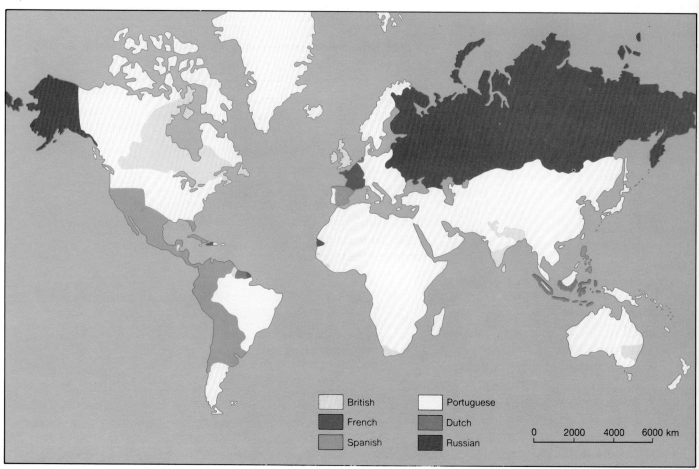

British　　　Portuguese

French　　　Dutch

Spanish　　　Russian

0　　2000　　4000　　6000 km

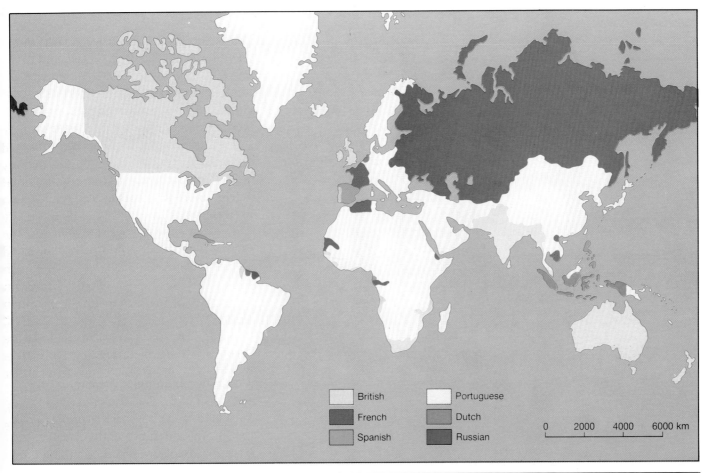

Empires in 1880.

colonies are millstones round our neck.'

On the other hand, many ordinary people were interested in the colonies as somewhere to settle. Life was becoming quite hard for working people in many European countries, partly because of a fast increase in the population. And so the idea of emigrating to other parts of the world became quite popular. Some figures show this very vividly. For instance, the population of England and Wales in the year 1821 was 12 million. The same number of people emigrated between 1821 and 1910. Most European emigrants went to North America, South America, South Africa, Australia, New Zealand and Siberia. The populations of these countries increased from 5.6 million in 1810 to 200 million in 1910.

Explorers and missionaries were also interested in visiting some lands. In the nineteenth century Africa was a mysterious place – the 'Dark Continent'. Because

In the middle of the nineteenth century Livingstone was a great hero in Britain. This was for a number of reasons. First, when he returned from his expeditions he made great speeches and wrote books about Africa. Secondly, his mission in life was to end conflict and slavery in Africa and convert the peoples to Christianity. He was once described as 'a perfect Christian gentleman'. When he plunged into the centre of Africa, he lost touch with the outside world; there were no radios in those days. While Livingstone was on one such expedition an American newspaper editor had the idea of sending one of his correspondents, H M Stanley, to find him. It made a great story. When Stanley met Livingstone, as shown in this drawing, he uttered the words that have become so famous: 'Dr Livingstone, I presume'.

The expanding frontiers

When Europeans first settled in vast countries like North America, Siberia and Australia – they settled in narrow strips of land. Later the edge, or 'frontier' as it was called, was pushed further out. Frontiers were expanded for various reasons:

1 Curiosity – to explore the further regions.

2 Need for land – as more settlers arrived more land was needed especially for farming.

3 Gold – the discovery of gold, especially in the USA and Australia, was a great incentive.

Let us look at two examples, Siberia and Australia.

Siberia is, of course, part of Asia. European Russians started to explore and settle there as early as about 1600. Within two hundred years almost all had been occupied. The Russians even had Alaska (which they sold to the USA in 1867). In the nineteenth century the Russians concentrated on obtaining land in two main areas:

1 The Far East, on the borders of the Chinese province of Manchuria. The great Pacific port of Vladivostok was founded in 1860 (the name means 'domination of the East').

Missionaries in the nineteenth century. Since the time of St Paul Christianity has been spread by the work of missionaries; people convinced that Christianity is the only true religion. Many have suffered (even torture and death). So they had to be tough and dedicated. There were probably more Christian missionaries throughout the world in the nineteenth century than at any other time. Missionaries also helped to spread their own language and trade from their home country, helping in the spread of colonies.

of diseases and the difficulties of crossing deserts and penetrating jungles, Europeans knew very little about the interior. The most famous explorer was David Livingstone. He was a doctor and a missionary who devoted over thirty years of his life to mapping vast areas of southern and central Africa. Missionaries followed the explorers in order to convert the African people to Christianity. They also devoted great efforts to converting Indians and Chinese. The missionaries believed that these people were 'heathen' and had to be 'saved'; and many had little sympathy for, or interest in, local customs.

In the nineteenth century Russia was shown in pictures as a dangerous bear. Britain was always a lion. This *Punch* cartoon, drawn in 1886, shows how the British saw Russia as threatening various countries.

ON THE PROWL.

2 Central Asia. Large areas were conquered from the local peoples so that by about 1880 the Russians had reached the borders of Afghanistan. Many people in Britain were worried that the Russians were advancing dangerously close to India. It looked almost as if war might break out between Britain and Russia in 1885 because of this. And the problem provided the background to *Kim*, a famous story by the English writer, Rudyard Kipling.

The first European settlement in Australia was in 1788. In that year a colony was founded at Botany Bay in New South Wales for convicted criminals. The town of Sydney grew up near this colony. A few other towns were founded in the 1820s; for example, Brisbane in 1826 and Perth in 1829. But few emigrants were attracted to Australia. However, more people moved to Australia after 1830 for several reasons:

1 Sheep farming was developed (mainly for wool) after 1830.

2 Farming for meat production became even more important after 1880 with the invention of refrigeration ships.

This kind of farming needs large areas of land. Australia could provide that. By 1880 all but the really desert areas of western and northern Australia had been explored.

3 The discovery of gold, especially in Western Australia in the 1850s, helped attract people to Australia.

Even so, the population of Australia remained very small – only 1.2 million in 1861 and still under 4 million at the end of the century.

China

In the nineteenth century Britain gained a colony in China. This was Hong Kong; and Britain is due to return it to China in 1997. By the 1880s it had become a prosperous town and port. How Britain obtained Hong Kong is an interesting story.

The East India Company traded not only in India, but also in China. Tea and silk were particularly popular. Unfortunately, there was very little that the Chinese wanted to buy in exchange. However, at the end of the eighteenth century

Population in millions

	1881	1981
Britain (people)	29.7	55.7
Australia (people)	2.7	15.0
(sheep)	65.0	137.0

Notice that:
1 Australia is thirty times the size of Great Britain.
2 In both 1881 and 1981 there were about 24 sheep for every human in Australia.

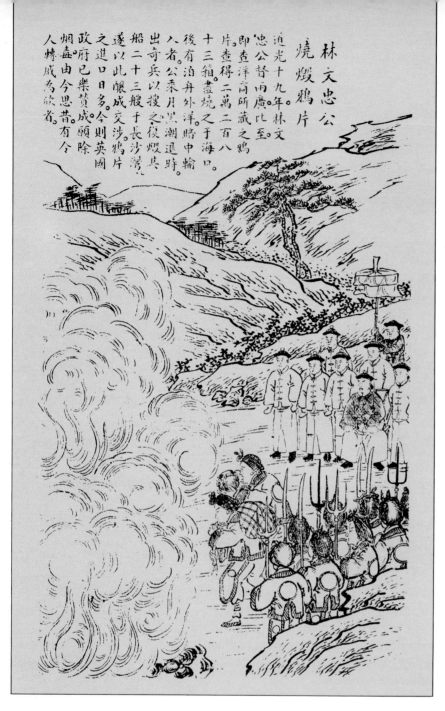

林文忠公
燒燬鴉片

道光十九年林文
忠公督兩廣比至
即查洋商所藏之鴉
片查得二萬二百八
十三箱盡燒之于海口。
後有泊舟外洋潮退時
者公乘以奇兵以搜之復燬其
八片船
出之進二口十三日多
遂以此釀成沙
之船二十三般交
政府已樂贊成今
煙毒由今思昔有
人轉成為故省。

When the Chinese Emperor appointed Lin as Commissioner, Lin set about destroying stocks of opium. This is a Chinese drawing of the time showing him doing it. The centre of the opium trade was Canton. Within two months of his arrival Lin had arrested 1,600 people involved, destroyed 42,741 pipes used for smoking, and confiscated 38,460 lbs of opium. Lin tried to be fair but firm with the English merchants supplying the opium. The war broke out when a Chinese man was killed by British sailors in a brawl. Lin wanted the sailors to be punished by the Chinese; the British refused. Lin cut off supplies of food to the British in Canton. The British replied by sending an army and navy.

the Company started to supply something the Chinese wanted – opium. The opium poppy was grown in Bengal. First of all the Chinese used opium as a medicine to relieve pain. Then people started smoking it for pleasure. Many became addicts. The British merchants supplied more and more – 1,000 chests in 1767; 40,000 in 1838.

By then drug addiction was so serious that the Chinese Emperor appointed a man called Lin as Commissioner, to put an end to the opium trade. Lin even wrote to Queen Victoria:

'The wealth of China is used to profit the barbarians [*uncivilized people*] ... By what right do they in return use the poisonous drug to injure the Chinese people? ... Let us ask, where is their conscience?'

The letter was received by the British Foreign Office. They ignored it. Britain wanted more trade with China and thought of the Chinese as rather backward people who could be treated without consideration. On their side the Chinese thought all other people were uncivilized barbarians and really did not want to know about them or have much to do with them.

The quarrel became worse and eventually a war broke out – known as the 'Opium War'. It lasted from 1839 to 1842. The Chinese were so ignorant about other countries that Lin seriously believed that he could defeat the British army by stopping their supplies of tea and rhubarb – they would collapse from thirst and constipation! Because of their superior weapons the British easily won.

As a result of the war China was forced to open up five of her ports to British trading ships and to give the island of Hong Kong to Britain. And the opium trade continued. By the end of the century other western countries were forcing China to trade. ☐

1 Make a list of the colonies still ruled by Britain today. What other European countries still have colonies?
2 Draw up a table listing the arguments for and against European countries having colonies. Indicate your own ideas as well as those in this Chapter. (Also refer to page 133.)
3 Imagine you are a weaver in England in 1840 but out of work. You decide to emigrate. Write a letter to a friend explaining where you are going and why. (You may find it helpful to refer to pages 30–44 as well.)
4 Look at the pictures on pages 23 and 24. Do you think that the African people were pleased or not to have Europeans in their lands? Give reasons for your answer.

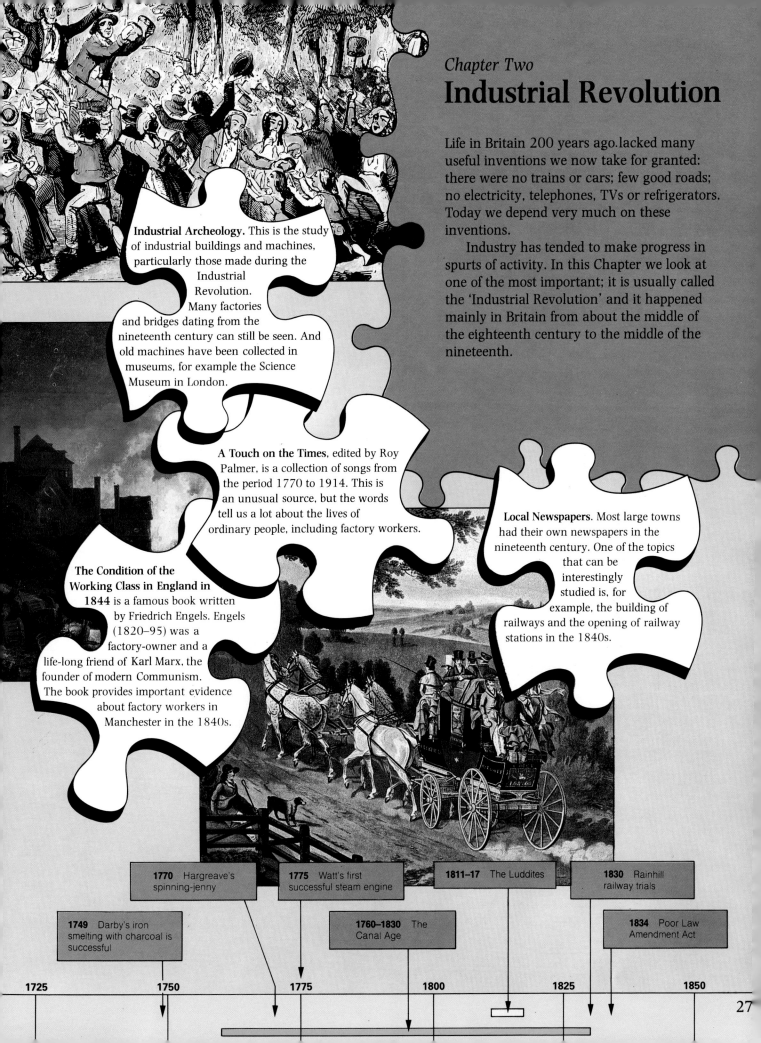

Chapter Two
Industrial Revolution

Life in Britain 200 years ago.lacked many useful inventions we now take for granted: there were no trains or cars; few good roads; no electricity, telephones, TVs or refrigerators. Today we depend very much on these inventions.

Industry has tended to make progress in spurts of activity. In this Chapter we look at one of the most important; it is usually called the 'Industrial Revolution' and it happened mainly in Britain from about the middle of the eighteenth century to the middle of the nineteenth.

Industrial Archeology. This is the study of industrial buildings and machines, particularly those made during the Industrial Revolution. Many factories and bridges dating from the nineteenth century can still be seen. And old machines have been collected in museums, for example the Science Museum in London.

A Touch on the Times, edited by Roy Palmer, is a collection of songs from the period 1770 to 1914. This is an unusual source, but the words tell us a lot about the lives of ordinary people, including factory workers.

Local Newspapers. Most large towns had their own newspapers in the nineteenth century. One of the topics that can be interestingly studied is, for example, the building of railways and the opening of railway stations in the 1840s.

The Condition of the Working Class in England in 1844 is a famous book written by Friedrich Engels. Engels (1820–95) was a factory-owner and a life-long friend of Karl Marx, the founder of modern Communism. The book provides important evidence about factory workers in Manchester in the 1840s.

1749 Darby's iron smelting with charcoal is successful

1770 Hargreave's spinning-jenny

1760–1830 The Canal Age

1775 Watt's first successful steam engine

1811–17 The Luddites

1830 Rainhill railway trials

1834 Poor Law Amendment Act

1725 1750 1775 1800 1825 1850

'Workshop of the World'

Causes of Industrial Revolution in Britain:

1 **Agricultural Revolution.** Improvements in crop production and quality of livestock meant more food was available. So more people could be employed in factories rather than on the land.
2 Important inventions were made, and could be applied to industry because money could be borrowed at low interest.
3 There were large amounts of coal and iron in Britain. Coal was important for steam-power and smelting iron. Iron was important for making machines, trains, ships.
4 Lancashire's damp climate was good for cotton manufacture: the most important industry.
5 British traders and manufacturers could make easy profits by forcing colonies (especially India) to buy goods.

Below are two descriptions of the same place – Manchester. The first was written by Daniel Defoe in 1725:

'... Manchester, one of the greatest, if not really the greatest mere [*small*] village in England.'

The second appeared in an article in *The Morning Chronicle* in 1849:

'Considerably within two-thirds of a century the scattered villages of Manchester, Salford, Hulme, Pendleton, Charlton and two or three others, became the vast cotton metropolis [*city*] which has lately succeeded in swaying [*greatly influencing*] the industrial and commercial policy of England.'

These accounts were written only 124 years apart. Obviously great changes had taken place between 1725 and 1849. What had happened? An 'Industrial Revolution'.

It is only about a hundred years ago that the term 'Industrial Revolution' was invented. A 'revolution' in history means a rapid, violent change, as we shall see in Chapter 3. By using the same word to describe industrial change we are empha-

sizing how *rapid* these changes were compared with slower changes over previous centuries. We are also emphasizing how many people suffered because of the changes, although many eventually benefited. Some historians think the comparison is not a good one: that the changes were not really *that* fast and that the poverty and hardship of the working-class was as great *before* the Industrial Revolution as it was during it. However, changes *did* take place. And they happened at first mainly in Britain.

Britain became, in the words of Disraeli, (the nineteenth-century politician), 'the workshop of the world'. She also became the most prosperous country in the world; one historian estimated that Britain as a whole was four times more wealthy at the end of the nineteenth century than at the beginning. What changes led to this wealth? We will look at them under three headings: inventions; transport; living and working conditions.

1 Explain in your own words what the Industrial Revolution was and why it happened.
2 Do you think it was an advantage for Britain to be 'the workshop of the world'? Explain your reasons.

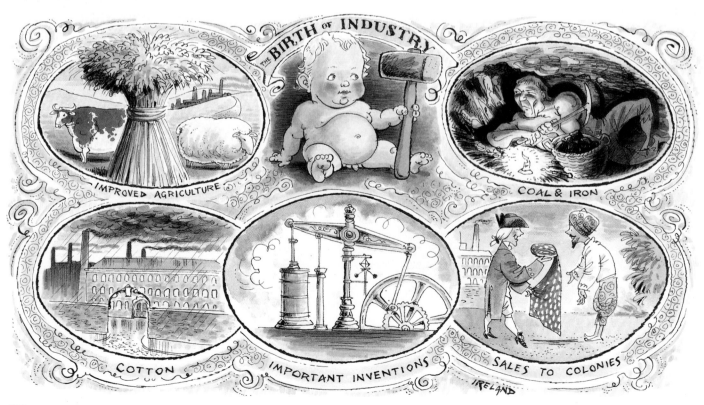

THE BIRTH OF INDUSTRY

IMPROVED AGRICULTURE

COAL & IRON

COTTON

IMPORTANT INVENTIONS

SALES TO COLONIES

IRELAND

Inventions

Iron and steel

Iron is mined from the earth in the form of 'ore'. Ore is a naturally-occurring rock made up of minerals from which metal can be extracted. Extracting the metal is done by melting the ore. This process is called 'smelting'.

Until the eighteenth century, the only suitable fuel for smelting iron ore in a furnace was *charcoal*. As charcoal was difficult to make (it is the black porous remainder of partly-burnt wood) and wood was becoming scarce, iron was very expensive. During the first half of the eighteenth century a father and son, both called Abraham Darby, experimented with *coal* as a fuel. But, compared with charcoal, it left far too many impurities in the iron. Their solution lay in using not coal but *coke*. Coke is the solid substance left over after heating coal. By 1749 the son was successfully producing good quality iron cheaply by using coke and a strong blast from a steam engine. A third generation Abraham Darby built the first iron bridge in 1779. It can be seen at the little town called, appropriately, Ironbridge.

As good quality iron became more available, people experimented with

The Darby's iron-smelting works at Coalbrookdale, Shropshire, in the late eighteenth century.

Iron production in Britain, 1720–1870.

different uses. Most famous was 'Iron-Mad' Wilkinson. He inherited an iron-works from his father and during his life he experimented with iron for an incredible range of items. As his business expanded, his founderies produced cannon which helped the Duke of Wellington to defeat Napoleon's army. He also built iron furniture; an iron ship; and he supplied Paris and New York with miles of iron waterpipes. He was even buried in an iron coffin! And he was such a powerful personality that when he died in 1808, a legend grew up that in 1815 he would rise from this iron coffin to visit his blast furnaces! A large, but disappointed, crowd gathered on the supposed day of resurrection!

It was people like this who gave Britain a strong lead in iron production against her competitors. Important iron works were developed in the Ruhr in Germany and in eastern France in Lorraine. Yet neither country was producing more than a quarter of Britain's output of pig iron in 1870.

Textiles

Before the Industrial Revolution the most important cloth produced in Britain was wool. Indeed, in the sixteenth century so much arable land was being taken over for wool production that the complaint was made that 'sheep devour man'! In the Industrial Revolution there was a change-over to a greater production of cotton cloth, made from the raw cotton which became available in large amounts from the southern states of the USA (see page 99).

Making cloth from wool or cotton involves two main processes: first the wool or cotton has to be spun into a thread; then the thread has to be woven into cloth. Before the Industrial Revolution it was very common for these processes to be undertaken in the workers' homes. This was called the 'domestic system'. Merchants would supply the wool or cotton; the thread would be produced on a spinning-wheel; and the cloth would be woven on a hand-loom.

Throughout the eighteenth century various machines were invented to make each of these two processes faster, particularly for cotton, which spins a stronger thread than wool. Many people contributed different techniques, though only a few became famous (see opposite).

These new inventions could not, of course, be used in ordinary cottages:

1   Rivers were needed for water-power.
2   Coal was needed for steam-power.
3   The power from the water, or steam, could only be made to drive the spinning-frames and weaving-looms by using complicated and large machinery.

So the new machinery was installed all together in large buildings. This is how 'factories' developed. But people at the time tended to use the old word 'mill' to describe a factory and it is still used today, especially in Lancashire and Yorkshire.

Centre; Cotton textiles as a percentage of all exports, 1760–1830. Notice how the value of cotton exports from Britain increased in this time. By 1830 cotton exports accounted for nearly two thirds of Britain's total exports. *Below*; amount of cotton used in English factories, 1800–1880. Notice the growth in cotton manufacture from the 1820s. The dip in the graph in the 1860s was known as the 'cotton famine', caused by the American civil war (Chapter 5). The Northern fleet blockaded the Southern States preventing their export of cotton. Despite the dreadful hardships caused to the Lancashire cotton workers, they continued to support the Federal side in the war out of sympathy for the slaves on the cotton plantations.

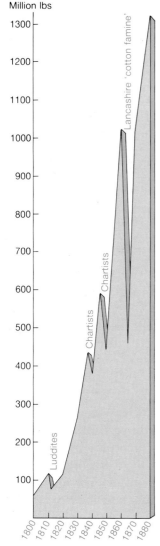

Amount of cotton used in English factories, 1800–80
Million lbs

Cotton textiles as a percentage of all exports

Year	%
1760	1%
1770	2%
1780	3%
1790	7%
1800	15%
1810	39%
1820	53%
1830	62%

Below; Engraving of an early industrial scene. Notice the combination of the old and the new: sailing ships and steam ships; agricultural land just across the river from smoke-belching factories; hills within view of the warehouses.

Weaving, 1840   Spinning, 1850

Spinning and weaving inventions

1733 John Kay's flying shuttle

This enabled the weaver to pass his shuttle automatically and quickly across the loom.

But, as more and more flying shuttles were introduced, the supply of yarn from traditional spinning-wheels could not keep pace . . .

John Kay was the son of a Colchester woollen manufacturer. But his father's weavers became so worried that his invention would put them out of work that he had to flee to France. There he was paid a small pension for making shuttles and he died in France, embittered by the ingratitude of his own countrymen.

Speed

1770 James Hargreaves's spinning jenny

This enabled the spinner to spin several threads at once. It was a great success: about 20,000 spinning jennies were in operation in Britain by 1788. (In comparison, France, with three times Britain's population, had only 900.)

But these machines still required human muscle-power for their operation . . .

James Hargreaves was a weaver who lived in Blackburn, where he worked for Robert Peel (the father of the man who became the founder of Britain's police force – 'Bobbies' – and prime minister). It is said that he named his invention after his wife, Jenny.

1768 Richard Arkwright's water-frame

This was a spinning-machine powered by a water wheel.

Later these machines were adapted so that they could be driven by steam power.

Richard Arkwright started life as a barber, then set up shop as a wig-maker in the industrial town of Bolton, where naturally he heard talk about different textile machines. With partners he set up his own factories, became prosperous and was eventually made a knight.

Power

1784 Edmund Cartwright's power-loom

This was a weaving machine powered by a water wheel.

Later these machines were adapted so that they could be driven by steam power.

Edmund Cartwright was a clergyman who became interested in problems of weaving when talking to some manufacturers while on holiday. He lost huge sums of money in the course of trying to develop his loom, partly because hand-loom weavers set fire to the factory he set up as they were afraid his invention would put them out of work.

Steam power

The most important invention of the Industrial Revolution was an efficient steam-engine – to replace the limited muscle-power of men and animals and the unreliable power of wind and water. Only then could new machines, like spinning-jennies and power-looms, have any real advantages over the old.

During the second half of the eighteenth century many factories relied on water power. Here is an extract from a letter showing one of the disadvantages of this method:

'There is not a single water mill now at work in Staffordshire, they are all frozen up, and were it not for Wilkinson's steam mill the poor nailers [*makers of nails*] must have perished; but his mill goes on rolling and slitting ten tons a day ... and thus the employment and subsistence [*wages for food and general living*] of these poor people are secured.'

It is sometimes said that James Watt invented the steam-engine, after watching the pressure of steam lift a kettle lid that was boiling in the kitchen. In fact the first steam-engine was made in Britain nearly forty years before Watt was born and, in any case, the principle of steam power had been known for centuries. Indeed, by the time Watt was a young man there were many steam-engines being used in Britain. These had been designed by Thomas Newcomen and were used to operate pumps for draining water from flooded tin and coal-mines. Nevertheless, James Watt's work was extremely important. So it is worth telling the story of his inventions and of his collaboration with Matthew Boulton and John Wilkinson. (The letter which we have just quoted was written by Boulton to Watt and refers to a factory owned by John 'Iron-Mad' Wilkinson.)

James Watt was born in Glasgow in 1736. He soon showed an interest in mechanical things. At the age of nineteen he moved to London to serve an apprenticeship as a maker of mathematical instruments. Ill health prevented him from completing his apprenticeship, but when he returned to Glasgow the following year, he was lucky to get a job – a good one at that. He was appointed as instrument-maker in the Department of Natural Philosophy (that is, Physics) at Glasgow University. One of the pieces of equipment in the department was a model of a Newcomen engine. It broke and Watt was asked to repair it. He started to think how the efficiency of the engine could be improved.

One Sunday in 1765 he had an idea. Newcomen's engine used a lot of coal because the cylinder had to be constantly cooled (see below). Watt's idea was to have a separate condenser cylinder. The problem was, how to make such an engine. Eventually he persuaded the owner of an ironworks a few miles away, near

Both the Newcomen and Watt engines worked on the same principle. Steam pushed the piston up. When the steam was cooled and condensed to droplets of water the piston dropped back into the cylinder. As a result the pump rod went up and down. Watt made the engine more efficient by adding a condenser. The steam was drained off there and the cylinder itself could therefore be kept hot. Newcomen's engine is shown below, left; Watt's engine is shown below, right.

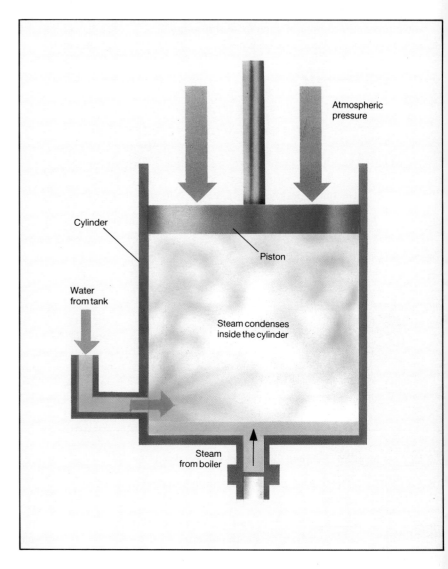

Atmospheric pressure

Cylinder

Piston

Water from tank

Steam condenses inside the cylinder

Steam from boiler

Falkirk, to work with him. But in 1773 they went bankrupt. At this point Matthew Boulton came on the scene. He had an engineering works at Soho in Birmingham, had experience with steam-engines, and had faith in Watt. In 1774 Watt became Boulton's business partner and carted his engine, named 'Beelzebub', to Birmingham. Once there, he was able to make important improvements, especially by using more accurately hollowed-out cylinders, supplied by Wilkinson. In 1775 Watt produced his first engine which he could sell – and it used only a quarter the amount of coal as the Newcomen engine! The Boulton-Watt order-book started to fill up very quickly.

But Watt's engine, like Newcomen's, could produce only an up-and-down movement (see below). So it could only be used as a pump. If it was to be used to drive machinery, it would have to be made to produce a *circular* or rotary movement. During the 1780s Watt worked on other inventions. In 1785 the first rotary steam-engine was at work in a cotton mill. By the end of that year 47 had been supplied to cotton mills and 11 to breweries. Watt's patent (or copyright) expired in 1800 so that after that date other manufacturers could copy his design. By then over 300 had been supplied from the Soho works.

Efficient steam-engines could, of course, be used for many purposes. The nineteenth century became the great age of steam. By 1850, 90 per cent of cotton mills in Britain were powered by steam. Steam-driven ships were soon produced. Indeed, the first commercial service was provided from 1807 between Albany and New York along the Hudson River by the steamship *Clermont*, which was powered by an engine supplied by the Soho works in England. However, besides the effect on the textile industry, the biggest effect of the steam-engine was on land transport with the development of railways. □

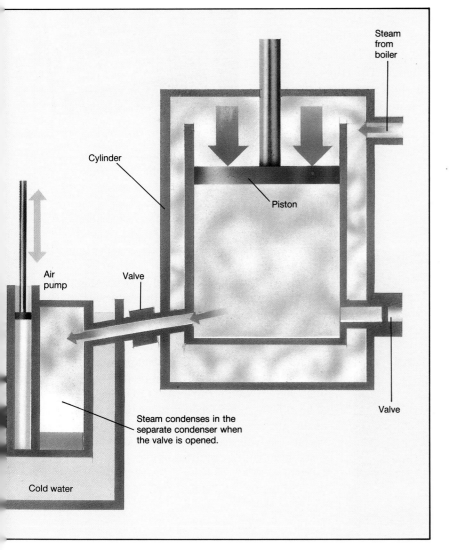

Steam from boiler

Cylinder

Piston

Air pump

Valve

Steam condenses in the separate condenser when the valve is opened.

Valve

Cold water

1 Look at the pictures on page 31 and read the description of factory conditions on pages 41–42. How far do you think the pictures give an accurate impression of work in textile factories?

2 If you could have been one of the inventor-engineers in the Industrial Revolution, which one would you most like to have been? Explain your reasons for your choice.

3 Draw graphs of cotton and iron production in Britain from 1820 to 1850. Work out the percentage increase for each and state which is the largest increase. To work this out use the following equation: increase (i.e. higher number minus lower number) divided by lower number, multiplied by 100 gives the percentage increase.

4 Steam is no longer used for power today. Make a list of what have replaced it and explain their advantages.

Transport

Before the arrival of locomotives and railways, overland travel was limited to roads and rivers and canals.

Opposite: by the 1830s the speed of coach journeys had improved enormously, as this picture shows. By that time travelling in this way had become so popular that there were over 3,000 coaches in Britain.

Roads

There had been no decent roads in Britain since the days of the Romans. By the late eighteenth century, most roads were in an appalling condition. In dry weather they were full of grooves – some over one metre deep! In wet weather, particularly in clay regions, roads became seas of sticky mud. In 1768 Arthur Young (see page 55) wrote:

'Of all the cursed roads that ever disgraced this kingdom in the very ages of barbarism, none ever equalled that from Billericay to the King's Head at Tilbury. It is for near twelve miles so narrow that a mouse cannot pass by any carriage; I saw a fellow creep under his waggon to assist me to lift, if possible, my chaise [*light horse-drawn carriage*] over a hedge. The ruts [*wheelmarks*] are of an incredible depth ... And ... I must not forget the eternally meeting with chalk-waggons, themselves frequently stuck fast till a collection of them are in the same situation, and twenty or thirty horses may be tacked to each to draw them out one by one.'

The London to Brighton Mail Coach. Notice that some people are seated outside, on top of the coach – very uncomfortable in bad weather (some people even froze to death on winter journeys!). A man called Shergold wrote about Brighton in about 1850 and made this interesting comparison between stage-coaches and trains as ways of travelling:

'In the coach you saw men and their faces, and acquired some information; in the railway carriage, you learn nothing except the number of persons killed or injured by the last accident. A young man who entered the coach at eight o'clock in the morning at Brighton took his seat, perhaps opposite a young lady whom he thought pretty and interesting. When he arrived at Cuckfield he began to be in love ... and when he gave her an arm to ascend the steep ridges at Reigate Hill, he declared his passion, was accepted and they were married soon after. Nothing of this sort ever occurs on railroads.'

Gradually, however, the roads were improved: partly by travellers paying tolls so that money was available for repairs; partly by improved techniques of surfacing. Most important was the work of John Macadam. He was appointed Surveyor-General of British roads in 1815. He improved the technique of laying stones for road surfaces. This was later improved even more by the addition of tar – 'tar-Macadam', or 'tarmac' for short.

Taking advantage of these improved roads, a great coaching industry grew up, at first for a fast postal service and then for people to travel. The hey-day of the stage-coaches was the period from 1820 to 1840. The combination of coaches, skilled coachmen and teams of horses caught the romantic imagination, still remembered on many a Christmas card. Speed and regularity of travel were dramatically improved, as you can see (left). A much more important means of transporting *heavy* goods were the canals.

In recent years travelling along the canals has become very popular for holidays, especially in brightly-coloured barges. A few are even used to carry passengers like buses. This is a photograph of one of these, taken on the Cauldon Canal in Staffordshire in 1981.

Canals

Before improved roads and before there were railways, it was easier to transport goods by water than by land:

1 For towns and cities on the coast, the sea could be used and in the eighteenth century there was a great deal of coastal traffic: for example, Newcastle supplied coal to London by sea.

2 For inland areas, water transport depended very much on rivers but these had many disadvantages: they were winding, they had strong currents, and their levels varied with the season. It was also difficult to transport large and heavy loads by river.

Yet the Industrial Revolution substantially increased the need for *bulk* transport: coal and iron had to be delivered somehow to the factories; and manufactured goods had to be delivered somehow from the factories to the market place. Canals provided the ideal alternative to rivers:

1 Canals could be built to connect towns which needed to use water-transport.

2 The level of the water would not change with the seasons.

3 There were no awkward currents in canals.

4 Canals were straight and had no obstructions like low bridges.

Canals also had an important advantage over *roads*. Canal barges could carry more than waggons; a waggon could carry just over half a ton on soft roads, a canal barge could carry 50 tons!

The first canal was built in England in the sixteenth century. But there were not nearly enough. Many canals were built between 1760 and 1830, especially in the Midlands and north of England. There was so much enthusiasm for building canals in the 1790s that it was called a 'canal mania'. And it was not just the factory owners who benefited; ordinary, working people did too. Commenting particularly

'Canal in the Air'. The two major figures in canal building, each quite extraordinary in his own way, were the Duke of Bridgewater and James Brindley.

The Duke owned coal-mines at Worsley. But he had two problems: first, the mines were constantly being flooded; secondly, it was very expensive to transport the coal to Manchester, even though it was only seven miles away. His estate manager hit upon the idea of digging a channel from the mines; this would drain the water from the coal-face and create a canal at the same time. The Duke was enthusiastic. Eventually, the canal stretched from Manchester to Merseyside. The cost was enormous: about £200,000; and the Duke became a figure of fun because of the shabby clothes he wore in order to save money for his pet scheme. The man whose services he obtained to build the canal was equally strange.

James Brindley was 43 when the partnership began in 1759 (the Duke was 23). Brindley started work as a wheelwright but soon became interested in mechanical problems. He was illiterate and had no training in engineering; he made no drawings or mathematical calculations; but he had a genius for knowing what would work and for solving practical problems. Whenever he came up against a difficulty he would take himself off to bed to concentrate – sometimes for as long as two or three days – until he had cracked it!

One of the most remarkable stretches of the Bridgewater Canal was the Barton Bridge over the river Irwell, shown in this engraving. This is the reaction of someone who saw it soon after it was opened: 'At Barton Bridge he has erected a navigable canal in the air ... Whilst I was surveying it with a mixture of wonder and delight, four barges passed me in the space of about three minutes, two of them being chained together, and dragged by two horses.'

The canal was a huge success: the price of coal in Manchester was halved and the Duke reaped a small fortune. This success encouraged others, and so began the great age of canals.

on the Grand Trunk Canal between the Trent and the Mersey, Thomas Pennant wrote in 1872:

'The cottage, instead of being half covered with miserable thatch, is now covered with a substantial covering of tiles or slates, brought from the distant hills of Wales or Cumberland ... Places which rarely knew the use of coal are plentifully supplied with the essential article upon reasonable terms.'

Some canals were not profitable but during the period when they were extensively used, they all reduced transport costs substantially. By the beginning of the nineteenth century Britain had 2,200 miles of canals. However, like the stagecoaches, the canal barges were soon replaced by the train.

Railways

Railways developed in the early nineteenth century by the combination of three skills:

1 Wheeled vehicles on metal rails.
2 Steam power to drive a vehicle (see pages 32–33).
3 Bridges, tunnels, embankments and cuttings built across the country to keep the railway lines level.

In the eighteenth century horse-drawn waggons running on rails were quite common at coal-mines. Then, with the development of steam power, stationary engines were built to haul waggons along by cables.

From 1800–30 a number of locomotives were built, though they were slow, unreliable and used a lot of coal. It was George Stephenson and his son, Robert who were the most important for improving efficiency. George Stephenson worked as a boy and young man operating machinery at coal-mines. He gained valuable experience (and a fine reputation) mending Watt steam-engines used for pumping and winding. He built his first locomotive in 1814: its maximum speed was 4 m.p.h.! Then, in 1825, he was appointed as engineer to build a railway

from Stockton to Darlington. This was the first line to use locomotives. Later on he built the Manchester-Liverpool railway for which his son, Robert, built the 'Rocket'. Later in life Robert built railways and bridges. His most famous bridge is over the Menai Straits to Anglesey.

In the early years there was considerable suspicion and opposition to trains. People foretold terrible effects: that trains rushing through the countryside would turn cow's milk sour; that the smoke would cause lambs to be born black; that passengers' lungs would be damaged by the speed. Here is a report of a ride on the Liverpool–Manchester railway just before its official opening:

'I had the satisfaction, for I can't call it *pleasure*, of taking a trip . . . [at] twenty miles an hour . . . it is really flying, and it is impossible to divest [rid] yourself of the notion of instant death to all upon the least accident happening. It gave me a headache which has not left me yet.'

Tough opposition came from the land-owners who objected to railways passing through their land. Many drove hard bargains in selling their land to railway companies and made great fortunes in the process. One landowner was paid £120,000 for property valued at £5,000!

However, by the 1840s, opposition was being overcome. The speed with which people could now travel became an advantage. Compare the times for the journey between London and Manchester in the graph (page 38).

Many lines were built in a short space of time: in 1843, 1,900 miles of line were

The Rainhill Trials. As late as 1830 there was still doubt as to whether developing steam locomotives would be worthwhile. By the 1820s businessmen were complaining about the high costs of transporting goods on the Bridgewater Canal. But would railways be any cheaper than canals? A railway was built between Manchester and Liverpool. But how should waggons be moved on this railway – by horse, stationary steam engine, or locomotive? To prove the case for the locomotive, trials were arranged.

The competing engines were assembled on 18 September 1830 before a huge crowd of excited spectators. Each locomotive had to make ten double journeys along a 1¾ mile line of level track. The drawing shows the locomotives which competed in the Rainhill Trials. The competition was easily won by the 'Rocket, an engine built by Robert Stephenson – it was the only one not to break down! People were convinced, and railways and locomotives were built at a tremendous rate over the next twenty years.

But the Rainhill Trials were marred by a sad accident. There were many important people at the ceremony, including the Prime Minister, the Duke of Wellington. At one point another Tory politician, William Huskisson, walked across the track to shake hands with the Duke. *The Manchester Guardian* recorded what happened then:

'. . . herald sounds announced the approach of the Rocket engine, on the opposite rail; a cry of danger was instantly raised. . . . The unfortunate gentleman became flurried . . . he missed his footing . . . and on falling to the ground, part of his person extended on the other rail, and the Rocket coming up at the instant, went over his leg and thigh, and fractured them in a most dreadful manner.' Huskisson died later that day.

open; by 1850, 6,600 miles. The lines were built by many different companies with no real co-ordination. Once plans were drawn up and approved by Parliament, an army of navvies would be set to work levelling ground, digging cuttings, throwing up embankments, constructing tunnels, laying track. These workmen were called 'navvies' as an abbreviation for 'navigators' – men originally recruited to build the canals along which barges were 'navigated'. Thousands of navvies were recruited; and they had a fearsome

37

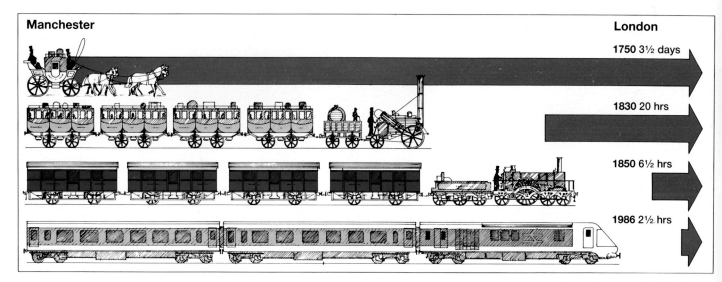

Manchester   **London**

1750 3½ days

1830 20 hrs

1850 6½ hrs

1986 2½ hrs

reputation. Here are some extracts from a description written in 1851:

'Rough, alike in morals and in manners ... impetuous, impulsive and brute-like ... Many of them lived in a state of intoxication until their money was spent, and they were again obliged to have recourse to labour ... The dread which such men as these spread throughout a rural community was striking.'

Trains, of course, had a great effect on the country. Heavy goods could be transported quickly and cheaply; people could live outside the centre of a city and travel to work – so suburbs developed rapidly; and even quite poor people could travel to seaside resorts for holidays. There were three classes of travel. Originally the third-class carriages were merely waggons with neither seats nor roofs. But an Act of Parliament was passed in 1844 which

Journey times, London-Manchester, 1750–1986

Railways in the mid-nineteenth century. In 1843, 1,900 miles of lines were open in Britain. By 1850, 6,600 miles of track, most of Britain's main lines had been built. Note that most railways had been built in northern Europe and that railroad construction in the USA was just beginning. (In 1850 the USA had only about 50 per cent more than Britain's mileage of track; by 1890 it had more miles of track than all European countries together!)

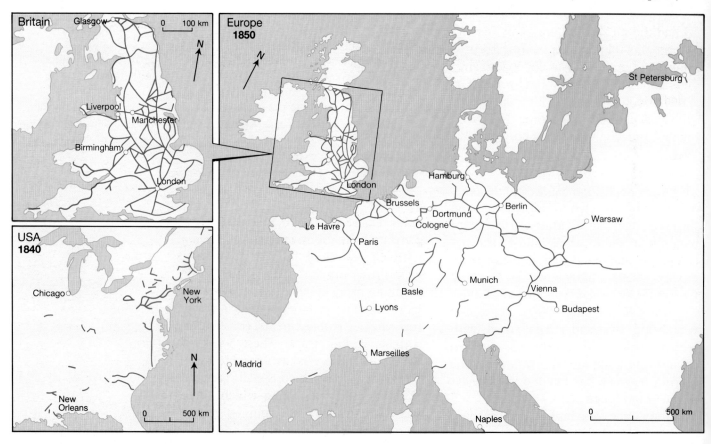

In the mid-1840s there was a railway mania involving a lot of financial speculation in buying land and building lines. Some people made fortunes, others were ruined. George Hudson, known as the 'Railway King', was the most famous. He became Mayor of York and an MP. At one time he owned a fifth of the country's railway system. This *Punch* cartoon shows even the aristocracy kneeling before the new 'king', who is attended by a railway worker. Mr Punch looks out from a painting in some astonishment! But Hudson tried to control too much with too little money. His business collapsed and shareholders were ruined

required both seats and protection for third-class passengers, who were to be charged one penny per mile. One town that quickly developed as a holiday centre because of the railway was Brighton – 'London by the sea' as it came to be called. Over 1,000 people travelled from London to Brighton on Easter Monday, 1844. A cheap-day excursion ticket at its cheapest (in 1861) could be bought for two shillings and sixpence (that is $12\frac{1}{2}$p)! ☐

One of the greatest engineers of the nineteenth century was Isambard Kingdom Brunel. He was justly famous in his own lifetime for a great variety of constructions. These included: the Clifton Suspension Bridge at Bristol; Box Tunnel near Bath; the *Great Eastern* steamship.

The *Great Eastern* was a fantastic enterprise; an iron steam-ship, almost six times bigger than the largest iron ship then built. But Brunel had been too ambitious. Commercially she was a failure: partly because there were not enough passengers at the time to fill her 4,000 berths; partly because of her reputation as being an ill-fated ship. She took months to launch, getting stuck in the mud at Millwall dock, and one of her boilers blew up on her maiden voyage, killing five people. The photograph shows Brunel at the launching in 1857.

1 Draw up lists of the advantages and disadvantages of travelling by road, canal and railway in 1840.
2 Imagine you were born in 1752. You make two journeys from London to Manchester – one when you are eight years old, the other at the age of seventy eight. Describe your two journeys to your grandchildren explaining the changes you noticed both in the journeys and in the appearance of Manchester. (See also page 28).
3 You are a friend of a navvy. Write a letter (which he has dictated to you) to his family in Ireland describing his life and work during one week.
4 Look at the *Punch* cartoon above. How has the artist managed to show how important George Hudson was?

Geography

Before the Industrial Revolution East Anglia, Sussex, and the West Country were large centres of British Industry (see maps). The emphasis then was on woollen manufactures and the smelting of iron with charcoal. The Industrial Revolution brought many changes – with a much greater emphasis on cotton and coal. New coalfields were opened up to meet the increased demand. As steam power was introduced for driving factory machinery, factories came to be built near coalmines. Also, cotton manufacture needs a damp atmosphere. The old industries declined and new industrial and mining areas rapidly grew – in South Wales, the Midlands and the North.

Britain had, and still has, large amounts of coal – and quickly became by far the biggest coal producer in the world. For example, by 1870 Britain produced *nine* times as much coal as France and nearly *four* times as much as Germany and the USA each produced (see graph).

However, conditions in the mines were extremely unpleasant. Winding gear was used to lower people into the mines and pumps were used to drain water. But apart from these, very little machinery was used. Men hacked the coal from the face with picks; and women, adolescents, children and ponies hauled the wagons of coal along the rails in the underground galleries. These galleries were so low-roofed that small people were often needed for this purpose; and the heat in these confined spaces was such that they had to work stripped to the waist, boys and girls alike. By the middle of the nineteenth century a quarter of a million people were employed in the coal industry.

As the Industrial Revolution got under way, large numbers of workers were needed – not just in the mines, but also in the factories, which were built in places near the coal-mines. For example, the population of Manchester increased from 41,000 in 1774 to 187,000 in 1821. At

Main industries in Britain, c.1720 and c.1790. Notice how different industries and different places became important as a result of the Industrial Revolution.

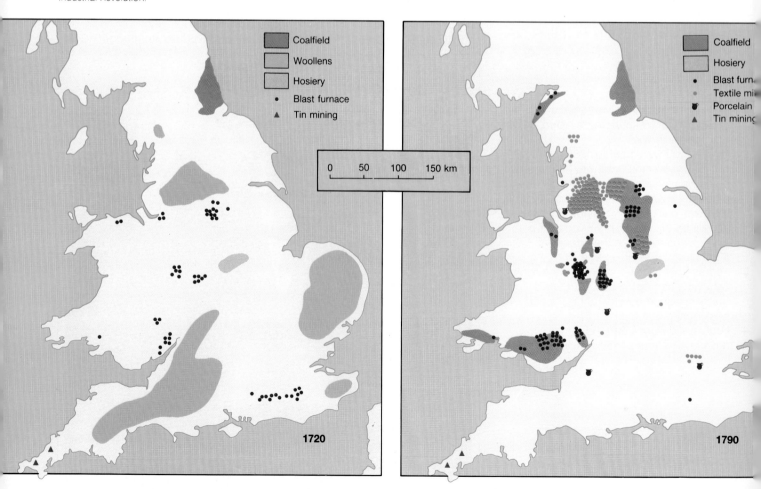

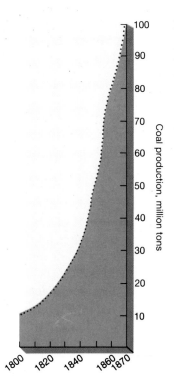

Coal production in Britain, 1800–70.

first there were very few people living in or near the new industrial areas, so where did these workers come from? In 1833 the Factory Commission (see page 78) received this evidence from one of its witnesses:

'A good many from the agricultural parts; a many from Wales; a many from Ireland and Scotland. People left other occupations and came to spinning for the sake of high wages. I recollect shoemakers leaving their employ and learning to spin; I recollect tailors; I recollect colliers; but a great many more husbandmen [*farmers with a small-holding*] left their employ to learn to spin.'

The Industrial Revolution brought about sharp divisions in England, between the industrial north on the one hand, and London and the rural south on the other. Also, class divisions became so much more obvious that the British politician, Disraeli, subtitled his novel, *Sybil*, 'The Two Nations' – the rich and the poor.

Factories

In order to make the most effective use of the new machinery the workers were gathered together into buildings called factories. They varied in size: some employed hundreds of men, women and children; others were very small. The main aim of most factory owners was to make large profits. So they made their workers work long hours and in unhealthy and often dangerous conditions.

Many people were shocked by these conditions (see Chapter 4). Many pamphlets, letters and reports were written: these provide us with some vivid descriptions. Here is an extract from a pamphlet written in 1832 about Manchester cotton factories:

'The population employed in the cotton factories rises at five o'clock in the morning, works in the mills from six till eight o'clock, and returns home for half an hour or forty minutes to breakfast.

This is Newcastle-upon-Tyne in 1848, a typical factory town during the Industrial Revolution. Notice the smoke obscuring the sun; the train on the viaduct; and the closely packed buildings.

This meal generally consists of tea or coffee, with a little bread ... The operatives return to the mills and workshops until twelve o'clock, when an hour is allowed for dinner. Amongst those who obtain the lowest rates of wages this meal generally consists of boiled potatoes ... melted lard and butter are poured upon them, and a few pieces of fried bacon are sometimes mingled with them. At the expiration of the hour, they are all again employed in the workshops or mills, where they continue until seven o'clock or a later hour, when they generally again indulge in the use of tea, often mingled with spirits accompanied by a little bread. Oatmeal or potatoes are however taken by some.'

41

In many factories workers were fined very heavily for breaking any of the stern rules.

Wages varied between nine and twelve shillings a week (that is 45 to 60p)! Average spending for a small family might be something like £3 per week.

So it is clear that everyone, even children, had to work. The excessive hours meant that they were in a state of sleepy exhaustion most of the time. One report in 1833 described how 'I have seen them fall asleep and they have been performing their work with their hands while they were asleep'. It is not surprising that accidents were common. Here is an extract from an enquiry made in 1832:

'Questioner: "Had any of them [i.e. children] an accident in consequence of this labour?"
Father: "Yes, my eldest daughter when she went first there ... the cog caught her forefinger nail and screwed it off below the knuckle, and she was five weeks in Leeds Infirmary."
Questioner: "Were her wages paid during that time?"
Father: "As soon as the accident happened the wages were totally stopped".'

Working conditions in many factories were indeed both dangerous and unpleasant. Moving parts of machinery had no protective guards or fences. Small children were employed to crawl around the moving machinery to clean. Factories were often dirty, badly ventilated, and with low roofs. It was rare to find somewhere to wash, despite the dirt and heat (often almost 30°C in cloth factories). Indeed, in one factory in the 1820s on a list of fines, there was a deduction of 1/- (5p) for any worker found washing in factory hours!

Housing

Because working hours were so long there was not much time left for travelling to and from the factory. As a result houses were built nearby so the working families could walk to work. But the houses were cramped and crowded.

Here is a description of one of the slum houses. The town is Stockton and the report was written in 1842:

'Shepherd's Buildings consist of two rows of houses [forty-four in all, each of two rooms, with twenty-two cellars used as separate dwellings] with a street seven yards wide between them ... There are no yards or out-conveniences: the privies [lavatories] are in the centre of each row, about a yard wide: over them is part of a sleeping-room ... in the centre [of the street] is the common gutter, or more properly sink, into which all sorts of refuse are thrown: it is a foot in depth. Thus there is always a quantity of putrifying matter contaminating the air.'

Conditions in some places were even worse than that! Engels, the friend of Karl Marx (see page 66), described a place where 'privies are so rare ... that they are either filled up everyday or are too remote for most of the inhabitants to use them'; human excrement oozed about the stinking alleys.

The factory areas of industrial towns were grim, poor and harsh to live in. Tall factory chimneys belched evil smoke and the streets were filthy. Here is a description written in 1845 of such a scene, taken from Disraeli's novel *Sybil*:

'There were no public buildings of any sort; no churches, chapels, town-halls, institutes, theatre; and the principal streets in the heart of the town in which were situate [to be found] the coarse and grimy shops ... were equally narrow and if possible more dirty [than the slum area].'

Poverty and unemployment

Some working-class families in the early nineteenth century existed on the very verge of starvation. Here is an eye-witness account of conditions in Colne in Lancashire in 1842:

'I visited 88 dwellings, selected at hazard. They were destitute of furniture save old boxes for tables or stools, or even large stones for chairs; the beds were composed of straw and shavings.'

At nearby Accrington he discovered that a number of people ate only on alternate days and kept themselves alive by boiling nettles. Many of those who suffered most were handloom weavers, whose skills were no longer wanted when power-looms were installed in the factories.

Several groups of people experienced hunger and felt that their livelihood was being threatened at least partly by the introduction of labour-saving machinery. As a result, there were three main out-bursts of violence in the first half of the nineteenth century involving the smash-ing of machines.

1   'Luddism', 1811–17. The Luddites named themselves after a legendary and mysterious figure, Ned Ludd. Many of those involved worked in the hosiery industry of the north midlands.

2   'Captain Swing' Riots, 1830–32. Agricultural workers in south-east England claimed to follow the equally mysterious Captain Swing. They smashed agricultural machinery.

3   'Plug Riots', 1842. Attacks on steam-powered machines in the north of England (see page 77).

From Tudor times each parish was made responsible for looking after its poor. Workhouses were built for those who could not make ends meet. However, by the early nineteenth century many people were receiving poor relief without having to live and work in the workhouses.

In 1834 the government stopped this arrangement by a new law called the Poor Law Amendment Act. Anyone wanting assistance had to enter the workhouse, where conditions were made deliberately harsh. The aim was to dissuade 'the idle and the dissolute' from applying. Once in

Conditions in slum houses like these were appalling; often very damp and crowded. It was common for people to sleep three or four to a small bed.

Handloom weavers: employment. Handloom weavers could not compete with the factories. You can see from this graph that the numbers employed declined rapidly 1830–60.

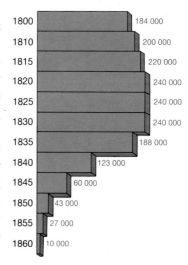

Year	Employed
1800	184 000
1810	200 000
1815	220 000
1820	240 000
1825	240 000
1830	240 000
1835	188 000
1840	123 000
1845	60 000
1850	43 000
1855	27 000
1860	10 000

the workhouse husbands and wives were separated; inmates could not receive visitors or go out without written permission; and it was intended that the administrator should be 'the hardest taskmaster and the worst paymaster'. The trouble was, many honest workers, like the handloom weavers, wanted nothing more than employment for a decent wage. And so the workhouses became hated as utterly unjust.

As a result of the Industrial Revolution many engineers, factory-owners and businessmen became rich – there is no doubt about that. But historians have argued about whether the working-class were better off before or after the Industrial Revolution. After all there was a great deal of poverty before the Industrial Revolution. The main difference lay more in unemployment. Before the Industrial Revolution people could usually earn something, even in the most difficult times, or at least grow some vegetables.

But, after the Industrial Revolution when the workers in a factory town were thrown out of work, there was little hope of any income. They could not help themselves; they were dependent on the employers. □

1 Find out about the effects of the Industrial Revolution where you live. Make lists of what you can still see (e.g. a factory, a railway). And, if you can find a history of your town or village, look up information about what it was like in about 1700. Make a list of the changes you think have been caused by the Industrial Revolution.

2 Study the maps on page 40 and the graph on page 41. What can you learn from them about coal production in England from 1720 to 1870?

3 The date is 1860, you are forty years old. Write an account of a typical day when you worked in a cotton-mill at the age of ten.

4 Write a conversation between a handloom weaver and his wife in 1840 on whether they should enter the workhouse or not.

The workhouses were so hated that they were called 'Bastilles (page 45). This drawing appeared in the *Illustrated London News* in 1842. It shows an angry crowd attacking the workhouse at Stockport. They are taking bread from the stores because they are hungry.

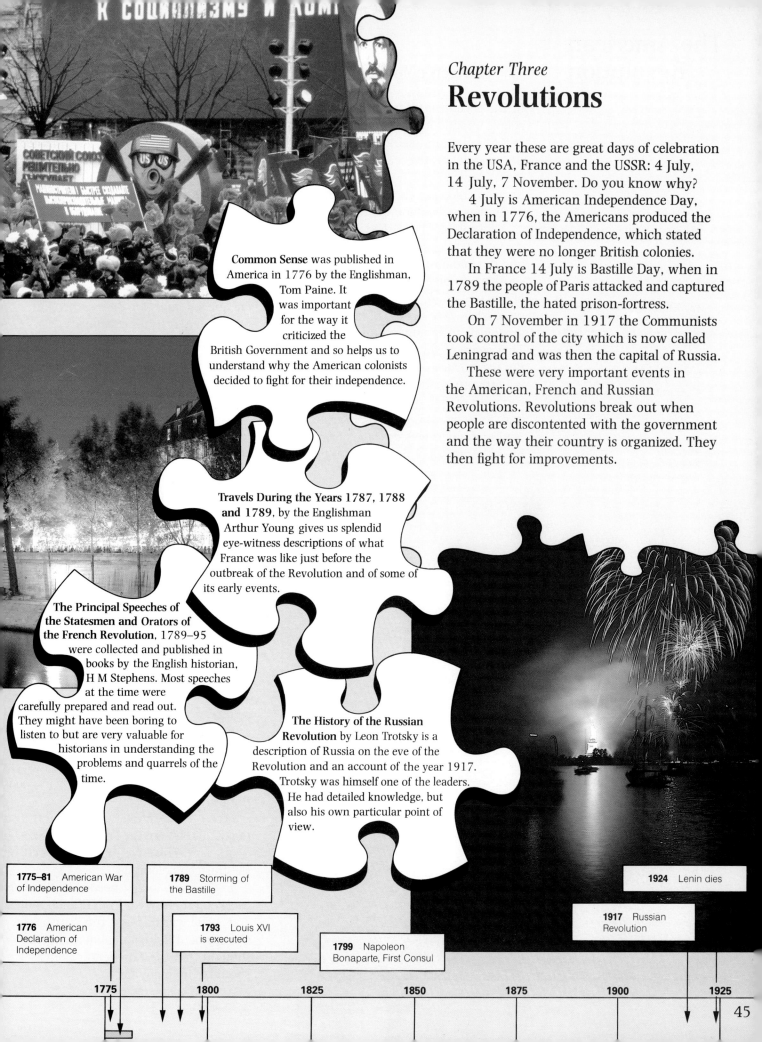

Chapter Three
Revolutions

Every year these are great days of celebration in the USA, France and the USSR: 4 July, 14 July, 7 November. Do you know why?

4 July is American Independence Day, when in 1776, the Americans produced the Declaration of Independence, which stated that they were no longer British colonies.

In France 14 July is Bastille Day, when in 1789 the people of Paris attacked and captured the Bastille, the hated prison-fortress.

On 7 November in 1917 the Communists took control of the city which is now called Leningrad and was then the capital of Russia.

These were very important events in the American, French and Russian Revolutions. Revolutions break out when people are discontented with the government and the way their country is organized. They then fight for improvements.

Common Sense was published in America in 1776 by the Englishman, Tom Paine. It was important for the way it criticized the British Government and so helps us to understand why the American colonists decided to fight for their independence.

Travels During the Years 1787, 1788 and 1789, by the Englishman Arthur Young gives us splendid eye-witness descriptions of what France was like just before the outbreak of the Revolution and of some of its early events.

The Principal Speeches of the Statesmen and Orators of the French Revolution, 1789–95 were collected and published in books by the English historian, H M Stephens. Most speeches at the time were carefully prepared and read out. They might have been boring to listen to but are very valuable for historians in understanding the problems and quarrels of the time.

The History of the Russian Revolution by Leon Trotsky is a description of Russia on the eve of the Revolution and an account of the year 1917. Trotsky was himself one of the leaders. He had detailed knowledge, but also his own particular point of view.

1775–81 American War of Independence

1789 Storming of the Bastille

1924 Lenin dies

1776 American Declaration of Independence

1793 Louis XVI is executed

1917 Russian Revolution

1799 Napoleon Bonaparte, First Consul

1775 **1800** **1825** **1850** **1875** **1900** **1925**

45

The American Revolution

The thirteen colonies

In the seventeenth century a number of people, mainly from Britain, sailed across the Atlantic, and settled in America. By the middle of the eighteenth century, these settlements were organized into thirteen colonies. The total population in 1776 was 2·5 million.

The colonies flourished. The northern colonies developed ship-building and trading; the middle colonies, farming; and the southern colonies, tobacco and rice plantations (see map). The American colonists were also very proud of the way they arranged their government and laws. They were meant to be ruled by Britain. But the journey across the Atlantic took so long that the colonies had to be allowed to run most of their own affairs. Each colony had its own assembly (or parliament). And in many towns decisions were made by gathering all of the citizens together.

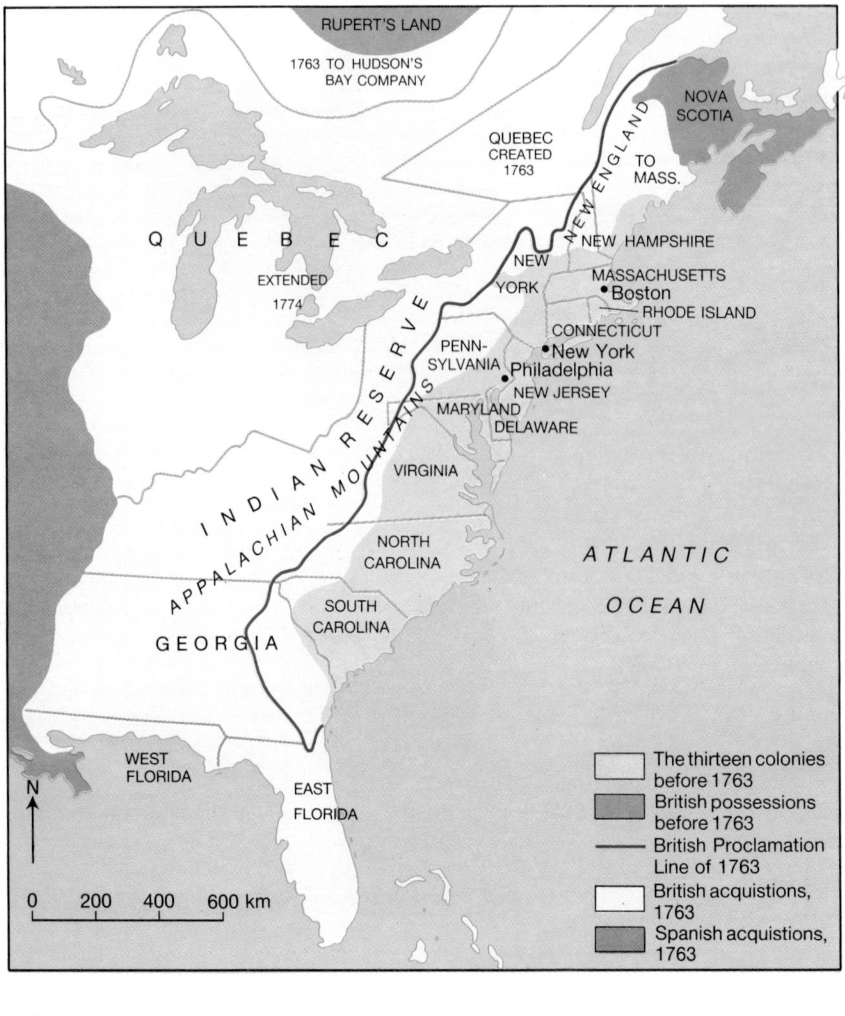

The quarrel with Britain

Thomas Jefferson, one of the most brilliant of the American colonists, and later President of the USA, wrote a pamphlet in 1774 in which he summed up what many in America were thinking: that they had a right to live their own lives. He wrote:

'America was conquered, and her settlements made and firmly established, at the expense of individuals, and not of the British public. Their own blood was spilt in acquiring lands for their settlement, their own fortunes expended [spent] in making that settlement effectual [successful]. For themselves they fought, for themselves they conquered, and for themselves they have a right to hold.'

As the colonists became stronger and more prosperous they became more self-confident. A letter written by a farmer in 1764 ends with the following words:

'For my part I am resolved to contend [fight] for the liberty delivered down to me by my ancestors; but whether I shall do it effectually or not, depends on you, my countrymen. "How little soever one is able to write, yet when the liberties of one's country are threatened, it is still more difficult to be silent."'

They became irritated that they were 'bossed about' by the British Government. Then, in the middle of the eighteenth century the British Government tried to tighten its control. It sent out governors to each of the colonies to overrule the assemblies. It tried to force the colonists to trade only with Britain and only in goods the British wanted.

We saw in Chapter 1 how the British took Canada from the French in the Seven Years War. This had important effects on the thirteen colonies:

1   They no longer needed British help to defend themselves from French attack.

2   The war had cost the British Government a great deal of money. It thought that the American colonists should help to pay for it.

The thirteen colonies. Notice that they vary a great deal in size. The present capital city of Washington was built later, named after the famous first President of the USA. The main towns at the time of the Revolution are marked. The Proclamation Line was announced by the British Government in 1763. It forbade the colonists from acquiring any more land to the west of the Appalachian mountains for fear of angering the Indians. Instead, the Proclamation angered the American colonists.

RUPERT'S LAND
1763 TO HUDSON'S BAY COMPANY
NOVA SCOTIA
QUEBEC CREATED 1763
TO MASS.
NEW ENGLAND
QUEBEC
EXTENDED 1774
NEW HAMPSHIRE
NEW YORK
MASSACHUSETTS
• Boston
RHODE ISLAND
CONNECTICUT
PENN-SYLVANIA
• New York
• Philadelphia
NEW JERSEY
MARYLAND
DELAWARE
INDIAN RESERVE
APPALACHIAN MOUNTAINS
VIRGINIA
NORTH CAROLINA
ATLANTIC OCEAN
SOUTH CAROLINA
GEORGIA
WEST FLORIDA
EAST FLORIDA
N
0   200   400   600 km

The thirteen colonies before 1763
British possessions before 1763
British Proclamation Line of 1763
British acquistions, 1763
Spanish acquistions, 1763

The Seven Years War ended in 1763. During the next few years the British Government kept on introducing new taxes. Each new tax roused the Americans to fury. The cry went up, 'No taxation without representation'. In other words, why should the Americans pay taxes imposed by a parliament in London where there were no American MPs? There were angry demonstrations, particularly in New England and British troops were sent to keep order. In 1770 British soldiers opened fire on some Boston townsfolk who had taunted and jostled them. Five Bostonians were killed. News of the 'Boston Massacre' angered the Americans even more.

In the same year the British Government decided to abolish all the unpopular taxes – except the tax on tea. But by now the colonists were too angry to be satisfied by this. In December 1773 three tea-ships put in to Boston harbour. Many townspeople, disguised as Indians, clambered on to the ships.

This cartoon shows the main actions taken by the British which particularly angered the American colonists and so led directly to protests, demonstrations, and then to the outbreak of fighting. Proclamation Act: see map. Stamp Act and Townshend Duties: taxes. Declaratory Act: Stamp Act (taxes on legal documents and newspapers) was abolished but the British Government declared their right to impose taxes. Boston Massacre and Tea Party: described in text. Intolerable Acts: to punish Massachusetts, included closing the port of Boston.

This is how the mate of the *Dartmouth*, one of the three ships, described what he saw:

'Between six and seven o'clock this evening came down to the wharf [*dock*] a body of about *one thousand people*. Among them were a number *dressed and whooping like Indians*. They came on board the ship, ... and they unlaid [*opened*] the hatches and went down the hold, where was eighty whole and thirty-four half chests of Tea, which they hoisted upon deck, and cut the chests to pieces, and hove [*threw*] the Tea all overboard, where it was damaged and lost.'

This 'Boston Tea Party' was an important act of defiance. The Americans would *not* drink tea whose price included a tax. The British Government hit back: the port of Boston was closed and public meetings in the town were forbidden.

In 1767 and 1773 the British Parliament passed Tea Acts. These gave great trading advantages to the East India Company, yet the American colonies still had to pay a tax on tea. This picture shows ladies in North Carolina writing out a pledge not to drink tea. *'We, the ladies of Edenton, do solemnly engage not to conform to the pernicious custom of drinking tea.'* The most famous event in the protest campaign was the 'Boston Tea Party' when chests of tea, valued at that time at £18,000, were destroyed.

The outbreak of war

This was too much for the Americans. Representatives from twelve of the thirteen colonies met at Philadelphia to organize protest and resistance against the British. This meeting was called a 'Continental Congress'.

The situation was tense. In April 1774 General Gage, Governor of Massachusetts, sent troops to take control of a depot of arms and ammunition at Concord (see map, page 51). This was to prevent the colonists from taking weapons. A man called Paul Revere galloped round the countryside warning that British troops were on the march. Some local farmers formed up with their muskets on the village green at Lexington to meet the British troops on the morning of 19 April. Firing started and fighting lasted throughout the day as the British 'redcoat' soldiers pushed on to Concord. As an American poet, Emerson, wrote much later:

'Here once the embattled farmers stood,
And fired the shot heard round the world.'

The American War of Independence had started. It was also to become, for the colonists, the American Revolution.

The Declaration of Independence

The war started as a struggle by the Americans for fairer treatment from the British Government. On their side, the British Government of George III and his ministers thought that the Americans were being unreasonable. Some Americans soon came to believe that there could never be agreement – the colonies had to break free of all British control.

Many colonists wished at first to be loyal to Britain. But some were won over to the idea of independence by a pamphlet called *Common Sense*. It was published in January 1776, and during that year it is estimated that $\frac{1}{2}$ million copies were sold! It was written by Tom Paine. Paine was born in England, where he earned a living

The Declaration of Independence was drawn up by a small committee. This picture was painted about fifteen years after the event, by a former officer in the Revolutionary army called John Trumbull. After the war he set about commemorating some of the main events in paintings. This painting shows the committee presenting their document to the full Continental Congress (representatives from the colonies). Of the five members, Thomas Jefferson was the most important. He is shown fourth from the left. Standing next to him at the end is Benjamin Franklin. Franklin was a scientist as well as a politician. He invented lightning conductors. During the War of Independence he was the Ambassador for the Americans in Paris. He persuaded France to help, eventually by declaring war on Britain.

first as a maker of ladies' underwear, then as a customs official. But he was much more interested in politics. In 1774, at the age of 37, he decided to emigrate to America, where he wrote his popular pamphlet and as a result earned the title 'Godfather of America'.

Meanwhile the Continental Congress was meeting again in Philadelphia. After emotional discussions, it was decided to make a formal statement of independence. It was composed mainly by a brilliant young man called Thomas Jefferson. It is known as 'The Declaration of Independence'. It is written in rather difficult language. However, it is so important that we must quote some parts.

It starts by declaring 'that all men are created equal' and that 'their Creator' has given them the 'Rights' of 'Life, Liberty and the Pursuit of Happiness'. It goes on to state that if any government tries to take away these rights, 'it is the Right of the People to alter or abolish it'. The Declaration claims that the aim of 'the present King of Great Britain' has been 'the establishment of an absolute Tyranny over' the colonies. There follows a list of the ways in which the British Government treated the Americans as if they were not

equals and deprived them of life, liberty and happiness. It concludes by declaring 'That these United Colonies are, and of a Right ought to be Free and Independent States'. The Declaration was announced by the ringing of the famous Liberty Bell, which can still be seen in Philadelphia.

Thomas Jefferson was probably the most remarkable of the 'Founding Fathers' of the USA. Like George Washington, he came from Virginia. He wrote most of the Declaration of Independence and became an active politician. He was the third President (1801–9). He was a great believer in democracy; he believed that the ordinary people knew what was best. In 1787 he wrote in a letter:

'I have no fear but that the result of our experiment will be that men may be trusted to govern themselves without a master. Could the contrary of this be proved, I should conclude, either that there is no God, or that he is a malevolent [evil] being.'

Jefferson was also a very able scientist and architect.

The fighting

The war lasted for six years from 1775 to 1781 and became quite complicated, involving other countries as well as Britain and the American colonies.

The man appointed to be commander of the American army was George Washington. But first he had to form an army, which would be far from easy:

1 the colonies did not have uniforms, weapons or money;

2 the motley bands of men who joined him did not have proper military training;

3 the men had great distances to travel to join the army: the colonies covered 800,000 square miles (sixteen times the size of England).

A writer described the army with which Washington vainly tried to defend Philadelphia in 1777 as 'ragged, lousy, naked regiments'. But the Americans did become good at what we today call 'guerrilla warfare'; they used speed and knowledge of the country to outwit their enemy. By contrast, the British army and commanders were slow and blundering.

This is how one famous American historian has described the two sides.

'The British could beat or scatter the Americans in battle but could not round them up wholesale or prevent their gathering again quickly to renew the struggle. They could make marauding [*destructive*] expeditions into the back regions of South Carolina, North Carolina, and Virginia, but they could not occupy those regions and hold them in subjection [*under complete control*] against the bands of American troops skilled in guerrilla warfare.'

In the first year of the war the British General Howe missed a splendid opportunity of a decisive victory in New England. Washington wrote: 'All winter we were at their mercy'. But Howe allowed Washington's army to retreat intact.

Still the Americans suffered many defeats. And Washington's ragged army suffered dreadfully in its primitive camp in

This cartoon from the *Westminster Magazine* appeared in 1775. It shows King George III being driven by Pride and Obstinacy over the edge of a chasm. In the background America burns. Many in Britain believed that the king and his advisers were misgoverning the country and in particular were mishandling the American crisis. These critics included the great Elder Pitt, Earl of Chatham, who had won Canada for Britain (see Chapter 1). He is shown on the extreme right, hobbling on crutches because of his severe gout. He made several speeches in the House of Lords. During his last he collapsed, and he died a few weeks later.

The Spirit of '76. This is a famous picture painted a century after the Declaration of Independence. Notice the look of heroic determination on the face of the central figure, and the wounded man in the corner saluting the marchers. Those who enthusiastically supported independence were called 'Sons of Liberty'.

During 1776–77 Washington was forced to retreat southwards, abandoning the cities of New York and Philadelphia to the British general, Howe. Washington set up winter quarters for 1777–78 in the valley of the river Delaware, called Valley Forge. This picture shows them there. Starving and freezing, his men were close to mutiny.

the winter of 1777–78 in Valley Forge. Many, in despair, deserted.

But meanwhile, the British made another mistake which gave the colonists a vitally important victory. The British General Burgoyne collected in Canada a large army of British and German soldiers (mercenaries, hired for the purpose) and Indian warriors. He started to march south. General Howe should have marched north from New York to meet him. He did not. American troops under General Gates caught Burgoyne's army in the forests and forced them to surrender at Saratoga.

The main battles. After the skirmishes at Lexington and Concord, American troops besieged Boston. This led to the first main battle of the war. The Americans occupied Bunker Hill overlooking Boston. The British general, Gage, ordered his men to capture it. The British redcoats slowly marched up the hill in beautiful parade-ground order. The Americans shot them. The British re-formed and advanced again. The British eventually took the hill but lost 1,054 men compared to the Americans' 441. The British tactics were wrong for fighting a 'guerrilla' war, but they never fully learned the lesson. The map also shows how Washington had to retreat in 1776–77 (during which time there were several other battles). Notice too the route taken by Burgoyne from Canada.

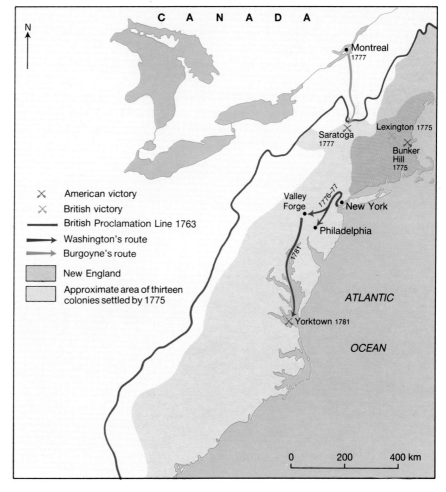

Saratoga was a great blow to British pride. But more than that. Britain's old enemy, France (and later, Spain and Holland), now agreed to join in the war to help the Americans. The French supplied money and soldiers and their navy made it increasingly difficult for the British to supply their armies across the Atlantic.

The British now tried to take control of the southern colonies. In his home state of Virginia, Washington trapped a British army under General Cornwallis at Yorktown at the end of a long peninsula. And there were no British ships available to rescue them. Cornwallis surrendered on 19 October 1781.

George Washington was the great hero of the American Revolution. He was born in 1732 in the colony of Virginia, where his great-grandfather had first settled 79 years before. George farmed the estate at Mount Vernon and became a Colonel in the army. He became Commander-in-Chief of the American army and the first President of the USA (1789–97). He created a successful, disciplined and trained army from the volunteers who joined him. Myths grew up about Washington which made him seem super-human. One story was about him chopping down his father's favourite cherry-tree. Although afraid of his father's anger, he confessed to what he had done, adding, 'Father, I cannot tell a lie, I did it with my little hatchet.' Historians have tried to discover what the real Washington was like. He was not in reality such a paragon of virtue: he gambled, swore, drank and lost his temper!

This picture shows Washington at Yorktown. With the help of the French he forced the British army to surrender there. He is shown in the centre of this painting shaking hands with the young French Commander, the Marquis de Lafayette.

Britain admits defeat

At the surrender ceremony at Yorktown Cornwallis ordered the British band to play mournful music. In particular he asked for an old nursery rhyme called *The World Turned Upside Down*. Some of the lines are as follows:

'If buttercups buzz
after the bee;
If boats were on land,
churches on sea;

If summer were spring
and the other way round
Then all the world would be upside down.'

If a collection of American colonists could defeat the British, the world *must* be upside down!

The British Prime Minister, Lord North, realized that the Americans had won. He resigned. In 1783 a peace treaty was signed in which Britain officially recognized American independence.

Many people in Britain believed that the thirteen colonies had been 'lost' because of incompetence. The army had been incompetent in not defeating Washington at the beginning; and the Government had been incompetent in even allowing the quarrel to break out into war at all. Some Americans wished to be loyal to Britain. Many of these loyalists even fought on the British side, and after the war many fled to Canada and Britain.

The loyalists were unpopular with their fellow American colonists and many suffered insults and injury. For example, the famous English writer, Leigh Hunt, described the experiences of his father, a Philadelphia lawyer:

'Early one morning a great concourse [crowd] of people appeared before his house ... They put him into a cart ... and, after parading him about the streets, were joined by revolutionary soldiers with drums and fife ... My father ... had a narrow escape from tarring and feathering ... [He bribed the guard and escaped;] he went first t

Barbados [*in the West Indies*], and afterwards to England, where he settled.'

On the other hand, most Americans believed that the British had lost all claims to loyalty by their actions. Before the war started, they thought the British were unfair. During the war, they were outraged by the savage brutality of the British troops, (especially those from the German state of Hesse). This point is made in the Declaration of Independence in connection with loss of life. King George III is accused of 'transporting large armies of foreign mercenaries to compleat the works of death, desolation and tyranny, already begun'. The strength of feeling once the war had started, is illustrated in this comment by a British writer in South Carolina:

'Even in their dresses the females seem to bid us defiance; . . . they . . . take care to have in their breast knots, and even on their shoes something that resembles their flag of the thirteen stripes. An officer told Lord Cornwallis not long ago, that he believed that if he had destroyed all the men in North America, we should have enough to do to conquer the women.'

However, most modern historians believe that the American colonies were bound to demand their independence whatever policies the British Government used. They had become too developed and prosperous – too 'grown up' to be kept under the control of Britain.

The American Constitution

The thirteen colonies had successfully rebelled against the Government of Britain, but they had no real government of their own. In 1781 Articles of Confederation were signed to try to bring the thirteen States together to a certain extent. But in practice they all remained independent of each other. After the war the problems became very clear. Each State had its own army, some even had

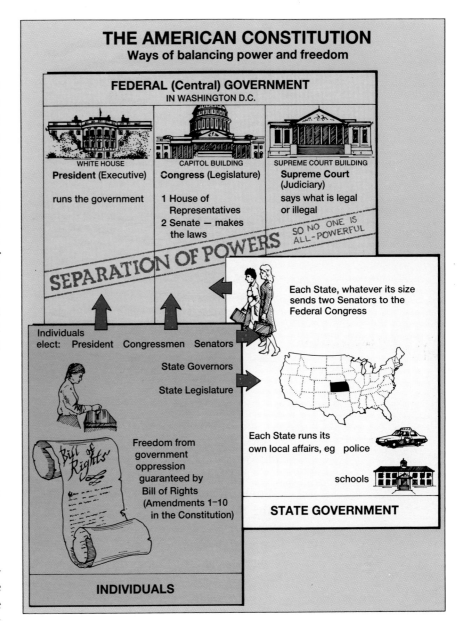

THE AMERICAN CONSTITUTION
Ways of balancing power and freedom

FEDERAL (Central) GOVERNMENT
IN WASHINGTON D.C.

WHITE HOUSE
President (Executive)
runs the government

CAPITOL BUILDING
Congress (Legislature)
1 House of Representatives
2 Senate — makes the laws

SUPREME COURT BUILDING
Supreme Court (Judiciary)
says what is legal or illegal

SEPARATION OF POWERS — SO NO ONE IS ALL-POWERFUL

Individuals elect: President Congressmen Senators
State Governors
State Legislature

Freedom from government oppression guaranteed by **Bill of Rights** (Amendments 1–10 in the Constitution)

Each State, whatever its size sends two Senators to the Federal Congress

Each State runs its own local affairs, eg police
schools

STATE GOVERNMENT

INDIVIDUALS

The American Constitution: how the US system of government works.

their own little navies. There was no common currency. Pairs of neighbouring States quarrelled over their frontiers. It was obvious that some form of central government was needed.

In May 1787 representatives from twelve of the States met at Philadelphia to draw up a 'Constitution' (that is, rules for government) for the whole country. George Washington, who represented Virginia, was chosen to preside over the gathering. Two particular problems faced this Convention, as it was called:

1   How could they make sure that the big states would not control the new central government at the expense of the small ones?

US flags in 1777 (*above*) and today (*below*).

2 How could they balance the powers of the central government with those of the individual States?

By September the Constitution was finally written. It was then presented to the thirteen States for their approval. A great debate then developed. Some people argued that the central or federal government, which the Constitution proposed to set up, would be dangerous – it would destroy the freedom of the States. Eventually it was agreed that amendments should be added, listing all the freedoms that should be preserved. This collection of ten amendments came to be called the 'Bill of Rights'. The new system of government came into being in 1789. On 30 April in a great ceremony in New York the first President of the USA took the oath of office. He was George Washington (see page 52).

Was it really a Revolution?

The Americans had won independence from Britain. But were the changes enough to call them a 'Revolution'? For example, there were still many poor people in America and there were still slaves, especially on the southern plantations. But even so, the separation from Britain was used as an opportunity to introduce many reforms (changes).

Some states now allowed more people to vote in elections. The property of the loyalists, many of whom were wealthy, was taken by other people. Class differences between people steadily became less. The freedom of people to worship as they pleased was proclaimed. In particular, the listing of rights and freedoms in the Declaration of Independence and the Bill of Rights was a very important step – and not just for the Americans. The idea that people could live in equality and freedom was exciting for people in other countries too, especially in Europe where these rights were not enjoyed. Thousands of Frenchmen fought in America: many were present at Yorktown. They helped Americans to enjoy rights which they did not have in their own home country. These comparisons helped prepare the way for the next major revolution, this time in France. Only two and a half months after Washington became the first President of the USA, the people of Paris stormed the Bastille. The French Revolution had begun. ☐

1 Compare the 1777 and present-day American flags (above).
a) Why are there a different number of stars on the two flags?
b) How many stripes are there? What do they represent?

2 Imagine you are a citizen of Boston, living there in 1774. Write a letter to the Governor of Massachusetts setting out all your complaints.

3 Pictures can be drawn or painted for propaganda, that is to give a point of view rather than the complete truth. Study the pictures on page 50 and explain what messages each of the artists was giving.

4 Imagine you are a British MP. Write a speech to give in the House of Commons in 1783 to defend the Government's handling of American colonies since 1763.

The French Revolution

Life before the Revolution

During the years 1787, 1788 and 1789 an Englishman named Arthur Young travelled widely throughout France. He knew a lot about agriculture and was very interested to see everything wherever he went. What is more he wrote a detailed account of his journeys. This is what he had to say about the poorest people living in the province of Brittany:

'The people almost as wild as their country, and their town of Combourg one of the most brutal, filthy places that can be seen; mud houses, no windows, and a pavement so broken as to impede all passengers ... The poor people seem poor indeed; the children terribly ragged, if possible, worse clad than if with no clothes at all; as to shoes and stockings, they are luxuries.'

In contrast the royal family and the rich nobles lived lives of almost unbelievable luxury. It is difficult to compare eighteenth-century money with today's. The basic unit was the livre. An ordinary farm labourer would earn about 30 livres per year. A wealthy lady would often spend 1,500 livres for a ball-gown. And Queen Marie Antoinette spent 150,000 livres having some gardens changed in style!

Although the *gap* between the richest and the poorest was big, the *division* of wealth was not that clear cut. There were great variations in wealth among the various groups of people: the clergy,

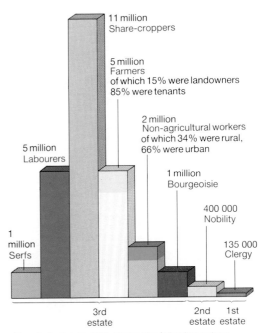

French Society in 1789. Notice the following points:
   1 The privileged classes numbered only just over half-a-million, or about 2 per cent of the population.
   2 The great majority of the population lived and worked in the countryside – over 80 per cent.
   3 The largest group were share-croppers; peasants who rented their land and often their tools from the landowner paying a proportion of their crop to him.

nobles, merchants, craftsmen, peasants. There were poor nobles and rich peasants, for example! But this sort of variation is not really surprising when you think what a large population France had: at the end of the eighteenth century France had 26 million people, compared with Britain's 9 million.

French Government

France was governed by the king, who claimed that he had complete power to rule because his power was given to him by God. This belief was called 'the Divine Right of Kings'. From 1774 to 1792 the King was Louis XVI. He was advised by a Council of Ministers, who looked after the various parts of government (such as foreign affairs and taxation).

There were also 'parlements' (important not to translate this word as 'parliament'). There was a parlement in Paris for the whole of central France and there were parlements for each of the provinces (e.g. Normandy, Brittany). They were really law courts. But, in addition, they had the responsibility of registering royal

This print is of *The Three Estates* and is in the French National Library. It condemns the social system before the Revolution. Legally the country was divided into three groups called 'Estates'. The first was the clergy, the second was the nobility, and the third was all the rest. The first and second Estates had many privileges. As a result, the others, especially the millions of poor peasants, suffered. For example, the landowner considered he owned all the wild animals and birds on his land. The peasant could not even protect his crops from being eaten by birds or rabbits, as shown in this print.

Many were charmed by Marie Antoinette, especially when she first arrived in France in 1770, aged 15, to marry Louis, then heir to the throne. One of the most famous books on the French Revolution was written in 1789–90 by a British MP called Edmund Burke. In a famous passage he wrote, 'I thought ten thousand swords must have leaped from their scabbards to avenge even a look that threatened her with insult. – But the age of chivalry is gone.'

In fact she was empty-headed, interested in frivolous pastimes and court gossip. She became hated because she was an Austrian (a country which had been an enemy of France for centuries). One story, almost certainly untrue, relates her reply when she heard that the people were hungry: 'They have no bread? Then let them eat cake!'. This portrait, by Louise-Elizabeth Vigée-Lebrun, shows Marie Antoinette with her three children. The elder boy died after a long illness in 1789; the younger boy died six years later of tuberculosis caused by his atrocious treatment in prison. Only the girl survived the Revolution. Marie Antoinette was herself executed during the Terror.

decrees. They could refuse to do this and so defy the king if they wished.

One of the most important, difficult and unpopular tasks of government, then as now, was increasing taxes. The French Government had three main sources of income:

1 Various personal taxes on an individual's wealth.
2 Customs duties on goods imported into the country.
3 Internal taxes. For example, there was a tax on salt, very important as a preservative in days before refrigeration. But different provinces imposed different amounts of tax!

Criticism and discontent

During the eighteenth century many people became very discontented. There were several reasons for this. One was that many of the wealthiest people – the nobles – did not have to pay taxes. Queen Marie Antoinette was unpopular and Louis XVI was an incompetent king. The parlements felt that they should have more power. Many of the successful and wealthy businessmen and merchants resented the privileges and airs and graces of the nobles. The poorer peasants and town-workers had to pay taxes while the nobility did not. They suffered hardship when bad harvests led to an increase in the price of bread, their main food.

A number of remarkable writers expressed the rising discontent in their books. Criticism of the government and the unfair class system became increasingly bitter as the century wore on. The ideas of the writers were eagerly discussed, especially in Paris and other cities. And many people were excited by the ideas about liberty and equality which the American Revolution had encouraged.

A play called *The Marriage of Figaro* (later made into an opera by Mozart) was written by a man called Beaumarchais. It

This is a rather flattering official portrait of King Louis XVI. He was a simple man who could not cope with the crisis of the Revolution. The Emperor of Austria described him as 'rather feeble, though not an imbecile'! His main interests were making keys and locks, hunting and eating; he had a vast appetite! He believed that he was king by Divine Right and that it was his duty to God to keep his royal power.

A Salon. During the eighteenth century it became popular for the educated people in towns to meet to discuss the new ideas about reforming society. These meetings were called Salons. This picture shows a Salon arranged by Mme Geoffrin in 1755. The person marked is Jean-Jacques Rousseau. He wrote a book in which he declared, 'Man is born free, and everywhere he is in chains.' He died before the Revolution but was considered a hero by the revolutionaries. However, before the Revolution, Voltaire was much more famous. Indeed, he was so critical of the Church in particular that he was often in trouble. His fame is indicated in this painting: it is his bust which seems to preside over the meeting from its pedestal.

was he who had persuaded the Government to help the American colonists in their war with Britain and organized the shipping of supplies of ammunition, guns and equipment to them. The character of Figaro is a cheeky person and in the course of the play he says of his master, a rich nobleman, 'What have *you* done to deserve such advantages? Put yourself to the trouble of being born – nothing more! For the rest – a very ordinary man!' The play opened in Paris on 27 April 1784. News leaked out that it was daring. The theatre was besieged by crowds throughout the day. It was the biggest theatrical success of the century in France.

The crisis of 1787–89

By the mid-1780s the French Government was bankrupt: it was spending more than it was collecting in taxes. The main reason for these difficulties was the huge expense of the fighting against Britain on the side of the Americans.

Ministers put forward schemes. But the real problem was that the Third Estate were paying as much as they could and the clergy and nobility refused to be taxed.

Several parlements stirred up trouble: they objected to the reform schemes and organized noisy demonstrations in the streets against the king's ministers.

A demand grew up that the problem should be tackled by the States-General. This was a kind of Parliament made up of representatives of the three Estates. But the last time it met was in 1614! However, elections were arranged. Lists of grievances were drawn up for the representatives to take with them when they eventually arrived at the States-General.

The opening was arranged for 5 May 1789 in a large building near the royal palace at Versailles, a few miles from Paris. Disagreement between the Third Estate and the rest immediately broke out. Was it going to be possible to attack privileges? The representatives of the Third Estate met on their own; called themselves the 'National Assembly'; and invited anyone from the other two Estates to join them. The situation was tense. Would they be allowed to become an effective Parliament? Would the King use force to evict them from their meeting-place? The King moved troops to the Paris area.

Many of the working-people of Paris and other towns were shopkeepers, craftsmen, apprentices. (There were very few factories as we know them today.) These were the people who went on to the streets to demonstrate in times of crisis. They were called 'sans culottes'. This was because they wore trousers and not the aristocratic knee-breeches (culottes). When groups of them demonstrated they were called 'the crowd'. These prints, which are in the French National Library, are called 'A sans-culotte and his wife'. The man is wearing a 'red cap of liberty' to show his support for the Revolution. They each wear a red, white, and blue rosette in their hats. These were the colours of the Revolution. The tricoleur, still the flag of France today, was invented by the revolutionaries: white from the old royal flag, and red and blue, the colours of Paris. Notice the weapons they are carrying.

Moderate Revolution, 1789–92

On 14 July 1789 the people of Paris brought about a dramatic change. Partly to support the National Assembly, partly in fear for their own safety, they gathered and attacked the Bastille. Louis XVI now had to decide whether to accept reforms drawn up by the National Assembly or cause bloodshed by using soldiers against the Assembly and Paris. He did what was expected: he dithered!

Another reason why the people of Paris were on edge was that the harvest of 1788 had been disastrous. By the summer of 1789 stocks of grain were low and the price of bread exceptionally high. On 10 June, Arthur Young, then in Paris, noted, 'the want of bread is terrible; accounts arrive every moment from the provinces of riots and disturbances.' Rumour had it that the Government was hoarding grain. In the countryside the fear was even more intense. People came to believe that the Government had a plan to starve the

Reforms of the French Revolution, 1789–91. Liberty and Equality were mentioned in the Declaration of Rights. The idea of Fraternity developed later.

FEUDALISM ABOLISHED

FRANCE DIVIDED INTO DEPARTMENTS WHICH STILL EXIST FOR LOCAL GOVERNMENT

FEUDAL DUES

FRANCE

LIBERTY EQUALITY FRATERNITY

FARM FOR SALE 5,000 Fr

LAND SOLD FROM THE CHURCH AND NOBLES WHO EMIGRATED IN FEAR

DECLARATION OF THE RIGHTS OF MAN AND THE CITIZEN

1791 – NEW FORM OF GOVERNMENT: THE KING HAD TO SHARE POWER WITH THE LEGISLATIVE ASSEMBLY (PARLIAMENT)

IRELAND

people into submission. Panic seized the peasants. They armed themselves for defence, then attacked châteaux in attempts to burn the hated papers listing the feudal dues (payments). For not only did the peasants have to pay taxes to the Government, they had also to make payments to their local Lord. This was a left-over from the medieval feudal system (see Book 1). The peasants were forced to work on the Lord's land and to pay a part of their own produce to the Lord.

On 5 October 1789 a crowd, many of whom were women, marched from Paris to Versailles. They went to fetch the royal family to Paris where they could keep an eye on them! The next day a bizarre procession wound its way back to Paris, where the royal family took up residence in the old Tuileries Palace.

Meanwhile the National Assembly (which also moved to Paris in October) was passing a very large number of reforms. By 1791 many changes had been made to make France a more efficient and fair country. And there had not been a great deal of bloodshed. But France would not be able to settle down and enjoy these advantages if the King did not accept a great reduction in his power. Louis would not. Instead, he planned to join Marie Antoinette's brother Leopold, the Emperor of Austria, to ask for his help. One night in June 1791 he and his family fled in disguise from the palace. But they were caught before they could cross the frontier and were escorted in disgrace back to Paris.

The Storming of the Bastille. It is sometimes said that the people of Paris attacked the Bastille, burnt it down and released all the prisoners inside. History is full of such myths and one must always read critically. Not everything you read is necessarily true:

1 You can see from this painting that the Paris crowd were considerably strengthened by soldiers and even some cannon.
2 It is hardly likely that such massive stone-work would have burned very easily! In fact it took demolition contractors months to destroy it.
3 The Governor in fact surrendered and lowered the drawbridge to allow the crowd in.
4 In the words of one historian, 'The prisoners who poured out of the dungeons of the Bastille consisted of four forgers, two lunatics, and a dissipated young nobleman.'

The fall of the Bastille was important not for what the Paris crowd achieved but rather as a great symbol that the old system was beginning to crack. And Louis XVI, typically, did not understand its importance. When told of the events that evening of the 14 July he said, 'But, that's a revolt.' 'No, Sire,' replied his informant, 'It's a revolution!'

The guillotine was used for executions, especially in Paris during the Terror. It was a more humane way of killing than the previous forms of execution. In Paris the guillotine was set up in one of the main squares of the city and the victims were taken there from the prisons in a cart. Many gathered to watch the beheadings. Some of the women took their knitting! – and became notorious as the 'tricoteuses'. Another myth of the Revolution is that all the victims were aristocrats. In fact, the majority were ordinary people.

Increased violence, 1792–94

Fears now grew again. The King could not be trusted. Would Leopold now invade France? Discussions about these problems took place in Paris in various political clubs that had sprung up since 1789. The most important and famous was the Jacobin Club.

In April 1792 war broke out between France on the one side and Austria and Prussia on the other. The French army did badly and the German armies invaded. The people of Paris feared for their safety. When the leading members of the Paris Clubs told the people that their danger was the fault of the King, they reacted with bloodthirsty violence. In August the crowd, with soldiers and artillery, attacked the Tuileries Palace and slaughtered the 600 members of the King's Guard. The royal family were put in prison.

The following month the crowd burst into prisons containing opponents of the Revolution. Over 1,000 prisoners were massacred. An eye-witness called Restif de la Bretonne, wrote this about the killing of the Princesse de Lamballe, friend of Marie Antoinette:

'Then one killer seized her, tore away her dress, and ripped open her stomach … I fainted. When I returned to my senses, I saw the bloody head. Someone told me they were going to wash it, curl it, stick it on the end of a pike, and carry it [round the streets].'

The period of really bloody revolution had begun.

In January 1793 Louis XVI was executed. Other countries, including Britain, soon declared war, horrified at the way the French Revolution was developing and fearing discontented people in their own countries would copy

In 1789 Maximilian Robespierre was a lawyer in the northern province of Arras. He was elected to the States General. But he made a bigger name for himself in Paris as a journalist and by making speeches in the Jacobin Club. From 1793 to 1794 he was the leading member of the Committee of Public Safety, which then governed France. He was always prim and proper in manner and dress and believed that it was his duty to rid France of wickedness. He earned the nickname of 'The Incorruptible' because he was never known to take a bribe. He tried to replace Christianity with the worship of a kind of vague Supreme Being. He presided over a great festival to launch this. He wore a new sky-blue coat. He was wearing this when he was arrested, as is shown in this engraving. Robespierre was blamed for making the Revolution fanatical. In fact, he was struggling conscientiously with huge problems.

the French. Many in France were also horrified. Protests against the Government in Paris led to civil war in some provinces, especially in the west.

For a year, from the summer of 1793, France was governed by a group of men called the 'Committee of Public Safety'. The most important was the Jacobin, Robespierre. Most of the others were also members of the Jacobin Club. They had huge problems: war, civil war, food shortages, inflation (i.e. decline in the value of money). They introduced conscription (compulsory military service) to try to stem the invading armies. And they introduced the 'Terror'.

The 'Terror' was an attempt to frighten the people of France into active support and defence of the Revolution. Spies denounced anyone who criticized the Government. The prisons were filled to overflowing. 'Traitors' had to be executed. And so they were. Historians have had difficulty in calculating the numbers who suffered. Probably 300,000 were arrested. In Paris alone 1,251 people were executed from March 1793 to June 1794; and from June to July 1794, 1,376. In one *month* more people were executed than in one whole year!

You can see from these Paris figures how the Terror was being horrifyingly stepped up in the summer of 1794. Many people, including leading politicians, became scared that they would be next. To put an end to the slaughter Robespierre was arrested, as you can see in the engraving. Somehow his jaw was shattered by a pistol shot. The next day, 28 July, he was taken to the guillotine. The nineteenth-century English historian, Carlyle, describes vividly how the executioner, 'Samson wrenched the coat off him; wrenched the dirty linen from his jaw: the jaw fell powerless, there burst from him a cry; hideous to hear and see … Samson's work done, there bursts forth shout on shout of applause.' The Terror was at an end.

War, 1792–99

After the first set-backs, the French army was remarkably successful and at the end of 1792 captured quite a lot of land. Then, after set-backs again in 1793, the French won the battle of Fleurus and resumed their advance in 1794. Present-day Belgium and Holland were captured.

During the years 1796–99 the most famous French General was Napoleon Bonaparte. He defeated the Austrians in a series of battles in Italy. He then sailed for Egypt, which he captured. However, his army was stranded there when the British admiral, Nelson, destroyed many of his ships in the Battle of the Nile.

Settling down, 1794–99

Life in France became more relaxed after the death of Robespierre and the Battle of Fleurus: both the Terror and the threat of invasion were at an end. But the problem still remained: how should France be governed? From 1795 to 1799 the country was governed by a Committee of Five Directors and an Assembly of Five Hundred.

However, there were still difficulties. Some people wanted the monarchy to be restored; others wanted more reforms for

The famous British Admiral, Lord Nelson, won three great naval battles: the Nile (1798), Copenhagen (1801), and Trafalgar (where he was killed, 1805). In the first of these he caught the French fleet at anchor at the mouth of the River Nile in Egypt, as this painting shows. Only four of the seventeen French warships escaped. Notice the tricoleur flags on the French ships.

'Bonaparte, the Saviour of France'. This allegorical picture shows France as the maiden being pulled to the edge of the pit by the evils of Revolution. Bonaparte saves her from destruction and turns her back to the virtuous ladies, Justice and Abundance. The propaganda is not very subtle!

revolutionary changes there also. In fact, the French Revolution was one of the most important events in modern history.

These are some of the changes which it brought about:

1 Most countries in Europe at the time had monarchs. By executing their king the French introduced the alternative system of a 'republic'. In other words, what the government does is to be decided in a democratic way by the ordinary people. The people were to be sovereign.

2 The revolutionaries also produced the idea of 'nationalism'. This is the idea that a people should be proud and united and govern their own land.

3 It was also now recognized that jobs should be done by the most able people – especially in government and the army. Appointments of aristocrats were replaced by 'careers open to talents'.

4 The Revolution also started a new era in warfare. Until this time wars were fought by relatively small professional armies. The Revolution introduced the idea of 'total war'. Men were forced by conscription to fight in the army and civilians were organized in an efficient way to make equipment and weapons for these large numbers. ☐

the benefit of the poor people. France generally was unsettled. There were constant rumours of plots. In the meantime, Bonaparte had been able to make good his escape from Egypt. On 9 November 1799 he used soldiers to drive out the Five Hundred from their meeting-place. A new government was set up of three Consuls. Bonaparte was First Consul. In practice he soon became dictator. The Revolution was at an end.

Why was the French Revolution important?

Leaving aside the military battles, the French Revolution was a much more violent affair than the American. Furthermore, as the French captured other European countries they introduced their

1 Draw up a time-chart listing in order all the dates (with their events) for the French Revolution. Do not forget to use the information with the illustrations as well as the text.

2 If you had been a working-class person in Paris during the Revolution would you have joined in the demonstrations like the attacks on the Bastille, the march to Versailles, the prison massacres, and the attack on the Tuileries? Explain your reasons.

3 Write the script of a dialogue between a Royalist and a Jacobin arguing whether it was right that Louis XVI was executed.

4 You are an American in France in August 1794. Write a letter home comparing what you have seen of the French Revolution with the American Revolution. Say whether you believe that the Revolution has been more of a benefit or a calamity for France.

5 Do you think that the artist of the picture above was a supporter of Napoleon Bonaparte or an opponent? Explain your reasons.

The Russian Revolution

Government of the Tsar

Over a century after the French Revolution a revolution broke out in Russia. And there were uncanny similarities. For example, the ruler was a weak man and his wife was hated because she came from an enemy country.

The ruler of Russia before the Revolution was called the Tsar. This title came from the Latin word 'Caesar' and means 'Emperor'. The Tsar from 1894 to 1917 was Nicholas II. He tried to rule conscientiously but he was rather weak. Also he did not understand that times were changing and that the old ways of government would no longer do. The Tsar was an autocrat, that is, he had complete control of the Government. When Nicholas came to the throne there was no parliament in Russia. If any changes were to be made the Tsar had to issue a 'Decree'.

Five years before he became Tsar, Nicholas met Alix. She was a German Princess and a grand-daughter of Victoria, the British Queen. Nicholas fell deeply in love with her. But there were doubts whether they could marry because, naturally, she was not a member of the Russian Orthodox Church. However, she eventually changed her religion, they were married, and she became the Tsarina Alexandra.

Most of the people in Russia were deeply religious. They believed that the Tsar ruled by the will of God and honoured him as 'the little father of the Russian people'. On the other hand, many believed the Government to be bad and blamed the Tsar's advisers and ministers. During the century before the Revolution in 1917 various political parties and groups were organized to try to bring about reforms. Some used violence. For example, Nicholas' grandfather, Alexander III, was killed by an assassin's bomb. The twelve-year old Nicholas watched by his grandfather's bedside as he died of his horrible wounds. The Government's reaction to these opponents was to arrest as many as possible. A large police force, called the 'Ochrana', was built up.

The family name of the Tsars was Romanov. Neither Nicholas nor Alexandra enjoyed government or court life. This picture shows the royal family in 1916. The boy in the middle is Alexis, the Tsarevich, that is, the heir to the throne. He suffered from haemophilia. This is a disease which prevents the blood from clotting. Any cut or any bruise which caused internal bleeding could therefore be extremely dangerous. He even had to be exceptionally careful when he played.

Two years after this photograph was taken all the members of the royal family were killed (see page 70). For some months they had been allowed to live in the town now called Sverdlovsk. But, in July 1918, they were taken down to the cellar of the house and shot. Their bodies were cut up, burnt, and thrown down an old mine shaft. However, there were rumours that one daughter, Anastasia, escaped. For many years afterwards several women in various countries claimed to be this princess.

How the people lived

Russia is a huge country – it is 17 per cent of the land area of the world! Many different kinds of people live there. At the beginning of the twentieth century about 80 per cent were still peasants. And many of these were very poor, using very primitive methods of cultivation. In contrast many of the aristocratic landowners were very rich, living off the rents paid by the peasants.

However, by about 1900, Russia was starting to develop heavy industries. Many factories and railways were built. More and more people started to work in industry. And because these industries were in towns, the numbers of people living in towns also increased.

Some of the town workers and their families lived in terrible conditions. By the early years of the twentieth century strikes were becoming very frequent in attempts to win improvements.

Effects of wars

In 1904 war broke out between Russia and Japan. The Russian army and navy were both defeated. This seemed to prove the incompetence of the Tsar's Government. So many demonstrations and strikes occurred in 1905 that the events of that year can be described as a Revolution.

In January a huge, peaceful crowd led by a priest, Father Gapon, went to the royal palace in St Petersburg (now Leningrad, then the capital of Russia). They wished to present a petition to the Tsar. Soldiers fired at point-blank range. Hundreds were killed, thousands wounded. It was called 'Bloody Sunday'.

In the summer the sailors of the battleship *Potemkin* (pronounced Pot-yom-kin) 'mutinied', that is, rebelled against their officers and took control of the ship. People in the port of Odessa supported them. Later a very famous film was made about these events. There are some vivid images in the film such as the sailors' food – meat which is so old and rotting that it is covered with crawling maggots!

As a result of these events the Tsar agreed to the calling of a 'Duma', a kind of parliament. But it had little power, and few reforms had been introduced when, in 1914, Russia became involved in the First World War against Germany and Austria (see Chapter 6).

Within a year the inefficiency of the Russian army was obvious. Many soldiers were being killed and those who could, were retreating rapidly. There was chaos. Ammunition was not reaching the soldiers in the front line. Food was also becoming scarce, mainly because great numbers of peasants and horses were drafted from the farms into the army. By October 1917 one general reported how serious the situation was:

'The Commander in Chief of the Western Front reports to you that, following threats by the starving population of the city and district to loot and burn down the army storehouse, the commander of the Vyazma garrison ordered seven wagons of flour to be removed from the storehouses and made available to the population ... However, the Ministry of Food evidently does not realize the seriousness of the situation at the front.'

By 1917 many army units and warships were in a state of mutiny.

Industry developed later in Russia than in some west European countries like Britain. However, by the 1880s, scenes like this one of a factory were becoming quite common. Many factories were organized in the capital, St Petersburg, and in Moscow. The combined populations of these two cities increased by two-and-a-half times from 1881 to 1917 – from 1.65 to 4.1 million. This shows how the number of people available to work in factories grew at the turn of the century.

This photograph was taken in about 1910. It shows the inside of one of the best textile factories in Russia at the time. It was at Kineshama on the River Volga, about 200 miles north-east of Moscow.

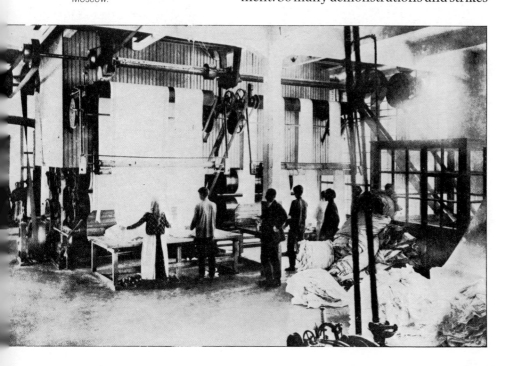

Unfortunately for the Tsar the discontent led to criticisms not just of ministers but of the royal family itself. In the summer of 1915 Nicholas took personal command of the army. He could therefore be personally blamed for the defeats. While he was away from the capital (now renamed Petrograd because 'St Petersburg' sounded too German) the Tsarina was in charge of the Government. But she came from Germany, the very country Russia was now fighting. Furthermore, Alexandra came under the spell of a strange holy man called Rasputin. Partly because of his influence she dismissed some of the most able ministers. And so the Government became even more inefficient.

Provisional Government

One of the little indications of Russian backwardness is that it was using an inaccurate calendar. As a result, Russian dates were thirteen days behind the rest of the world! In 1917 there were two revolutions. The first is called the 'February Revolution' but happened in March; the second is called the 'October Revolution' but happened in November! We shall use the correct dates here.

By March 1917 conditions in Petrograd were becoming very serious: food was in short supply and expensive; workers were striking and demonstrating in the streets; soldiers were refusing orders to disperse the crowds, even joining them. Local committees called 'soviets' were formed among workers, soldiers and sailors. It was Revolution. The President of the Duma sent a telegram to the Tsar: 'The government is absolutely powerless to suppress disorders. Nothing can be hoped from the troops of the garrison ... Officers are being killed.' Nicholas abdicated.

The Duma took control of the Government and appointed ministers. The most important was Alexander Kerensky. But in addition, representatives were elected for a soviet for the whole of Petrograd, and this came to control the capital. Soviets were also set up throughout Russia. The new group of ministers was called the Provisional Government because its main task was to draw up a constitution for a new permanent system of government. But in the meantime, it had the unenviable job of fighting the war and trying to maintain food supplies. Also, there were a number of people who wanted to set up a completely different government immediately.

Alexander Kerensky (1881–1970), head of the Provisional Government, July–November 1917.

Rasputin was one of the most bizarre characters to have had great influence in modern history. This is how one historian has described him: 'He seldom washed and he smelt vilely; at the table he plunged his greedy hands into his favourite fish soup; he was the kind of drunkard who smashes the furniture; he was blasphemous, vicious and obscene, and his lechery had a barbaric Mongolian quality that made him more like a beast than a human being.' And yet he had a great attraction to women including the Tsarina. Alexandra favoured him because he claimed to be a holy man and because he seemed to be able to ease the effects of Alexis' haemophilia. Rasputin's death was as weird as his life. By 1916 his influence on the government was so evil that a group of noblemen plotted to kill him. Prince Yusupov invited him to his house where he gave the strange holy man poisoned cakes and wine. These had no effect. So Yusupov shot him. Rasputin staggered, then attacked the nobleman. After more shots, he collapsed. He was dragged to the river and thrown in.

The Bolsheviks

The most important of these were the Bolsheviks. In the nineteenth century a German who lived much of his life in England wrote about revolutions. His name was Karl Marx. A number of Russians became interested in his ideas. They formed the Social Democratic Party, but they quarrelled and split into two. One group was called the Bolsheviks. Their leader was a man called Lenin.

The Bolsheviks devoted themselves to planning the overthrow of the Tsar and the creation of a Communist society where everyone would be equal. Naturally the Ochrana did their best to track down the Bolsheviks. Many fled from Russia. When the February Revolution took place, Lenin was in Switzerland. He was naturally very impatient to return to Russia to take control of the Revolution in order to bring about the kind of changes the Bolsheviks wanted. The Germans arranged for him to travel from Switzerland through Germany to Sweden and then to Russia. After all, if Lenin caused trouble for the Provisional Government, Russia would be thrown into even more chaos and be even less able to fight in the war. On 16 April Lenin arrived by train in Petrograd.

Bolshevik Revolution

Lenin was joined by other leading Bolsheviks. Most importantly Trotsky, who had been in exile in New York and who had previously disagreed with the Bolsheviks, returned to support Lenin.

Lenin appealed to the discontented soldiers, sailors, workers and peasants with two popular slogans:

'All Power to the Soviets';
'Bread, Peace and Freedom'.

Yet it was touch and go whether the Bolsheviks would be able to seize power. An attempt in July was a fiasco and Lenin had to go into hiding. Many other Bolshevik leaders thought that the time was not right. But Lenin was absolutely determined not to let the opportunity slip. Also Trotsky took control of the Revolutionary Military Committee, set up by the Petrograd Soviet, and organized armed Red Guards. Lenin returned to Petrograd. On the night of 6 November he wrote a letter to key Bolsheviks in which he declared:

'The situation is critical in the extreme. In fact it is now absolutely clear that to delay the uprising would be fatal ... The government is tottering. It must be *given the death-blow* at all costs.'

That same night the Red Guards started to put into effect the plan carefully prepared by Trotsky: key places, such as bridges, the telegraph station, the telephone exchange, and the railway stations were occupied. By the morning of 8 November the Winter Palace, headquarters of the Provisional Government, had been taken. The Bolsheviks were in control of the capital. Similar events took place throughout Russia. Within ten days the Bolsheviks had won.

Lenin became Prime Minister. Decrees were issued approving the peasants' seizure of land from the landowners and

Karl Marx was the founder of modern Communism. Together with his friend Engels he wrote *The Communist Manifesto*. This contains the famous words: 'Let the ruling classes tremble at a communist revolution. The proletarians have nothing to lose but their chains. They have a world to win. Working men of all countries, unite!' 'Proletarians' are the working-class people in the towns. Marx believed that they would become so discontented that they would some day, inevitably, rise up in revolution. As a result, all class differences would be abolished; Communism would be set up and be much fairer. It would follow the slogan: 'From each according to his abilities, to each according to his needs'. Marx is buried at Highgate Cemetery in London. His tomb, shown in this photograph, attracts many visitors.

This painting is based on a photograph taken in Moscow. Lenin's real name was Vladimir Ilyich Ulyanov. He adopted the name 'Lenin' when on the run from the Ochrana. He was born in 1870 in a small town on the River Volga. He studied law but soon became involved with the Social Democrat Party. His wife was a devoted helper in his revolutionary work. Both were arrested by the Ochrana. By 1900 Lenin was in Switzerland editing the party's newspaper, copies of which were smuggled into Russia. When the party split, Lenin became leader of the Bolsheviks. He also started a newspaper called *Pravda* ('Truth'). This is still the official Communist Party newspaper in Russia. Lenin was a man of great determination and will-power: determined to bring Communism to Russia. He once said, 'Soviets plus electrification equals Communism'. When he died in 1924 his embalmed body was placed in a tomb in Moscow where it is still visited by many people.

declaring Russian withdrawal from the war. Then an election was held. This had been arranged by the Provisional Government for a Constituent Assembly, that is a body to draw up a new constitution. But when it met there was a large anti-Bolshevik majority so it was disbanded. So much for democracy! But a few months later the promise of peace with Germany was honoured and the Treaty of Brest-Litovsk was signed by the two countries.

Like the storming of the Bastille in the French Revolution, the storming of the Winter Palace is thought of as the great heroic and symbolic act of the Russian Revolution. But we must beware of myths! This picture looks like a photograph taken at the time. In fact, the Palace was captured after dark, and by some sailors and Red Guards who found a back door left open! The defenders surrendered. This is in fact from a film made afterwards.

Civil War

However, the Bolsheviks were immediately involved in another kind of fighting: Civil War broke out inside Russia (see map). Many people disliked the Bolsheviks. Those who disliked them were:

1 People who supported the Tsar.

2 People who lost property when the peasants seized the land and when many firms were nationalized.

3 The Governments of the USA, Britain and France who felt let down by Russia making peace with Germany. People who oppose a revolution are 'counter-revolutionaries'. In the Russian Civil War the revolutionaries were called 'Reds' and the counter-revolutionaries, 'Whites'.

The Red Army eventually won because they had several advantages:

1 The soldiers of the Red Army were fighting to defend the Bolshevik Government which promised them a better life than they had had under the Tsar.

2 Trotsky was a brilliant Commander-in-Chief.

3 The White Armies were scattered and disorganized.

The Civil War was important because it made the Bolsheviks frightened and suspicious; of their enemies inside Russia, and of countries like America and Britain who had helped the White Armies.

The Government of Lenin

As soon as he became Prime Minister Lenin arranged for the Government to take control of much of the Russian economy. Big businesses were nationalized and the peasants were forced to hand over much of their grain. As a result many, especially peasants, lost the incentive to work hard. In 1921 Lenin had to allow the peasants to make a profit again by selling their produce.

There was so much opposition to the Bolsheviks that the Government decided that they must use force to take full control of the country. As early as

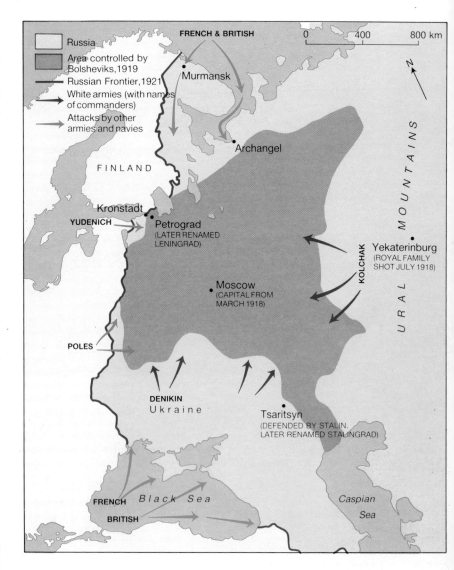

Above: Civil War in Russia. *Below*: The Communist Party (as the Bolsheviks became in 1918) was keen that the ordinary people should know what was happening and be persuaded to give their support. But many were illiterate. So the government relied on street posters. Some fine artists produced these. This one shows a Red Army 'wedge' attacking the Whites.

December 1917 Lenin set up the 'Cheka'. This word is an abbreviation, in Russian, for the 'All-Russian-Extraordinary Commission for the Struggle with Counter-Revolution and Sabotage'. In practice it became a secret police, every bit as inhumane and feared as the Tsar's Ochrana. Here is part of a report prepared in 1910:

'In 1918, persons arrested on the charges of counter-revolution, crime in office, speculation, use of forged and other people's documents, etc., numbered 47,348 ... During 1918 and 1919 7,068 persons were shot on the charge of counter-revolution...'

ПОМОГИ

...amine. Because the Civil War so quickly followed the First World War, agricultural production declined for many years. In a desperate effort to keep the armies and the towns fed the Government confiscated food from the peasants. In 1920 there was a severe drought, which reduced the production of food even further. A dreadful famine resulted in 1921. Many foreign organizations arranged to supply food: the American Relief Administration fed 3.75 million people; Save the Children Fund, over two hundred thousand. Yet the suffering was terrible; 10 million died. In a town in the Ukraine, for instance, a woman shopkeeper was sentenced to twenty-five years' imprisonment for selling human flesh. The picture is a famous poster appealing to people to succour the hungry. The caption says 'Help'.

Trotsky was one of the most brilliant of the revolutionaries, though he joined the Bolsheviks only in the summer of 1917. He played an important part in the 1905 revolution; he planned the Bolshevik takeover of Petrograd; he arranged the Treaty of Brest-Litovsk with the Germans; and he commanded the Red Army in the Civil War. During the Civil War he directed operations from a train, which for months was his home and headquarters. He was able to travel quickly to whichever front needed his leadership.

When Lenin died many thought that Trotsky would take over as leader of the Communist Party. In fact, he quarrelled with the Party Secretary Stalin and eventually he was forced into exile, after some journeyings ending up in Mexico. Stalin thought that he was a dangerous enemy even when he was so far away. As late as 1940 one of Stalin's secret agents made friends with Trotsky. One day he showed him some papers to read. While Trotsky was bending over, the man took an ice-pick from his pocket and smashed Trotsky's skull.

During his exile Trotsky wrote many books. One of his main ideas that he had for many years was that Communism would never be safe until other countries became Communist. Many people today still support Trotsky's ideas. They are called 'Trotskyists'. In Britain, those who dislike these extreme left-wing ideas call them by the nick-name 'Trots'.

Прежде

Один с сошкой, семеро с ложкой.

Теперь

Кто не работает, тот не ест.

This Russian cartoon was drawn in 1921 to show how the Revolution was supposed to have improved the lot of the peasants compared with the rich people (including the army officers and clergymen). The captions say: 'Then: One with the plough; seven with the spoon. Now: He who does not work does not eat.'

The head of the Cheka was Dzerzhinsky, 'a silent, gloomy man ... He signed scores of [death] warrants every day whilst sipping glasses of tea, always with the same gloomy air.' The activities of the Cheka became a Terror – to terrify the population into supporting the Bolsheviks.

To prevent the royal family from becoming the centre of opposition they were all shot in 1918. But discontent continued. In 1921 the sailors in the naval port of Kronstadt near Petrograd put forward demands for better conditions. The Government decided to reply with force. A battle took place in which many were killed. The Communist Government were now shown to be absolutely determined to keep power – even if they had to shoot the very sailors who had fought for the Revolution in 1917!

The following year the creation of the USSR was declared. These initials stand for the Union of Socialist Soviet Republics. And two years later Lenin died.

Why was the Russian Revolution important?

The October Bolshevik Revolution was one of the most important events in the history of the twentieth century. Until 1917 people had only *talked* about Communism. Now one country was trying to put theory into practice, though the Communists in the USSR realized that it would take a long time to make all the necessary changes.

For about thirty years the USSR was the only Communist country in the world. So it became, for many people, the model of what a Communist country was like. There were Communist Parties in many other countries and these wanted to copy the USSR. Other people disliked what was happening in the USSR and believed that Communism was wrong, even evil (see Chapter 8). But it was no longer possible to ignore the ideas of Karl Marx. ☑

1 List all the evidence from illustrations and quotations about the problem of food at the time of the Russian Revolution (pages 63–70). What do these sources tell you about the importance of the problem?
2 You are living in Petrograd. Write a letter to a relation living in another part of Russia describing what life was like in the city, including the main events, 1916–1921.
3 If you had been a sailor at Kronstadt would you have joined in the Revolution in March 1917, in November 1917 and the mutiny in 1921? Give your reasons for each.
4 Write speeches for two lawyers: one for the prosecution of Tsar Nicholas II, the other for his defence.

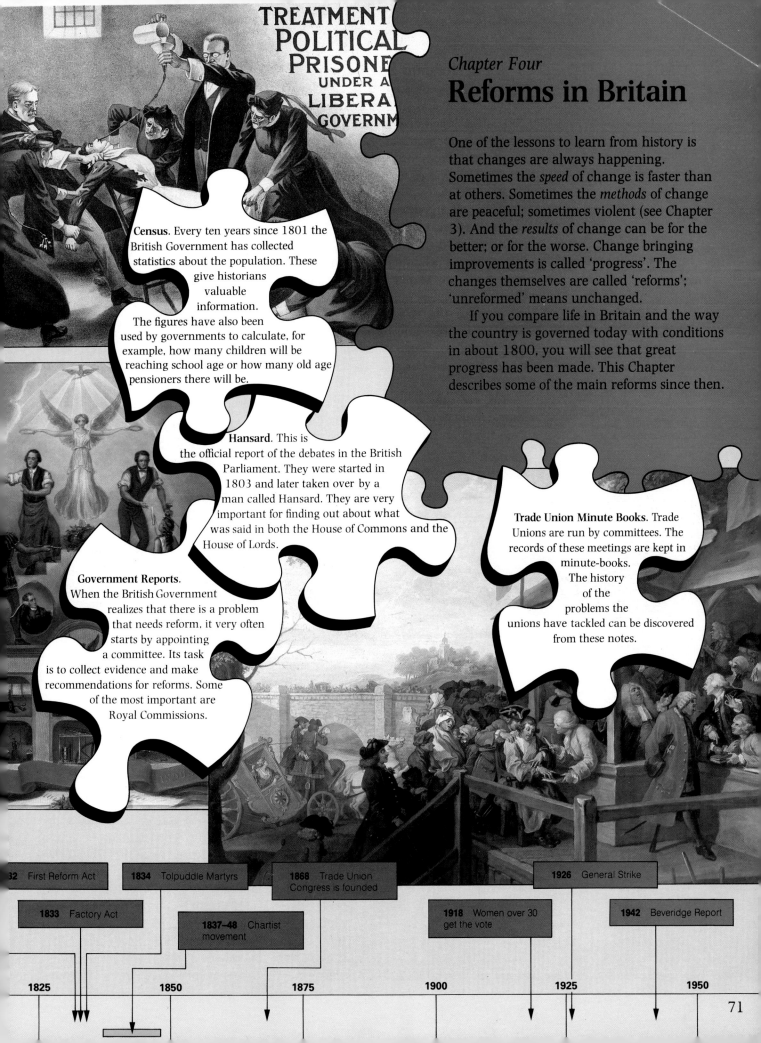

TREATMENT
POLITICAL
PRISONE
UNDER A
LIBERA
GOVERNM

Chapter Four
Reforms in Britain

One of the lessons to learn from history is that changes are always happening. Sometimes the *speed* of change is faster than at others. Sometimes the *methods* of change are peaceful; sometimes violent (see Chapter 3). And the *results* of change can be for the better; or for the worse. Change bringing improvements is called 'progress'. The changes themselves are called 'reforms'; 'unreformed' means unchanged.

If you compare life in Britain and the way the country is governed today with conditions in about 1800, you will see that great progress has been made. This Chapter describes some of the main reforms since then.

Census. Every ten years since 1801 the British Government has collected statistics about the population. These give historians valuable information.
The figures have also been used by governments to calculate, for example, how many children will be reaching school age or how many old age pensioners there will be.

Hansard. This is the official report of the debates in the British Parliament. They were started in 1803 and later taken over by a man called Hansard. They are very important for finding out about what was said in both the House of Commons and the House of Lords.

Trade Union Minute Books. Trade Unions are run by committees. The records of these meetings are kept in minute-books.
The history of the problems the unions have tackled can be discovered from these notes.

Government Reports.
When the British Government realizes that there is a problem that needs reform, it very often starts by appointing a committee. Its task is to collect evidence and make recommendations for reforms. Some of the most important are Royal Commissions.

32 First Reform Act	1834 Tolpuddle Martyrs	1868 Trade Union Congress is founded	1926 General Strike
1833 Factory Act	1837–48 Chartist movement	1918 Women over 30 get the vote	1942 Beveridge Report

1825	1850	1875	1900	1925	1950

The unreformed Parliament

People who live in small tribes or villages can gather together and have discussions and make decisions about matters that affect them. But it is impossible, of course, for a population of millions in a country such as Britain to govern themselves like this. The solution then is for people to elect representatives, to choose people to represent them and their views at a meeting. This is how Parliament gradually developed from the Middle Ages. Parliament then, as now, was made up of two different groups: the House of Lords (composed of Lords, some bishops and some judges); and the House of Commons (composed of elected Members of Parliament, MPs).

One of the ways Parliament had gained more power was by taking it away from the king. In this respect Britain had made much more progress by 1700 than other European countries. The French philosopher, Voltaire, wrote in 1733: 'The English nation is the only one on earth which has succeeded in controlling the power of kings by resisting them ... [and] has at last established this wise system of government ... in which the people share ...' However, by the end of the eighteenth century this 'wise system of government' was coming in for a great deal of criticism.

What was the 'system of government'? The basic arrangements for England and Wales (Scotland and Ireland were slightly different) were that each county elected two MPs, and each borough elected two MPs. A simple system. What was wrong with it? To answer that we need to ask three questions:

1   What kinds of towns were 'boroughs'?

Boroughs were those towns with a 'royal charter', that is a privilege given to them by the Sovereign enabling them to send members to Parliament. But very few towns had been given charters since the sixteenth century! So it was unfair. Large new industrial towns like Manchester, Leeds and Sheffield had no MPs (see map). What was even more ridiculous was that some places with hardly anyone living in them still had two MPs! For example Old Sarum, near Salisbury (Wiltshire), was a pile of ruins; and Dunwich (Suffolk), had fallen into the sea (because the coast had eroded)! As a result of this unfairness, Lancashire, for instance had 12 MPs (5 boroughs + 2 county members), whereas Cornwall had 44 (21 boroughs + 2 county members).

2   Who was allowed to vote?

The right to vote is called the 'franchise'. Who could vote varied, depending on whether you were in a county or a borough. County MPs were elected by landowners, and the franchise was the same in each county. But in the boroughs it was very complicated. Some were called 'corporation boroughs'; in these only members of the town corporation could vote. Some were called 'potwalloper

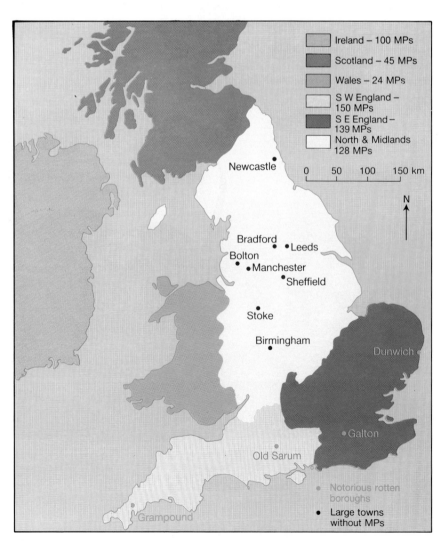

Some of the obvious faults in the system of parliamentary representation before 1832.

Ireland – 100 MPs

Scotland – 45 MPs

Wales – 24 MPs

S W England – 150 MPs

S E England – 139 MPs

North & Midlands 128 MPs

Newcastle

0   50   100   150 km

N

Bradford
• Leeds
Bolton
• Manchester
•Sheffield

Stoke

Birmingham

Dunwich

• Galton

Old Sarum

Notorious rotten boroughs

• Large towns without MPs

Grampound

'The Election' by the famous eighteenth-century artist, William Hogarth. Notice how most of the electors seem to be senile or crippled. The one in the centre of the picture is mentally very ill! Why do you think Hogarth portrayed them like that? Even though there were usually very few voters, the election took several days. What happened was:

1 The candidates made speeches.
2 The candidates and their agents tried to 'persuade' the voters in various ways.
3 The voters registered their right to vote.
4 Election was by show of hands.
5 If the result was disputed, a poll was taken (i.e. each voter's stated preference written down).

boroughs'; in these anyone who owned a fireplace on which to boil a pot could vote! There were several other kinds as well! And this, added to the fact that only adult males had the vote, meant that the majority of people in England and Wales could not vote. In fact by 1830, out of a total population of 19 million, only 435,000 people had the right to vote in England and Wales.

3 How were the votes cast?

Voters had to vote in full public view, not in secret as today. And since in many boroughs there were very few voters (most had fewer than 500) it was easy for candidates to bribe and bully the voters. Corruption was so obviously taking place in some towns that they were called 'rotten boroughs' (see map). In his novel, *Pickwick Papers*, Charles Dickens gave a vivid picture of a borough election. Half joking he wrote:

'Excisable articles [*those with a tax on them, i.e. alcohol*!] were remarkably cheap at all the public-houses; and spring vans [*comfortable vehicles*] paraded the streets for the accommodation of voters who were seized with any temporary dizziness in the head – an epidemic [*disease which spreads*] which prevailed among the

electors, during the contest, to a most alarming extent, and under the influence of which they might frequently be seen lying on the pavements in a state of utter insensibility.'

Protests

But the faults of this old parliamentary system were not funny for the poor and unemployed people who had no vote. They felt that the MPs chosen by this system were not interested in them or the terrible conditions in the industrial cities. A Declaration (statement) drawn up in Birmingham in 1830 expressed this view:

'That honourable House [i.e. of Commons], in its present state, is evidently too far removed in habits, wealth and station, from the wants and interests of the lower and middle classes of the people, to have any just views respecting them, or any close identity of feeling with them. The great aristocratical [*upper class*] interests of all kinds are well represented there ... *But the interests of Industry and of Trade have scarcely any representatives at all!*'

73

The Peterloo Massacre. This print appeared in the *Illustrated London News*. It was called, 'A View of St Peter's Place and Manner in which the Manchester Reform Meeting was dispersed by Civil and Military Power'. You can see the slashing sabres clearly. But note that the Government did not censor this picture, as might have happened in some countries. The massacre made a vivid impression. The poet Shelley wrote a bitter attack on the government called 'The Mask of Anarchy'. In it he urged the people to rise up in revolt. This is a famous line from it: 'Ye are many – they are few'. As recently as 1940 a journalist and novelist, Howard Spring, wrote a novel called *Fame is the Spur*. In this a sabre, taken by a demonstrator at Peterloo, is a constant inspiration to a politician to work for the interests of the ordinary people.

After the war with Napoleon in 1815 unemployment in Britain rose and the price of food increased. The working people were hit hardest. They started to hold demonstrations to protest at their situation. The most famous occurred in Manchester.

On Monday 16 August 1819 60,000 workers and their families gathered in an open space called St Peter's Field in Manchester. They had come to hear a famous speaker called 'Orator' Hunt speak to them about reforming Parliament. The organizers stressed the need for 'cleanliness, sobriety, order and peace'. The great gathering was in fact a very orderly meeting until things started to go disastrously wrong. The local magistrates were nervous. They feared violence and ordered the yeomanry (part-time soldiers) to arrest Hunt. But, of course, the crowd was densely packed. There was jostling. The magistrates ordered in the cavalry. These soldiers charged into the helpless throng of men, women and children, who became panic-stricken. The troops lashed out with their sabres. In a short time they had done their work. The crowd had dispersed – all, that is, save the eleven who were killed and the 400 wounded. The cavalry had quite evidently used the edges of their sabres to *cut*, not the flats of their blades to *hit* as their regulations said. They had obviously *intended* to kill and wound.

The meeting in Manchester took place four years after the end of the Napoleonic Wars so the Duke of Wellington's great victory at Waterloo was still fresh in people's minds. Why do you think the massacre at St Peter's Field was called 'Peterloo'?

The bloodshed was bad enough. But the Government made the situation worse by congratulating the magistrates for what they had done. Such an attitude just made it clearer that the House of Commons had to be reformed.

The Great Reform Bill

The 'Peterloo Massacre' did not stop the protests. Throughout the 1820s the demand for reform continued. Then in July 1830 a general election was held and there was much talk of the need to reform Parliament. In November the Prime Minister, the Duke of Wellington, made a speech. He said that he thought the British system could not be improved and that he would never introduce any reform. This utter refusal even to *consider* any changes shocked many people; some of the Duke's own supporters in the House of Commons voted with the Opposition; Wellington decided to resign.

In the early nineteenth century there were two main political parties in Britain: Whigs and Tories. The Tories, who were more opposed to reform than the Whigs, were very worried. They feared a revolution might break out in Britain as it had done in France from 1789 (see Chapter 3). They believed that by being firm (for example by punishing protestors) and by not introducing changes, the Government could stop a revolution happening. The leader of the Whigs was Earl Grey. He became Prime Minister when the Duke of Wellington resigned in 1830.

Grey realized it was dangerous to ignore the complaints about the way the House of Commons was elected. He set up a small committee to draw up a bill (a proposal to make changes) to present to Parliament. On 1 March 1831 one of the committee members, Lord John Russell, rose in the House of Commons to explain the changes they proposed. Most MPs expected to hear a scheme for very *minor* alterations of the system. Those Tories who were opposed to any changes at all were shocked by what they heard. Robert Peel warned that if the Bill was passed 'we shall have one of the worst despotisms [*rules by force*] that ever existed ... a parliament of mob demagogues [*trouble-makers*] – not of wise and prudent men'.

It was going to be difficult for the Whigs to get a majority in favour of their reforms. When a proposal to make changes is introduced into the House of

THE BOY-OF-ALL-WORK.

Lord John Russell (born in 1792) was Prime Minister twice: 1846–52 and 1865–66. At the time of the Reform Bill he was in the House of Commons because his title of 'Lord' was a 'courtesy title' (giving no right to sit in the House of Lords), which he had as the younger son of a Duke. One historian described him as 'A small, prim young man, with a large head and a precise, old-fashioned mode [*way*] of speech'. When further parliamentary reform was suggested in the House of Commons in 1837 he spoke against it. He called the 1832 Act a 'final measure'; for this he earned the nickname 'Finality Jack'. He became Prime Minister in 1846 and had a lot of other problems to cope with, as this *Punch* cartoon shows.

Commons, it is called a 'bill'. It has to pass three 'readings'. The most important of these is the second. If it passes the second reading, it is presented to a committee of MPs who make detailed suggestions for alterations. Then the bill is presented to the House of Lords for their approval and finally to the king or queen for the 'royal assent'. When the House of Commons voted on the second reading of the Reform Bill, it passed by a majority of one! But a few days later the Government lost a vote in the committee. Grey called a general election. Great excitement swept the country.

The Whigs won a clear majority; the Reform Bill passed the House of Commons; then in October it was rejected by the House of Lords. The ordinary people of Britain were furious. There were widespread demonstrations and riots in many towns. In London the windows of Apsley House, Wellington's house in Piccadilly, were smashed by an angry crowd. The Duke of Cumberland was dragged from his horse. The Archbishop of Canterbury was booed and jeered. The centre of Bristol was destroyed by fire by the rioters.

Throughout the winter and spring of 1831 and 1832 there was confusion. Eventually, King William IV promised Grey that he would create enough new peers to swamp the opposition in the House of Lords. The Tory Lords gave in.

The Great Reform Bill became law.

But the changes were really not all that great. When the new House of Commons met as a result of the new system of elections in 1833 the Duke of Wellington remarked, 'I have never seen so many bad hats [*unsuitable men*] in my life'. In fact, the kind of men who were elected were very similar to those elected *before* 1832. The number of voters was increased by less than 50 per cent – to 652,000. But there was still no secret ballot; bribery and bullying were still possible. More important than this slight increase in franchise was the redistribution of seats: 142 seats were taken from small and rotten boroughs and given to the new large towns like Manchester, Birmingham, Leeds, and Sheffield.

So, was the Reform Bill important after all? Yes – and mostly because it brought about changes. Now that *some* changes had been made, there could be no excuse for not introducing *more* in future. This, in fact, was just what many Tories had feared – the Reform Bill was only the start ... the thin end of the wedge.

Chartism

By the late 1830s many working and lower-middle class people had been disappointed:

1   Even after the Reform Act (1832) they were still not allowed to vote.

2   Their attempts to form trade unions (as we shall see later in this Chapter) were unsuccessful.

3   A lot more of them living in industrial towns became unemployed in 1837.

4   Those of them who were too poor to look after themselves had to live in work-houses. These were bitterly hated and called 'Bastilles' (named after the fearsome prison in Paris which was destroyed during the French Revolution, see Chapter 3).

In 1837 two London men, William Lovett and Francis Place, drew up a petition listing six demands for further Parliamentary reform. This list soon came to be called the 'People's Charter'; and those who supported it were called 'Chartists'. Throughout the country local societies

The six points of the Charter.

were organized to support the Charter; and people were persuaded to sign petitions in favour of the 'Six Points'. Those who gathered support were called 'missionaries'. Here is an extract from a letter written from Pontypool in 1839:

'The missionaries attend at public houses or beer shops where a party ... has been assembled. The missionary expounds [*explains in detail*] to them the grievances [*grounds for complaint*] under which they labour, tells them that half their earnings is taken from them as taxes..., that their employers are tyrants who acquire wealth by their labour.'

Large meetings were organized, particularly in the north of England in 1839. A petition with over 1 million signatures was presented to Parliament. It was rejected. The Chartist leaders then split up. Lovett wanted to continue with 'moral force' (i.e. peaceful persuasion). Feargus O'Connor, a fiery Irish journalist living in Leeds, wanted to use 'physical force' (i.e. violence). And in fact the rejection of the Charter did spark off violent demonstrations. The most serious one was in Newport, Monmouthshire. A second unsuccessful petition by the Chartists in 1842 was followed by the 'Plug Riots' (see page 44). Angry workers in Lancashire and the West Midlands removed the plugs from boilers, cutting off the steam power from the factory machines. The Chartist movement finally fizzled out with a third unsuccessful petition in 1848.

The Government and Parliament stubbornly refused the petitions and stood firm against threats of violent uprisings. Chartism seemed to have failed. Or had it? By 1918 five of their six demands had been put into effect. ☐

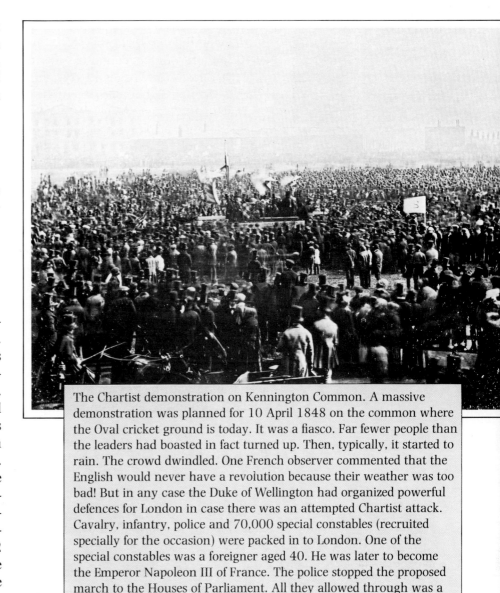

The Chartist demonstration on Kennington Common. A massive demonstration was planned for 10 April 1848 on the common where the Oval cricket ground is today. It was a fiasco. Far fewer people than the leaders had boasted in fact turned up. Then, typically, it started to rain. The crowd dwindled. One French observer commented that the English would never have a revolution because their weather was too bad! But in any case the Duke of Wellington had organized powerful defences for London in case there was an attempted Chartist attack. Cavalry, infantry, police and 70,000 special constables (recruited specially for the occasion) were packed in to London. One of the special constables was a foreigner aged 40. He was later to become the Emperor Napoleon III of France. The police stopped the proposed march to the Houses of Parliament. All they allowed through was a petition with five Chartist leaders. The Chartists' petition demanded further parliamentary reform. They claimed that 5,706,000 people had signed it. It was a great bulk of paper; it weighed 5 cwts 84 lbs (292 kg) and had to be carried in three cabs! When MPs eventually came to examine it, they discovered that it contained fewer than 2 million names. And even these included obvious forgeries like 'F M Duke of Wellington', 'Victoria Rex' (i.e. Latin for *King* Victoria!), 'Pug Nose', and others which the House of Commons Committee 'do not hazard offending the House and the dignity and decency of their own proceedings by reporting'! The House of Commons rejected it with jeers. This is the earliest photograph of a demonstration.

1 Imagine that you are living in 1831. Write a speech in favour of reforming Parliament.

2 Imagine you are living in London between 1830 and 1848 and keep a diary. Write out the main events you would have recorded in your diary during that time.

3 Make a list of the Chartists' Six Points. Explain why each was important. Why do you think that one still has not been put into effect?

4 Compare the picture and quotation on page 73. How reliable do you think each of them is as evidence of how elections were carried out at the time? Give your reasons.

Even though there were disappointments for the working classes in the 1830s and 1840s and they had to continue suffering very real miseries (see pages 43–44), some reforms were passed by Parliament.

During these twenty years in particular, there were some sincere and sympathetic people (factory owners, politicians and civil servants) who worked hard to improve the working and living conditions of ordinary people in Britain. People who devote their energies to the good of others are called 'philanthropists'. It is not possible to tell the stories of all of these philanthropists or of all the Acts of Parliament they managed to have passed. Improvements were made throughout the nineteenth century in education, lunatic asylums, safety at sea, conditions in mines, for example. But we can see what kinds of reforms were passed by looking at acts dealing with factory conditions and public health in the 1830s and 1840s.

Factory Acts

On 16 October a long letter appeared in the *Leeds Mercury*. It was a bitter attack on child labour in particular. Here is an extract:

'Thousands of our fellow-creatures and fellow-subjects, both male and female, the miserable inhabitants of a *Yorkshire town* ... are this very moment existing in a state of slavery, *more horrid* than are the victims of that hellish system '*colonial slavery*' ... The very streets ... are every morning wet by the tears of innocent victims at the accursed shrine of avarice [*greed*], who are *compelled* [*forced*] ... to hasten ... to those magazines [*stores*] of British infantile slavery – *the worsted [woollen yarn] mills in the town and neighbourhood of Bradford.*'

The letter was signed 'A Briton'.

Conditions were appalling in the textile factories of northern England in the early years of the nineteenth century (see Chapter 2). In 1830 two Yorkshire factory-owners launched a campaign to reduce the maximum number of hours to be worked in factories to ten per day. These men were John Fielden and Richard Oastler. It was Oastler who wrote the letter and signed it 'A Briton'.

A Royal Commission was set up to investigate conditions in factories. Many factory owners complained that if they were forced to reduce working hours they would be financially ruined. But several MPs, including Lord Ashley (later the Earl of Shaftesbury), took up the cause. As a result a Factory Act was passed in 1833; and from then on factory inspectors were to be appointed. They visited factories and made sure the terms of the new law were being obeyed.

However, those who wanted reforms

The Factory Act of 1833 (applied only to textile mills)
1 Children under 9 not to be employed
2 Children 9–13; 9 hours a day maximum
3 Young persons 13–18; 12 hours a day maximum
4 Children 9–13; 2 hours a day education
5 No one 9–18 to work at night
6 Factory inspectors appointed

in the factories, particularly Lord Ashley, were not satisfied. They still wanted working hours reduced to ten. Then another Factory Act was passed in 1844. This was important because it introduced safety regulations: dangerous machinery had to be fenced and no machinery was to be cleaned while it was moving.

In 1847, another act, introduced by John Fielden, reduced the working hours for women and young people to ten. The reformers had never thought they could get enough support for a bill reducing *men's* hours to ten. But they had hoped that employers would be forced to do this if the women and children were not available to do their own essential work – a preparation for the men's work. In fact, the factory owners still managed to keep their men working up to fifteen hours a day by introducing 'relay' (shift) systems for the women and children. However, in 1850 a further act reduced hours to $10\frac{1}{2}$ and forbade relay systems. It had been a long and difficult struggle; and even then, only certain kinds of factories were included. More reforms have been needed even up until today.

Public health

By the early nineteenth century it was clear that slum conditions in the industrial towns bred disease (see Chapter 2). Yet nothing was done about this problem until the 1840s. There were two main reasons for this:

1 No one fully understood why the really terrible diseases like cholera and typhus broke out. It was not until 1836 that deaths (and births and marriages) had to be registered (recorded). So until then there were no accurate statistics about the causes of death or the most unhealthy places. And doctors were too frightened to work with people who were suffering from such deadly illnesses. As a result scientific knowledge about disease was primitive. All that was noticed was that epidemics broke out when there was 'a great stink'; so it was thought that disease was caused by 'bad air'. No one

Lord Shaftesbury's funeral. Lord Ashley, who became the Earl of Shaftesbury in 1851, was the most famous of all nineteenth-century philanthropists. Huge crowds thronged in and outside Westminster Abbey for his funeral in 1885, as you can see from this drawing. Representatives from 232 organizations he had helped during his life were there – Female Inebriates, Unemployed Cab Drivers, Society for Suppressing the Opium Trade, Turkish Refugees, Sons of Poor Clergymen, to name only a few! The band of the Costermongers' Temperance Society played the March from Handel's oratorio, *Saul*.

Shaftesbury won such affection because his deep religious conscience drove him to devote his life to helping those in need. He was especially concerned about children. He believed passionately that members of the ruling class like himself must take responsibility for reforms. He believed that the working class themselves were quite unable to help themselves because they had no political power. His most famous reforms were those relating to boy chimney-sweeps, coal-mines and textile factories. But he was always aware that such reforms still left many evils. Just before he died he noted in his diary: 'I cannot bear to leave the world with all the misery in it'.

A poster warning of overcrowded church yards during the cholera outbreak in 1832.

CHOLERA.

THE

DUDLEY BOARD OF HEALTH,

HEREBY GIVE NOTICE, THAT IN CONSEQUENCE OF THE

Church-yards at Dudley

Being so full, no one who has died of the CHOLERA will be permitted to be buried after *SUNDAY* next, (To-morrow) in either of the Burial Grounds of St. *Thomas's*, or St. *Edmund's*, in this Town.

All Persons who die from CHOLERA, must for the future be buried in the Church-yard at Netherton.

BOARD of HEALTH, DUDLEY.
September 1st, 1832.

W. MAURICE, PRINTER, HIGH STREET, DUDL.

Edwin Chadwick lived for almost as long as the century; 1800–90! He was a great believer in the Government using its power to improve the living conditions of the ordinary people.

During the 1830s and 1840s he was very active. He was Chairman of the commission whose findings led to the 1833 Factory Act. More than anyone he was responsible for changes in the Poor Law in 1834 and setting up new workhouses. He was the first Secretary of the Poor Law Commissioners. He produced the important Report which led to the Public Health Act of 1848. As a result of this act the General Board of Health was set up, for which Chadwick worked as Secretary for six years.

When he retired he was a disappointed, hated and misunderstood man. He was so tactless and obstinate that he made many enemies. For example, he thought that the authorities were so inefficient in coping with an outbreak of Cholera in 1849 that he complained about their 'self-satisfied bumbledom'! Also his Poor Law did not really help the destitute people of the country at all! He was loathed by them as a 'monster in human shape'. Yet his work to improve public health was very important for reducing disease and saving lives. His Report has been described by one historian as a 'masterpiece'.

asked what caused the 'stink'. A poster issued at the time of a cholera outbreak carried the following advice:

'The principal Rules to be attended to for the PREVENTION of the Cholera are CLEANLINESS, EXERCISE AND TEMPERANCE. It has been remarked that most of those who have died were TIPPLERS [drinkers of alcohol], BEGGARS, AND IDLE PEOPLE.'

2 Even when it was realized that lack of clean water and proper sewerage systems led to disease, there was still resistance to reforms; because they would mean change and that would interfere with builders and owners of slums. And, of course, they would cost money!

But one man in particular was determined to do something. This was Edwin Chadwick. He wrote a superb pamphlet called *Report on the Sanitary Condition of the Labouring Population*. He collected a lot

of statistics, and his findings were quite shocking. He showed, for example, that the average length of life for 'mechanics and labourers' in the rural county of Rutland was 38, whereas in Bethnal Green, London, it was 16. He concluded that every year the 'loss of life from filth and bad ventilation are greater than the loss from death or wounds in any wars in which this country has been engaged in modern times'. Moreover, he argued that *preventing* the disease would cost less than the cost of *treating* and caring for its victims. So he recommended the provision of pure water-supply, flushing lavatories and underground sewerage pipes.

Chadwick's Report was published in 1842. It caused widespread interest. But it took six years for the Government to produce a Public Health Act. And the reform might not have come even then except that people were afraid of a new cholera outbreak. This epidemic had started in south-east Asia in 1840 and spread slowly westwards. In December 1848 it reached London.

That was the year the Public Health Act set up a General Board of Health. The General Board's job was to encourage local government authorities to improve health standards in their own areas. But progress was slow. The General Board was abolished in 1858 and some of its duties were taken on, appropriately perhaps, by the Privy Council (a group of senior politicians appointed by the monarch). By an act of 1866 sanitary inspectors were appointed; and by another of 1875, local medical officers of health were appointed. But it was not until well into the twentieth century that the majority of houses had their own water-supply and lavatories. □

1 Who do you think was the most important reformer among the following: Oastler; Shaftesbury; Chadwick? Give reasons.
2 Using the poster on page 79 write a short speech by Chadwick about public health.

Trade unions

Early failures

Even today it sometimes takes an Act of Parliament to get better working conditions. But it is more usual for workers to protest about conditions of work through their trade union. A trade union is an organization for workers in a particular trade or industry to make sure that the members have the best possible wages and working conditions.

The most powerful way of protesting and demanding changes is by striking (stopping work until demands are met)

But at the start of the nineteenth century trade unions were illegal. New laws called the Combination Acts were passed in 1824 and 1825. As a result there was a great increase in the number of trade unions and membership. An ambitious scheme was thought out by Robert Owen – he created the Grand National Consolidated Trades Union (GNCTU) in 1833. It boasted a membership of $\frac{1}{2}$ million. But it was too large to be properly organized and it soon collapsed.

In 1833, a few months before the creation of the GNCTU, a small group of agricultural labourers in the village of Tolpuddle in Dorset decided to form a union. The reason? Their wages had been reduced and they wanted to do something about it.

Their union rules stated 'That the object of this society can never be promoted by any act or acts of violence' and they condemned 'any violation (*breaking*) of the laws'. And yet ... an MP, John Roebuck, takes up the story:

'Six of these men were informed by the constable of the village, there was a charge against them at Dorchester, and requested them to go with him and answer it. The poor fellows, believing themselves perfectly innocent, told the constable they would go with him; and informed their wives and families that they would be back in the evening. The poor men never returned!'

It is fairly clear that the Dorset magistrates planned to 'get' the Tolpuddle men. This poster was produced on 22 February 1834 – just three days before they were arrested. Also, the law under which they were found guilty dated back to 1797 and was passed to deal with mutinies in the navy! No one expected it to be used against trade unionists. The Tolpuddle Martyrs have remained the greatest heroes of the trade union movement. The 150th anniversary of their conviction was celebrated in 1984.

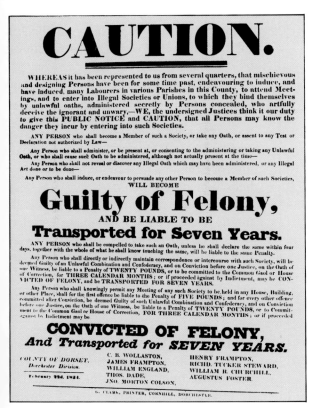

When British working men first started to organize trade unions there were fears that they might start a revolution. This cartoon shows a meeting in the 1830s where the trade unionists are drawn like the people who took part in the great French Revolution (compare the cartoons of the sans-culottes on page 59).

They were arrested and found guilty because they had taken an oath – they had promised to keep the rules of the union. They were sentenced to seven years' imprisonment in Australia! Huge demonstrations took place especially in London against this vicious sentence on the 'Tolpuddle Martyrs', as they were inevitably called. Eventually, the new Home Secretary, Lord John Russell, pardoned them; and they came back to England.

Growth of trade unions

During the thirty years after the Tolpuddle Martyrs case, more trade unions were formed. But things came to a head again in 1866–68.

For several years some unionists had been intimidating (that is, threatening) workers who did not belong to a union. These acts of intimidation were especially serious in Sheffield: they became known as the 'Sheffield Outrages'. In October 1866 the house of a non-union worker was even blown up by gunpowder. This led to a Royal Commission being set up in 1867 to investigate trade union affairs. They uncovered evidence of other unsavoury behaviour. In the same year the Lord Chief Justice declared that trade unions could not get their money back if their funds were stolen by a dishonest official.

Despite all this, the TUs survived – and for three main reasons:

1 In 1868 a number of unions formed the Trades Union Congress (TUC). There were two main aims: to improve the image of unionism; and to help individual unions.

2 The Royal Commission report was not as hostile as some unionists feared.

3 The Liberal leader, Gladstone, won the election of 1868. He decided to help the unions. Why was this? One reason was that many working-class people now had the vote, and unions were mostly made up of the working class.

The Trade Union Act of 1871, passed while Gladstone was Prime Minister, was the first of many Trade Union laws. The 1871 Act made unions legal and allowed them to keep their funds. Another act passed four years later, guaranteed them the right of peaceful picketing – to persuade workers to join a strike.

Membership card of the Amalgamated Society of Engineers. Trade unions only slowly recovered from the double blow of the Tolpuddle convictions and the collapse of the GNCTU. By the late 1860s there were still only about 0·25 million members (compared with 10·25 million a century later). In the 1850s 'new model unions' were gradually formed. They were more like friendly societies – to help their members when ill or out of work, for example. There were no oaths. And most were formed among skilled craftsmen. The first, formed in 1851, was the Amalgamated Society of Engineers. This elegant, coloured membership certificate shows that as an organization they were quite wealthy as a result of members' subscriptions.

Strikes

Trade unions spend most of their time and effort meeting with employers trying to come to an agreement. But if this does not work, then, as a last resort, they can organize 'strikes'. This means that members of the union stop work. (The word was first used in the eighteenth century: 'strike work' was used in a similar way to the phrase 'strike sail', used by sailors.) Strikes, or even threats of strikes, have sometimes brought about improvements.

By the 1870s and 1880s unskilled workers were also organizing themselves into trade unions: agricultural workers, dockers, railwaymen, for example. These people were more desperate to improve their wages and work conditions than the better-off skilled workers. This rise of 'the new unionism', as it was called, was marked by serious strikes, especially in 1888–89 and 1910–12.

But the most serious strike was in 1926. It began with a dispute in the coal mining industry. Until nationalization (that is, the Government became the owners) in 1947 the coal mines were privately owned. In 1925 the owners announced that they were going to reduce miners' wages. After unsuccessful discussions, in which the Government was also involved, the miners went on strike

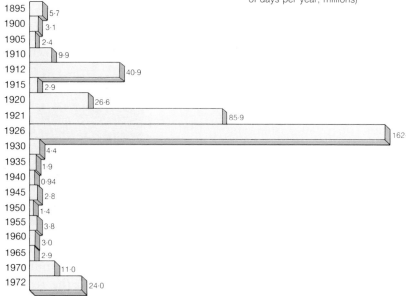

Total number of working days lost by strikes (number of workers on strike × number of days per year, millions)

Year	Millions
1895	5·7
1900	3·1
1905	2·4
1910	9·9
1912	40·9
1915	2·9
1920	26·6
1921	85·9
1926	162·2
1930	4·4
1935	1·9
1940	0·94
1945	2·8
1950	1·4
1955	3·8
1960	3·0
1965	2·9
1970	11·0
1972	24·0

on 26 April 1926. On 3 May the TUC called some other unions 'out' (on strike) in sympathy. The General Strike had begun.

Without trains, buses or lorries the country was in danger of grinding to a halt. The Government called for volunteers and used the army. People helped each other, especially if they had cars. Food supplies were somehow kept up – one of the biggest problems was how to distribute loads of potatoes! In some places demonstrating strikers clashed with the police or volunteer constables. Altogether 2 million workers were on strike. Baldwin,

Working days lost by strikes 1895–1972. The number of strikes that take place in a year is not the best way of telling how big the stoppage of work is. It is better shown by the number of working days lost, shown in this graph. Notice which were the worst years for strikes; the years immediately before and after the First World War.

A family making match-boxes in their home in Bow, East London, 1871. There was a very dramatic strike in 1888 – by the match-girls employed by Bryant and May in East London. They worked for little money on dangerous work. Contact with the phosphorus produced 'phossy-jaw' (the complete rotting away of the jaw). Encouraged by a woman journalist, they formed a union, went on strike, and marched in demonstration through London. Newspaper publicity and the pitiful sight of these sick, ragged girls and women won sympathy for them. Bryant and May were forced to improve the wages and conditions of work. The drawing shows the worst paid of all in the match industry – the box-makers. They earned 2¼d (less than 1p) for a gross (144) of boxes.

the Prime Minister, just waited. Behind the scenes Sir Herbert Samuel was showing more initiative. He was a Liberal politician and former Home Secretary; through his discussions with the TUC, they agreed to call off the strike on 12 May.

Some people felt at the time, and some historians have suggested since, that Britain had been dangerously close to revolution or civil war. Fortunately that did not happen. The danger and the attitude of the Prime Minister is shown by the following story. Baldwin, the Prime Minister, kept Winston Churchill (a member of his cabinet) 'busy' editing a Government newsheet. Baldwin described it as 'the cleverest thing I ever did: otherwise he would have wanted to shoot someone'!

But the trade union movement did suffer a great deal from the strike:

1   The TUC received nothing in return for calling off the strike. Many unions, especially the miners, felt betrayed.

2   Some unions were financially weakened because of all the 'strike-pay' (money paid to strikers) they had paid.

3   The Government passed a new law in 1927, the Trade Disputes and Trade Union Act. This made illegal any strikes made by one union in sympathy for another already on strike. (This Act was not repealed – abolished until 1946.)

Because dock-workers and lorry-drivers were not working during the General Strike, the supply of food to shops was a serious problem. The Government used volunteers and the army. This photograph shows a convoy of food vans driving along the East India Dock Road in London. The vehicle in front is an armoured car in case the convoy was attacked by strikers.

1   Explain why the Tolpuddle men were called 'martyrs'.
2   You were born in 1803. You started working in Manchester as an apprentice weaver but were out of work by 1819. Later you get work in a factory in Sheffield. Would you have attended the meeting in St Peter's Field; and would you have taken part in the 'Sheffield Outrages'? Explain the reasons for your answers.
3   Explain in your own words the meaning of the word 'strike'. What are the advantages and disadvantages of striking?
4   Compare the pictures on pages 81 and 82. Why do you think they give such different impressions of trade unions?

Skilful cartoonists often sum up the news in one cartoon. Their work can give us important evidence about the way ordinary people saw events. One of the most famous cartoonists in Britain this century was Low. These cartoons show how the public were affected by the General Strike. Low shows a sense of humour, although the strike was very serious. The country was divided. The Prime Minister, Stanley Baldwin, and his supporters believed that the strikers were threatening a democratically elected government. Baldwin said, 'The General Strike is a challenge to Parliament and is the road to anarchy and ruin.' The General Council of the TUC insisted that 'The sole aim of the Council is to secure for the miners a decent standard of life. The Council is engaged in an industrial dispute'.

Reforming Parliament again

Reform Acts and the Parliament Act

We have taken the story of trade unions into our own century. Now we retrace our steps and pick up the story of Parliamentary Reform after the collapse of Chartism.

The question of whether or not to let more people vote was debated several times in the House of Commons in the 1850s and 1860s. There was a lot of opposition. One Liberal MP, Robert Lowe, said that if the franchise was given to the working classes, this would 'add a large number of persons to our constituencies [*voting districts*], of the class from which if there is to be anything wrong going on we may naturally expect to find it.' A year later the Second Reform Bill was passed (1867). This gave the vote to householders and lodgers who paid at least £10 a year in rent. Some working-class people were now able to vote. A third Reform Act was passed in 1884–85 when Gladstone was prime minister. Voting by secret ballot was introduced in 1872.

By the early years of the twentieth century some men were being elected into the House of Commons who were particularly interested in the problems of the working class. The Labour Party was formed in 1900. But there was another obstacle to reforms: the House of Lords. A Liberal Chancellor of the Exchequer challenged the peers on behalf of the people. This was David Lloyd George. In 1909 he introduced a 'People's Budget'. In this he proposed to tax the rich in order to pay for pensions schemes for the unemployed, old or ill. The House of Lords rejected it. There followed a tense period. The king promised to create enough Liberal peers to swamp the opposition. The Lords gave way. Do you remember a similar crisis over the First Reform Bill (see page 76)?

In 1911 a Parliament Act was passed, which forbade the Lords to reject any bills passed by the House of Commons. From now on they could only *delay* anything they objected to.

Suffragettes

In the nineteenth century some men reformers had sympathy for women who were suffering hardships in factories. But very few thought that girls should be allowed much education; and certainly the idea that women might be allowed to vote was thought to be absurd. As late as 1912 a letter appeared in *The Times* newspaper over the signature of the eminent doctor, Sir Almroth Wright. He hinted at the then unmentionable subject of women's monthly periods:

'... no doctor can ever lose sight of the fact that the mind of woman is always threatened with danger from the reverberations of her physiological [*biological*] emergencies ... It is with such thoughts that the doctor lets his eyes rest upon the militant suffragist. He cannot shut them to the fact that there is mixed up with the women's movement such mental disorder.'

Courageous women campaigned for educational and political rights. Those who argued for the right to vote were called suffragists or suffragettes.

The 1867 Reform Act. There was uncertainty and nervousness about giving the vote to the working class, even the more wealthy among them, as in the Second Reform Act. The Prime Minister described it as 'a leap in the dark'. Robert Lowe sadly commented, 'We must educate our masters'. By this he meant that the extra people now allowed to vote must be given an education so that they could choose MPs wisely. *Punch* picked up the Prime Minister, Disraeli's comment and portrayed him as a horse carrying the country (Britannia) into the unknown thicket of reform.

A LEAP IN THE DARK.

Mrs Emmeline Pankhurst. The two most famous suffragettes were Emmeline Pankhurst and her daughter, Christabel. They were fiery speakers and Emmeline was a good organizer. When Emmeline died some of her devoted supporters gave her a military-style funeral. However, some of their statements and actions, particularly of the more emotional Christabel, lost them support. Many women disapproved of their violence. And even Lloyd George, who was quite prepared to be sympathetic, declared: 'They are mad, Christabel Pankhurst has lost all sense of proportion and reality.' The photograph shows Mrs Pankhurst being arrested in May 1914 after demonstrating outside Buckingham Palace.

('Suffrage' like 'franchise' means the right to vote). This letter shows the kind of prejudice that women had to put up with then. Can you think of any examples of discrimination and prejudice by men against women in Britain even today?

In 1903 Mrs Emmeline Pankhurst founded the Women's Social and Political Union. The struggle to win the vote was to be a hard and vicious one. At first the suffragettes tried to use peaceful methods; they heckled political meetings with shouts of 'votes for women' and chained themselves to railings, for example. But these tactics had no effect. So more violent methods were used, especially from 1912: they burned empty houses, rang false fire alarms; cut telephone wires; slashed paintings in art galleries; they even threw bombs. But the most dramatic action of all was by one suffragette, Emily Davison, who threw herself under the king's horse at the Derby and was killed. *The Daily Mail*, reporting the incident, described her as having a record of 'mad exploits' and as being 'the hottest of all Suffragettes "Hot-bloods"'. Whose side do you think the reporter was on?

Women who committed acts of violence were imprisoned. Some went on hunger strike (they refused to eat as a protest). Prison authorities then force-fed them: a rubber tube was forced down the women's throats, and liquid food poured down. But it was a dangerous procedure.

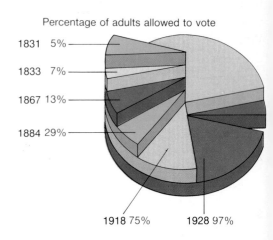

Percentage of adults allowed to vote

1831 5%
1833 7%
1867 13%
1884 29%
1918 75%   1928 97%

The pie chart clearly shows that Britain was not really a democratic country until the twentieth century.

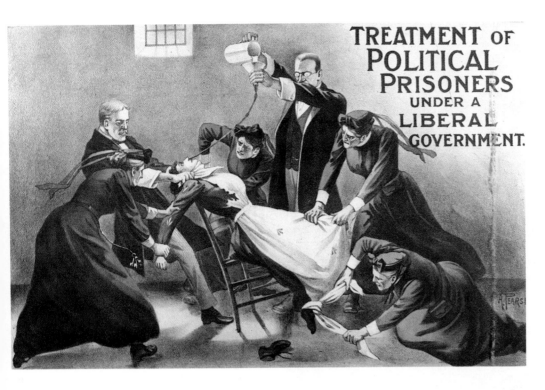

TREATMENT OF POLITICAL PRISONERS UNDER A LIBERAL GOVERNMENT.

This poster was produced by the suffragettes to show how horrible it was to be force-fed. It could cause pneumonia if the food entered the lungs.

So the Government passed an Act in 1913 allowing suffragettes, who were weak from a hunger strike, to be released from gaol. After they had recovered at home, they were arrested again. The Act was called the 'Cat and Mouse Act'. Why do you think that was?

A year later the First World War broke out. Women did valuable war-work – in factories, on farms, as police and on the buses. When the war came to an end the Government no longer dared prevent women from voting. In 1918 women over thirty received the vote; ten years later, women over twenty one. (British women had an advantage over French women, who had to wait until after the Second World War for the vote.) ☐

advantages of these methods. Can you think of any groups who use similar methods today?

5 Who is allowed to vote in elections in Britain today? Do you think that people should use their vote? Give your reasons.

This suffragette poster very clearly makes the point about the unfairness of women not being able to vote.

1 When the second Reform Bill was passed, Robert Lowe said 'Now we must educate our masters'. What do you think he meant and do you agree with him?

2 Look at the picture on page 86. Do you think that the photographer was sympathetic to Mrs Pankhurst or not? Explain your reasons.

3 You are a suffragette. Write a letter to your MP explaining why you think that women should be given the vote.

4 The suffragettes often used non-violent ways to make their protest. Explain the

87

The Welfare State

During the Second World War, William Beveridge was appointed as chairman of a committee to produce a plan for improved social welfare after the war. The committee produced a pamphlet called *Social Insurance and Allied Services*, more often known as the Beveridge Report. It immediately became a best seller – nearly 700,000 copies were sold in one year! It was so popular that for a time, in December 1942, when the Report was published, the war seemed almost forgotten as people talked just about the Beveridge Plan.

Wartime origins

By the Second World War (1939–45) the British people had seen about 100 years of social reforms. But there was still a lot to be done: there was still poverty, malnutrition, ill-health, insanitary homes and illiteracy. At the start of the war many children were evacuated from the big cities, especially London, in case they were killed or injured in air raids (see pages 131–32). Some of these children were not at all healthy and this came as a dreadful shock to the organizers of the evacuation scheme and the temporary foster parents with whom the evacuees lived.

It was obvious that, once the War was over, much more had to be provided in the way of social welfare – to give all people a reasonable life from 'the cradle to the grave'. The framework for these reforms was the famous Beveridge Report, which was described by the Minister responsible for this area of Government work in the following words: 'No document within living memory has made such a powerful impression, or stirred such hopes.' Beveridge wrote of five 'giants' to be tackled on the road of social progress: want, disease, ignorance, squalor and idleness (see cartoon).

The giant of ignorance was attacked before the others. In 1944 the President of the Board of Education, RA Butler, introduced an Education Act. Local Authorities were to provide schools suited to the 'age, aptitude and ability' of each child. From now on children were to attend 'primary' schools until the age of eleven. Then they were to transfer to secondary schools; the most academically-inclined to grammar schools (the fees for which were abolished); the others to secondary modern schools. The separation of children into 'grammar' and 'modern' schools was to become very controversial. Indeed the merits of 'selection' in comparison with 'comprehensive education' (schools for all pupils in a particular area) are still hotly discussed.

Labour Party reforms

A general election was held in 1945. Many believed that the Labour Party would be more likely to introduce reforms than the Conservatives. And so the Labour Party was voted in with a very large majority. Clement Attlee became prime minister. While he was PM, the following Acts were passed:

1　The Family Allowance Act, 1945 – the Government paid allowances (sums of money) to families with children.

2　The National Insurance Act, 1946 – the Government, employers and employees provided money for social services.

3　The National Health Act, 1946 – for free medical care.

4　The National Assistance Act, 1948 – payments to the specially needy.

The most controversial of all these was the National Health Act, which set up the National Health Service. The Minister responsible for this, the Welshman Aneurin ('Nye') Bevan believed passionately in its necessity. He said:

'No society can legitimately [*properly*] call itself civilized if a sick person is denied medical aid because of lack of means.'

This cartoon appeared in *Punch* to show that better education was needed. Before the Second World War the Labour Party had argued for 'Secondary Education for All' because most pupils left 'elementary' school at the age of 14 having been taught little more than the '3 Rs' (reading, 'riting, 'rithmetic).

Education became by far the most expensive service provided by local government. Old buildings and those destroyed by bombs had to be repaired or replaced. Also, there were more students in schools: plans were made to raise the school-leaving age (to 15, and eventually 16). And after 1945 people started having more babies again.

Spending on welfare and social services

	£m
1909	2
1914	21
1939	260
1950	1,500
1961	3,900
1968	7,900
1978	20,400
1985	52,600

For many years after the Second World War a great effort was made to build more houses and flats. They were needed for two reasons: to replace the terrible old slums many people were still living in (see page 42); and to replace the houses destroyed by bombing during the War. The photograph shows 'Nye' Bevan (with flower in button-hole) at an official opening of council houses in 1949.

Parliamentary		Social		Trade Unions	
1819	Peterloo Massacre	1830	Start of the 'Ten Hour' Movement	1824–5	Trade Unions made legal
1830–32	Campaign for Reform Bill	1833	Ashley's Factory Act	1833	Grand National Consolidated Trade Union
1832	First Reform Act	1836	Registration of births, marriages and deaths		
1837	People's Charter drawn up			1834	Tolpuddle Martyrs sentenced
1839	First Chartist petition	1844	Factory Act	1851	Amalgamated Society of Engineers founded
1842	Second Chartist petition	1847	Factory Act		
1848	Third Chartist petition	1848	Public Health Act	1868	TUC established
1867	Second Reform Act	1866	Public Health Act	1871	Trade Union Act
1872	Secret Ballot	1875	Public Health Act		
1884	Third Reform Act	1942	Beveridge Report	1888–89	Several strikes
1903	Foundation of the Women's Social and Political Union	1944	Education Act	1910–12	Several strikes
1911	Parliament Act	1945	Family Allowances	1926	General strike
1913	The 'Cat and Mouse' Act	1946	National Insurance National Health	1927	Trade Union Act
1918	Reform Act				
1928	Reform Act	1948	National Assistance	1946	Trade Union Act

The main 'mile-stones' in the reform movement in Britain, 1800–1950.

For the first time in history British people would be able to receive free hospital care, medicine, dental treatment and glasses. But Bevan had a fierce struggle with the medical profession, who were seriously worried that they would be made civil servants and lose professional control of medical services. Bevan won.

Modern disagreements

Although the Labour Party introduced these reforms, the Conservative Party came to accept them. However, by about 1980 the two main political parties were disagreeing on two important matters: the trade unions and the Welfare State.

The Conservatives believe the trade unions have been given too many privileges in law in the past and became too powerful. So, in the 1980s new laws were passed to reduce the right to strike. The Conservatives also now believe many parts of the Welfare State should be

changed; that people should take more responsibility for looking after themselves. Otherwise they worry that by the year 2000 (because there will be so many old age pensioners) the cost of pensions and the health service will be huge.

On the other hand, the Labour Party believe that the working class and poor should be looked after at least as well in the future as in the past. Some people also point out that several European countries now have better pensions and health schemes than Britain. This is partly because they are richer. Do you think that Britain should make changes? If so, what kinds? □

1 Make a list of reforms which you think Britain still needs. Explain why you thihk they are needed.
2 Look at the photograph on page 89. Why do you think Bevan was the minister responsible for housing? (You will need to read the text on that page as well.)

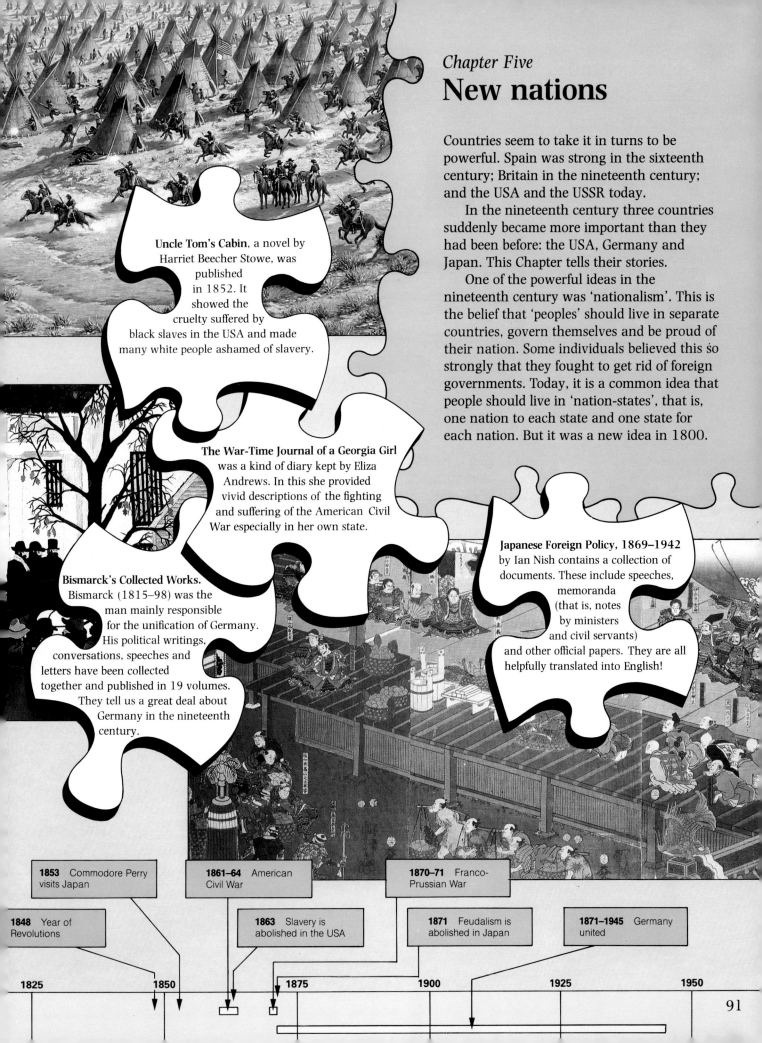

Chapter Five
New nations

Countries seem to take it in turns to be powerful. Spain was strong in the sixteenth century; Britain in the nineteenth century; and the USA and the USSR today.

In the nineteenth century three countries suddenly became more important than they had been before: the USA, Germany and Japan. This Chapter tells their stories.

One of the powerful ideas in the nineteenth century was 'nationalism'. This is the belief that 'peoples' should live in separate countries, govern themselves and be proud of their nation. Some individuals believed this so strongly that they fought to get rid of foreign governments. Today, it is a common idea that people should live in 'nation-states', that is, one nation to each state and one state for each nation. But it was a new idea in 1800.

Uncle Tom's Cabin, a novel by Harriet Beecher Stowe, was published in 1852. It showed the cruelty suffered by black slaves in the USA and made many white people ashamed of slavery.

The War-Time Journal of a Georgia Girl was a kind of diary kept by Eliza Andrews. In this she provided vivid descriptions of the fighting and suffering of the American Civil War especially in her own state.

Japanese Foreign Policy, 1869–1942 by Ian Nish contains a collection of documents. These include speeches, memoranda (that is, notes by ministers and civil servants) and other official papers. They are all helpfully translated into English!

Bismarck's Collected Works. Bismarck (1815–98) was the man mainly responsible for the unification of Germany. His political writings, conversations, speeches and letters have been collected together and published in 19 volumes. They tell us a great deal about Germany in the nineteenth century.

1853 Commodore Perry visits Japan	**1861–64** American Civil War	**1870–71** Franco-Prussian War
1848 Year of Revolutions	**1863** Slavery is abolished in the USA	**1871** Feudalism is abolished in Japan	**1871–1945** Germany united

1825	1850	1875	1900	1925	1950

A typical scene of a 'shoot-out' from a Western film called *Rio Grande*. This is the river which forms the boundary between the USA and Mexico. The people of Mexico speak Spanish and many have settled in the USA. That is why some characters in Westerns which are set near the Mexico border speak with a Spanish accent. A lot of Westerns were made in the 1930s and 1940s. One of the actors who played cowboys in some of them became President of the USA in 1981. This was Ronald Reagan.

Increase in population and in area of the USA, 1789–1850. In 1789 there were 3 million people to an area of 800,000 square miles. By 1850 there were 23 million people to an area of 2,920,000 square miles.

Go West, young man!

Most people have seen a 'Western', a film about adventures in the nineteenth century when the central plains and the western parts of the USA were being 'settled' by white people (that is, people were setting up home there). Most of these films were made in Hollywood and usually have the same sort of themes: a sheriff trying to keep law and order; cattle rustlers; wars between Indians and the army; stories of cowboys – 'goodies' and 'baddies' (who are usually wearing the black hats!). These films have given us the wrong idea about what life was *really* like. It was not all heroic shoot-outs with the 'goodies' always winning.

We left the story of America in 1789 (see Chapter 3). George Washington had just become President. The number of people living in the USA increased by

Settlers. The 'frontier' is what the Americans called the western edge of the land occupied by white settlers. As more settlers occupied new land, so the frontier moved westward. To this day many Americans are proud of the 'frontier tradition' – the tough, adventuring spirit which made the USA a country stretching across the whole continent. In many ways 'the frontier' became a myth; the bad aspects were conveniently forgotten.

great numbers (see cartoon, left). Why? It was partly because immigrants arrived from many European countries, mainly Britain, Ireland and Germany to settle in the USA. Extra land had been gained partly by buying it and partly by fighting for it in war.

To the west of the original thirteen colonies there was rich land – for hunting, farming, cattle-rearing and prospecting for gold. People with energy and clever ideas could sometimes make a fortune if they settled in these new lands. That is where the saying 'Go West, young man!' comes from.

First of all, trails (routes) were opened up by explorers and the pioneers, the early settlers. Their journeys were dangerous

Westward expansion.

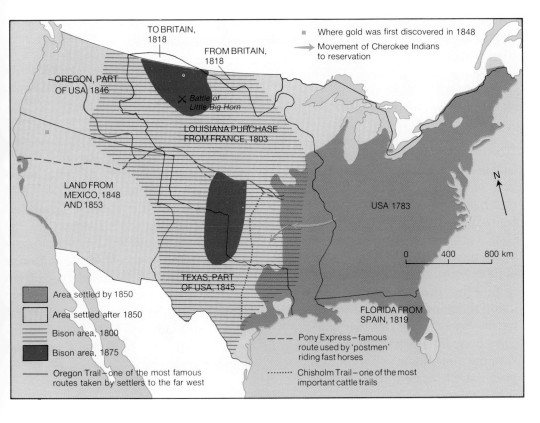

TO BRITAIN, 1818

FROM BRITAIN, 1818

■ Where gold was first discovered in 1848

→ Movement of Cherokee Indians to reservation

OREGON, PART OF USA 1846

✕ Battle of Little Big Horn

LOUISIANA PURCHASE FROM FRANCE, 1803

LAND FROM MEXICO, 1848 AND 1853

USA 1783

N

TEXAS, PART OF USA, 1845

FLORIDA FROM SPAIN, 1819

0   400   800 km

Area settled by 1850

Area settled after 1850

Bison area, 1800

Bison area, 1875

Oregon Trail – one of the most famous routes taken by settlers to the far west

Pony Express – famous route used by 'postmen' riding fast horses

Chisholm Trail – one of the most important cattle trails

THE INDEPENDENT GOLD HUNTER ON HIS WAY TO CALIFORNIA.
I NEITHER BORROW NOR LEND

This cartoon shows a quite wealthy person from the state of Missouri walking 2,000 miles with all his equipment to California in search of gold.

But in 1848, gold was found in the mountain-streams in California (see map)! The news spread fast. 1849 became the year of the 'gold rush'; 80,000 people poured west with dreams of fantastic fortunes. (The famous song 'Clementine' is about the daughter of a 'forty-niner'.) All these extra people had to have somewhere to stay; towns sprang up, dotted about the country. They also had to be fed; huge cattle farms were developed, especially in Texas, to supply meat. 'Cowboys' were the men who looked after these animals and accompanied them on the long and tedious and tiring journeys to the slaughter-houses in the north. A cowboy named Andy Adams described one of the hazards – lack of water:

'Good cloudy weather would have saved us, but in its stead was a sultry [*warm and humid*] morning without a breath of air, which bespoke [*showed it would be*] another day of sizzling heat. We had not been on the trail over two hours before the heat became unbearable to man and beast ... the cattle congregated into a mass of unmanageable animals, milling and lowing in their fever and thirst ... For the first time a fact dawned on us that chilled the marrow in our bones – *the herd was going blind.*'

Miners, prospectors (explorers looking for gold) and cowboys were often rough, tough and violent men. There were many criminals such as bank robbers, looters of stage-coaches and trains, cattle-rustlers. The USA grew so fast to the west that it was almost impossible to organize a proper police force. Each town had a sheriff and the railroad (railway) companies employed detectives.

Barbed wire was an especially important invention – it kept cattle within a particular area and stopped them from being stolen. Gradually the West became less wild. But the tradition grew up that people must have guns to defend themselves. To this day millions of American homes have guns.

and hard. They travelled in convoys of covered waggons. Much of the land was wilderness: if their horses or mules died, they would be helpless; they could die of hunger, thirst or snake-bites; and they could be attacked by Indians. Most of the settlers were looking for land to farm. Most did not make fortunes at all but led hard and lonely lives. Here are the re-collections of one woman who settled in Iowa:

'The drudgery was unending. The isolation was worse ... We had a good farm of rich black soil. But it is people that really make a country, not soil ... One of our neighbours let three years go by before she came to see us. All about the house, at first, was a tangle of hazel brush. It grew so close about us that the cows couldn't get between it and the house ... There was one terrible period when, for two years, I carried my little sick Carrie around with me on a pillow as I went from store to table or from room to room doing my work.'

Indians

The white people were not, of course, the original inhabitants of America. These were the Indians. They were called Indians because the first European explorers in America thought they had sailed round the world to India! Naturally, when white settlers took their land the Indians resisted. From the early seventeenth century there was fighting. There were hundreds of Indian tribes, or 'nations'. Each spoke different languages and had different customs.

Treaties were signed between the American Government and the Indians to safeguard their land, most white settlers despised the Indians as 'savages' and took their lands anyway. When the Indians made war to get back their lands, the Government had to use the army to try to defend the white settlers. Atrocities were committed on both sides: torture, scalping, massacres. The Indians had a hard time of it:

1   In the 1820s and 1830s the white Government started to 'resettle' some tribes much further west than their home-lands. Uprooted, they suffered immense hardship and many died in the winters on the bleak plains.

2   White men built railroads, which cut across their land and hunting grounds.

3   White men of the north mercilessly killed their American buffalo, or bison.

The Indian tribes of the plains (or prairies) depended on the bison for food (meat), clothes and shelter (hides). The white men also wanted the hides. They could be sold for a lot of money. They started killing the animals at an incredible rate. In the 1870s it is estimated that 2 million were being killed a year! You will probably have heard of 'Buffalo Bill'. That was his nickname, earned because he killed so many buffalo. His real name was William Cody. At one time he claimed to have personally killed well over 2,000 in a year! By the 1880s only a few were left in special conservation areas.

By this time too what remained of the Indian tribes were in protected reservations – most of the tribes had died or been killed. Some tribes had resisted into

A painting of the Indian Wars. From the early seventeenth century to the late nineteenth century there were wars going on between the white man and the Indian 'redskins'. Altogether about one hundred big battles took place. Some people have accused the Americans of 'genocide', that is, deliberately killing off most of the Indian people who lived there. The Indians managed to buy some guns, but they had no chance against the better weapons of the US army.

the 1870s. The Sioux were particularly willing to fight to defend themselves; and they were the tribe who inflicted the last defeat on the American army in the Indian wars. This is the story. The Sioux had been given land in Dakota in the north of the USA. But gold was discovered there and the Sioux lands were invaded by prospectors. The Sioux chief, Sitting Bull, decided to fight for his people. In June 1876 he cleverly ambushed a detachment of troops under the command of Colonel Custer at a place called Little Big Horn. Completely outnumbered, the soldiers had no chance. For his men and for the Colonel himself it was 'Custer's last stand'.

Slavery

Some of the earliest settlers tried to make Indians slaves. But the Indians would rather die. So Africans were transported across the Atlantic to be bought as slaves (see Chapter 1). By the end of the eighteenth century there were about $\frac{1}{2}$ million black slaves in the USA. Most of them were in just two states – Virginia and South Carolina.

Why were there more slaves in the south? Slaves were particularly useful in the huge plantations and those were mostly in the south. The plantations were used for growing rice, sugar and cotton, in particular. In 1793 a machine was invented which made it easier to process the raw cotton. So then many plantation owners changed over to growing cotton because it could now be more profitable. But they needed a lot of people to pick the cotton from the plants: so they bought more slaves. In 1790 there were about 700,000. By 1860 there were $4\frac{1}{4}$ million slaves in the southern states.

Some slaves were treated well by their owners, especially if they were house servants. Some were even allowed to go free by their master. But, whatever happened, they would always suffer humiliation as long as people thought of them as 'inferior'. (And a black person could never escape from the colour of his skin.) Even today there are still some people in the

USA who treat black people as inferior. This is partly because of their slave ancestors; partly because of the colour of their skin. This is a vivid example of prejudice.

But most slaves suffered from much more than just hurt pride. Their families were broken up; they were made to work intolerably hard; they were treated brutally, even killed sometimes if they tried to escape. Plantation-owners appointed overseers to be in charge of all the slaves – there might be up to 100 overseers working on one plantation. Some of them were brutal bullies. One white man from the north travelled around the southern plantations in the 1850s. He wrote of what he saw:

'The whip was evidently in constant use . . . I said to one of the overseers, "It must be disagreeable to have to punish them as much as you do?" ". . . I think nothing of it. Why, sir, I wouldn't mind killing a nigger more than I would a dog."'

Also in the 1850s the novelist Harriet Beecher Stowe wrote a book called *Uncle Tom's Cabin*. It immediately became a best seller – 300,000 copies were sold in ten months! The reason? It described in harrowing detail the miseries of southern slaves. Many white people in the north had no idea what was going on in the south. They were horrified at what they read. They were also ashamed and started to demand the abolition of slavery. Here is

Cotton production increased from £5 million in 1795 to £1,000 million in 1850. By 1850 the USA was providing seven-eighths of the total world supply. A few families made fortunes from 'King Cotton'. But this cheap, mass production depended on slaves. By the middle of the century there were so many slaves in the southern states that many areas had more slaves than white people.

The picture shows a cotton plantation on the banks of the Mississippi River in 1833. Notice the overseer on horseback supervising the slaves, and the paddle-steamer in the background.

a short extract from the book. Mrs Shelby is speaking to her husband, a slave-owner:

' "Mr Shelby, you cannot be serious."

"I'm sorry to say that I am," said Mr Shelby. "I've agreed to sell Tom."

"What! Our Tom? – that good faithful creature! – been your faithful servant from a boy! O, Mr Shelby! – and you have promised him his freedom, too, – you and I have spoken to him a hundred times of it. Well, I can believe anything now, – I can believe *now* that you could sell little Harry, poor Eliza's only child!" said Mrs Shelby, in a tone of grief and indignation.

"Well, since you must know all, it is so ..."

"Why sell *them*, ... if you must sell at all?"

"Because they will bring the highest sum of any – that's why ..." '

Origins of the Civil War

We saw at the beginning of this Chapter how the USA grew by gaining more and more land to the west. As people went to live in these new areas the lands became organized into new States and involved in the system of government. To start with, each State had the right to decide whether it would allow slavery or not in its own area. But, in 1820 a law was passed saying there should be no more slaves in the North. Even so, as each new territory to the North became part of the USA the question was asked, 'should slavery be allowed there?'

A bitter quarrel broke out in 1854 about slavery. Senator Douglas of Illinois, an energetic man, sometimes called the 'Steam-engine in Britches', produced a plan. He proposed that the prairie lands of the north be organized into two large territories called 'Kansas' and 'Nebraska'. The people who settled there should decide for themselves whether to have slavery or not. So, what was wrong with that? Well, it contradicted the law of 1820 which said there should be no more slaves in the North. Douglas became the most hated man in the North: his effigy was burnt on bonfires like Guy Fawkes; whenever he appeared at meetings he was hooted and jeered. The atmosphere became tense:

1 Fighting broke out in Kansas between settlers who supported slavery and those who opposed it.

2 People in the North organized themselves to help runaway slaves who escaped from the South.

John Brown. By the 1850s hatred had grown up between the North and the South. The North wanted to abolish slavery because they said it was evil. The South wanted to keep their slaves. They said the abolitionists had no right to interfere – it was none of their business. The story of John Brown provides a good example of this tension. He was very religious and believed that slavery was an 'abomination' (that is, evil in the sight of God).

In 1855 there were particularly serious quarrels in Kansas. In one incident Brown took a party of men, raided a settlement occupied by people in favour of slavery and murdered five men. He then fled to the North where he was welcomed as a hero. In 1859 he held a meeting and planned an uprising of slaves. He and seventeen followers attacked and captured an army weapons and ammunition store at Harper's Ferry in Virginia. The aim was to arm the local slaves. But the plan failed. Brown was captured and hanged. It was a crazy adventure. In the North John Brown became a martyr; in the South, people were scared that a slave revolt might succeed next time. The painting, done in the twentieth-century, shows Brown tied up and being taken by cart to the gallows.

Pennsylvania Academy of the Fine Arts, Lambert Fund Purchase

North versus South.

North ('Union' or 'Federal' side): depended on trade and industry; believed in equality; 23 States; 22 million people.
South ('Confederate' side): depended on agriculture; controlled by small number of aristocratic families; 11 States; 9 million people.

3 A new political party was created, called the 'Republican Party', whose aim was to end slavery. One of its first members was a man called Abraham Lincoln. In 1858 Lincoln competed with Douglas to be Senator for the State of Illinois. Their public debates centred on the question of slavery.

4 The following year John Brown led a mad-cap invasion of the South to free the slaves. He was captured and executed. But, as the famous song about him says, 'John Brown's body lies a-mould'ring in the grave, His soul is marching on.' He became a hero with the 'abolitionists', as those against slavery were called.

The USA was drifting into Civil War between North and South. Besides the question of slavery there were other differences which they quarrelled about. The North depended on trade and industry; the South, on agriculture; The North believed in equality and democracy; the South was controlled by a small number of very rich families.

The Presidential election was held in November 1860. Lincoln was the Republican candidate. Douglas was one of the other candidates. Lincoln won by a big majority. The Southern States were afraid that the President would abolish slavery, so they started to 'secede', that is they announced that they were no longer part of the USA. They called themselves the 'Confederacy' (that is, a losely joined collection of States). It seemed as if the USA could break up. The President had promised to protect the Union, the *United* States. Would he risk a civil war to bring the Southern States back? He kept Northern troops in Fort Sumter in South Carolina. In April 1861 it was surrounded by Confederates. Lincoln sent supplies by ship. Firing started. The garrison of the fort was forced to surrender. It was war.

Civil War

In the war the North was called the 'Union' or 'Federal' side; the South, the 'Confederate' side. The Confederate side was much smaller. The Union generals therefore expected a quick victory. But that was not to be. The Confederate armies fought well under two brilliant Generals: Robert E Lee and 'Stonewall' Jackson. Also, in order to increase the number of their soldiers the Confederates introduced 'conscription' (enforced service with the army) in 1862. This is what one soldier, Sam Watkins, thought of that:

'From this time on till the end of the war, a soldier was simply a machine, a conscript ... All our pride and valor [courage] had gone and we were sick of war and the Southern Confederacy ... The glory of the war, the glory of the South, the glory and pride of our volunteers had no charms for the conscript.'

The war lasted four years. During that time the Confederacy appointed their own President – Jefferson Davis. However, Lincoln still claimed that he was the President of the whole USA. These were the main campaigns of the war (see map):

1   The Union had almost the whole of the American navy. So they were able to blockade the South.

2   The Confederate states were then cut in two by General Grant who took control of the River Mississippi.

3   The Confederate capital was at Richmond in Virginia. But the Union armies failed to capture it. The Confederates were quite successful in battles in this eastern region.

4   Lee invaded Pennsylvania. The Federal General Meade marched to meet him. The two armies faced each other at the little town of Gettysburg where they fought a bitter battle that lasted three days; the biggest of the war. It was July 1863. Lee lost so many men he had to retreat. After two years of war, the South could not replace the killed and wounded with more men. It was now obvious that the North would win.

5   In November–December 1864 Major-General Sherman marched 'from Atlanta [Georgia] to the sea'. As the last verse of the well-known song explains:

'So we made a thoroughfare for
   Freedom and her train,
Sixty miles in latitude – three
   hundred to the main;
Treason fled before us, for resistance
   was in vain,
As we were marching through
   Georgia.'

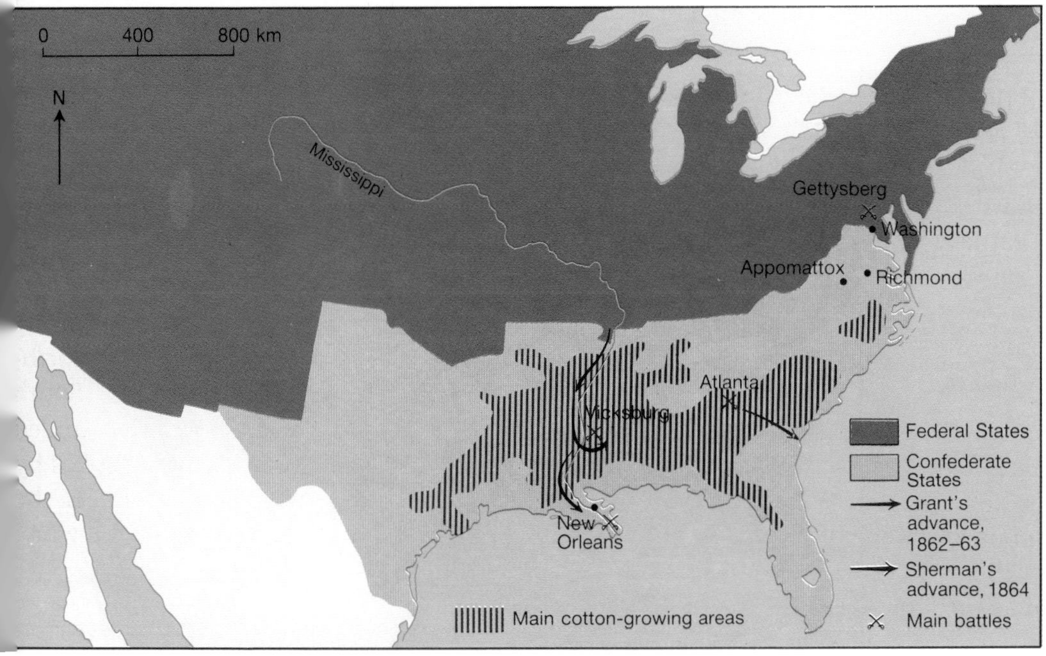

Civil War battles.

0 400 800 km	

N

Mississippi

Gettysburg
Washington
Appomattox   Richmond

Atlanta

Vicksburg

New Orleans

Legend	
■	Federal States
□	Confederate States
→	Grant's advance, 1862–63
→	Sherman's advance, 1864
‖‖‖	Main cotton-growing areas
×	Main battles

Civil War soldiers. Federal soldiers wore blue uniforms and Confederates, grey. They referred to each other as 'Yankees' (Federal) and 'Rebels' (Confederate). The American Civil War was one of the biggest wars of the nineteenth century. Infantry, artillery and cavalry were all involved. There were many acts of heroism. One of the most famous happened at the Battle of Gettysburg. On the third day of the fighting the Confederate General Lee decided to try to break the Federal line. 15,000 Virginians charged across a field to a wall defended by Federal infantry and artillery. Many fell; the rest advanced. The Federal guns fired at point-blank range; the remnants of the Virginian army clambered over the wall. More Federal troops were brought up; the Virginians had to retreat. Only 5,000 returned to their own lines.

His army burned and looted over this whole 60 by 300 miles area. It was a campaign that was not only cheerily remembered in the song; it left bitter memories of hatred in the South. This bitterness is revealed in a journal kept by a girl called Eliza Andrews. In it she wrote:

'About three miles from Sparta we struck the "burnt country", ... and then I could better understand the wrath and desperation of these poor people ... The fields were trampled down and the roads were lined with carcasses of horses, hogs, and cattle that the invaders ... had wantonly shot down, to starve out the people ... while here and there lone chimney stacks, "Sherman's sentinels", told of homes laid in ashes.'

6 Finally, Lee had to evacuate Richmond and then formally surrendered to Grant in a ceremony at Appomattox, on 9 April 1864. Other Confederate armies surrendered as the news spread.

When the war started it was uncertain whether the North really wished to abolish slavery altogether. In fact, in 1862 Lincoln wrote: 'My paramount object in this struggle *is* to save the Union, and it is *not* either to save or destroy Slavery'. But, on 1 January 1863 Lincoln issued a proclamation in which he declared all slaves

Nearly 3 million men served in the armies during the Civil War – about ⅓ of all adult white males. The photograph (*below*) was taken during the Battle of Gettysburg, July 1863. It shows a Confederate 'sharpshooter'. A sharpshooter was a rifleman who could shoot very accurately; a marksman or sniper.

in the Confederate states to be free. It was clear now that the war was about slavery as well as about keeping the USA as one country.

Lincoln also emphasized the importance of freedom in a speech in 1863. In November of that year a ceremony was held at Gettysburg for the dedication of a cemetery for those soldiers, Confederate as well as Union, who had fallen in the battle there in the summer. At the end of his speech, which came to be called Lincoln's 'Gettysburg Address', he said

'…We here highly resolve that these dead shall not have died in vain, that this nation, under God, shall have a new birth of freedom, and that government of the people, by the people, for the people, shall not perish from the earth.'

By the end of the war Lincoln had become a very famous and respected man. Five days after Lee's surrender to Grant, Lincoln went to the theatre in Washington. There he was shot dead by an assassin. He was the sixteenth President of the USA and, with Washington, accepted as the greatest.

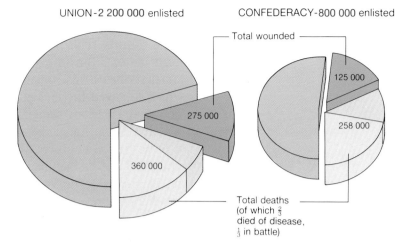

UNION - 2 200 000 enlisted   CONFEDERACY - 800 000 enlisted

Total wounded

275 000

360 000

125 000

258 000

Total deaths (of which $\frac{2}{3}$ died of disease, $\frac{1}{3}$ in battle)

Civil War casualties. Notice that nearly half the Confederate soldiers died or were wounded. Of the 600,000 who died about two-thirds died of disease; only one third were killed in battle.

Reconstruction

The slaughter and destruction of the Civil War left bitter memories and hatred, especially in the South. A civil war is the most horrible of all kinds of war for those involved. Terrible decisions have to be made. In the South particularly each young person had to ask himself questions like these: 'Shall I be loyal to the United States or to the Confederacy?'; 'Am I willing to kill other Americans?'; 'Am I willing to fight to defend slavery?'. What do you think *you* would have decided?

Because the war caused so much

The impressive Lincoln Memorial in Washington shows the respect the American people have for Lincoln. He was born in a typical log-cabin in 1809 in Kentucky. He became a lawyer. Lincoln was a tall, awkward rather untidy man. His enemies called him 'the gorilla'! But he was patient, tactful and hard working and he learned to make very moving speeches. He was one of four American Presidents (including Kennedy) to have been murdered. History never actually repeats itself. But, some of the similarities between the murders of Lincoln and Kennedy were quite uncanny:

1 Lincoln was elected in 1860; Kennedy in 1960.
2 Lincoln's assassin was born in 1839; Kennedy's in 1939.
3 Their successors as President were both named Johnson.
4 Lincoln's secretary was named Kennedy; Kennedy's secretary was named Lincoln.
5 Both men were shot in the head in the presence of their wives.
6 Both assassins were themselves murdered before they could be brought to trial.

hatred, it was important that the years immediately after it should be used to heal and reunite the country. This period was called 'Reconstruction'. But one American historian described it like this: 'The ten years which followed the end of the war were one of the darkest decades in American history.' What happened after the war left more hatred between North and South than the war had left itself.

So what did happen? The victorious North sent soldiers to occupy the South. Many people in the South were prohibited from voting and from helping to govern their own States. And the government of the South fell into the hands of three different kinds of people:

1 Blacks who had little education and no experience in government because they had only just been freed from slavery.

2 Corrupt Southerners, who merely wanted to make as much money for themselves as possible. They were called 'scalawags'.

3 Corrupt Northerners, who saw opportunities in the South for making money. They were called 'carpet-baggers'.

Because the freed slaves knew nothing about government, the scalawags and carpet-baggers took control, made fortunes for themselves and left the Southern States poor and in chaos. People in the South resented this. They came to hate the negroes who seemed to have become so important so quickly. In 1867 an organization was formed called the 'Ku Klux Klan'. They dressed in white robes and hoods and devoted themselves to prevent-

ing black people from having equality with Whites. They started terrorizing Blacks – beating, torturing and killing them. By 1877 the government of the South had returned to normal. But intense racial hatred remained. □

A carpet-bagger. Northerners who moved to the South to take over the state governments there were called 'carpet-baggers'. Because they left the North in such a hurry they were thought to have thrown a few clothes into a carpet-bag for the journey. Of course there were many honest people from the North who went to the South to help improve conditions: teachers, doctors, clergymen, for example.

1 The USA still has a 'Federal system' of government, (that is, the individual States in some ways govern themselves). List as many countries in the world today as you can which have a similar arrangement.

2 Compare the picture of cowboys on page 92 and the quotation from Andy Adams on page 94. Do you think that most 'western' films give accurate pictures of what the life of a cowboy was like? Give reasons for your answer.

3 Imagine you are a black person, born in 1800 and living in Virginia in 1870. Write an account of your life and thoughts about your experiences to tell your grandchildren.

4 Write out two speeches for lawyers, one for the prosecution and one for the defence of John Brown.

5 Write a newspaper report of *either*: a) the Battle of Gettysburg; *or* b) Sherman's march through Georgia.

This photograph shows a gathering of the Ku Klux Klan (KKK). The movement was active after each of America's serious wars: the Civil War and the two World Wars. It was at its strongest in the 1920s when it claimed to have 5 million members.

Germany

Germany in 1815

At the start of the nineteenth century almost the whole of Europe was controlled by the French Emperor, Napoleon. He was finally defeated at the Battle of Waterloo in 1815.

The important politicians met at a congress (or conference) in Vienna, the Austrian capital, to draw up a peace treaty. They had to divide up Napoleon's empire – to redraw many of the boundaries of Europe. One of the biggest problems was what to do about Germany.

Before Napoleon's time there was no state of Germany. At least, not in the same way as there was France or Britain, for instance. In the centre of Europe, where people spoke the German language, there were well over 300 states! Some were quite big, like Prussia, Austria, Bavaria; some were no more than independent cities. Germany could not go back to this chaos. Instead, the Congress of Vienna arranged that there should be only 39 German States.

These states were loosely joined in a 'Confederation' (the German word was 'Bund') (see map). Representatives of the 39 governments met together at Frankfurt in a kind of parliament called a 'Diet'. But the Diet had no powers. In practice each of the 39 states was independent and separate.

The president of the Diet was always the representative from Austria. Austria was a sprawling country. It included what is today Austria, Hungary, Czechoslovakia and parts of Poland, Romania, Italy and Yugoslavia (page 104). Only about one-third of this Austrian Empire was in the Confederation because many people in the Austrian Empire were not Germans. After Napoleon was defeated, Austria was the most powerful country in Europe. The Emperor did not want any change. The chief minister or Chancellor in 1815 was Prince Metternich.

Now, although the Austrian Empire was so powerful, there was another German state, in the north of the country, which was becoming strong. This was Prussia. It had an especially well-trained army (ever since the eighteenth century). It also owned the area of West Germany known as the Ruhr. This was to become the centre of German industry.

How to unify Germany?

Many people in the German Confederation did not like this system. They wanted a united Germany. It was fashionable at this time to be interested in Germany's past. Scholars studied the German language and the history and traditions of German people. For example, two brothers studied old myths – and even fairy stories. Their name was Grimm. It is because of their research that young children today can enjoy stories like 'Snow White and the Seven Dwarfs'.

At first the younger people were the keenest on unification. They accepted these new ideas more easily and enthusiastically than older generations. Students became especially interested; they organized secret societies to talk about ways of making Germany a united and democratic country. The two ideas of 'unity' and

Germany after 1815.

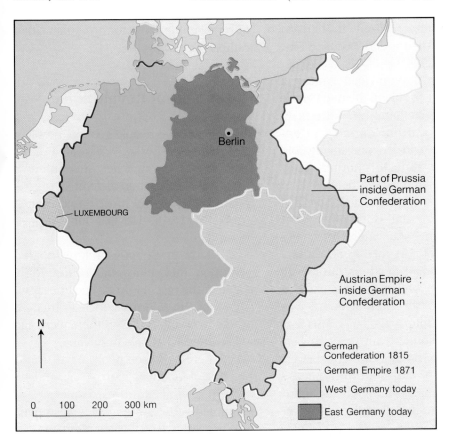

Berlin

LUXEMBOURG

Part of Prussia inside German Confederation

Austrian Empire inside German Confederation

N

0   100   200   300 km

German Confederation 1815

German Empire 1871

West Germany today

East Germany today

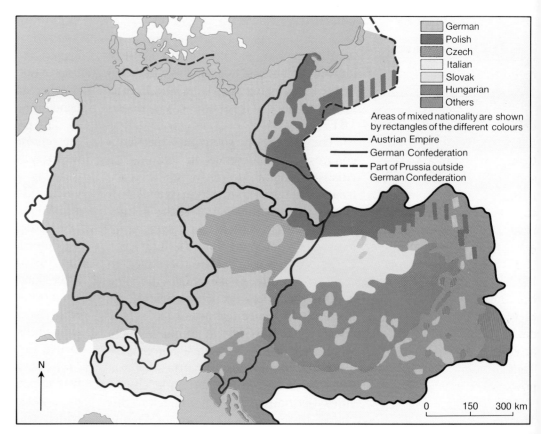

Legend:
- German
- Polish
- Czech
- Italian
- Slovak
- Hungarian
- Others

Areas of mixed nationality are shown by rectangles of the different colours
— Austrian Empire
— German Confederation
--- Part of Prussia outside German Confederation

0   150   300 km

N

'democracy' seemed to go together. The Emperor, kings and princes were not only preventing unification, they also kept backward the systems of government. Prince Metternich realized that these student societies were dangerous. So he made them illegal.

Keeping Germany divided caused a serious practical problem. It made trade difficult. In 1815 customs duties (taxes on goods passing from one country to another) had to be paid on goods being sold by one German state to another. They even had to be paid on goods being sold in the same state, e.g. by one half of Prussia to the other! The Prussian Government was particularly keen to sell more linen and corn. So some states in northern Germany agreed to get rid of customs duties. By 1834, 17 states had become part of a 'customs union' (the German word was 'Zollverein') (see map, page 107). This was the start of economic team work in Germany, similar to the Common Market we have in western and southern Europe today. It was an important start to building a united Germany. A British politician noted in 1840:

'It has done wonders in breaking down petty and local jealousies ... The *Zollverein* has brought the sentiment of German nationality out of the regions of hope and fancy into those of positive material interests.'

1848: Year of Revolutions

All over Europe people rose in revolt in most capitals. Berlin, Vienna, Prague; there was even another revolution in Paris. Metternich had defended the old system and was the most hated man in Europe in 1848. He fled for safety to England.

We saw in Chapter 3 how a great revolution took place in France. Many people in the rest of Europe became rather jealous of the reforms which France enjoyed as a result. By 1848 there were a lot of discontented people in Europe.

1   There had been poor harvests and the price of food was high.

2   In several countries people demanded better systems of government with properly elected parliaments.

3 There was strong nationalist feeling in several countries. Czechoslovakia and Hungary wanted to be independent of Austria, for example; and Germany wanted to be united.

All these disturbances provided an opportunity to unite Germany. So in May a kind of parliament for the whole of Germany met in Frankfurt. These professors, lawyers, doctors, businessmen set themselves the job of organizing a united Germany. But it was an impossible task really. Why do you think that was? Here are some reasons:

1 The Frankfurt Assembly was powerless. In fact, it had the reputation of being the most ineffective 'talking shop' in history. For over a year they just talked and did nothing. But then they could not do anything because they had no power. They would only be able to act when a powerful ruler supported them.

2 They quarrelled among themselves. They divided into 'Great Germans' against 'Little Germans'. The problem was: where should the boundaries of a new united Germany be? And, how much of the Austrian Empire should be included? The 'Great Germans' wanted all of Austria; but that would have meant having a lot of non-German people in Germany. The 'Little Germans' either wanted to exclude the Austrian Empire altogether, including the German-speaking members, or to split it in two. Obviously all these solutions had their problems.

3 They did not have a powerful leader, yet that was the only way to make progress. The Austrian Emperor made it clear that he would not take the lead. So the Frankfurt Assembly asked King Frederick William IV of Prussia to be Emperor of a united Germany. He replied with contempt that he would not 'pick up a Crown from the gutter'. In fact, it was not just that he despised the Frankfurt Assembly; he was also frightened that Austria would fight a war to destroy a new Germany controlled by her great rival, Prussia.

By 1849 the revolutions in Germany and throughout the Austrian Empire had been crushed and the representatives had gone home from Frankfurt. Obviously if they were to unite Germany they would have to use different methods.

Little Germans and Great Germans.

Prussia and Bismarck

Prussia had to fight three wars before Germany became united. Frederick William, the King who refused to become German Emperor in 1849, went insane. His successor was William I. He believed that Prussia had to be made stronger so it could bring about the unification of Germany. Soon after he became King he made Otto von Bismarck Prime Minister. He was Prime Minister of Prussia first, and then Chancellor of Germany for a total of twenty-seven years. He was one of the most important men in modern history.

Bismarck was born in 1815. He was a 'Junker' (that is, from a family of landed gentry), proud and hard-working, though not all that rich. He was intelligent, had considerable personal charm, and was very determined. He always seemed stern and in complete control when dealing with government work. This gave him the name 'Iron Chancellor'. In fact, he described himself like this; 'I am all nerves, so much so that self-control has always been the greatest task of my life...' He had a powerful temper which he had to struggle to control.

Bismarck was a heavily built man. And he put on more weight by too much eating and drinking. When he moved from his Berlin house, which had been his office, his store of wine had to be moved as well! He had 13,000 bottles! He once said that it was his ambition to drink 5,000 bottles of champagne during his life.

As soon as he became Prime Minister he made one thing clear. He believed in 'blood and iron'. That is, that war was the only way to get things done. He said:

> 'The great questions of the day will not be decided by speeches and the resolutions of majorities – that was the blunder of 1848 and 1849 – but by "iron and blood".'

One of the interesting but difficult questions to ask ourselves about history is whether great men like Bismarck plan exactly what they want to do. Or do they just take advantage of events as they happen? By 1871 Bismarck had united Germany. But when he became Prime Minister in 1862 do you think he *really* had a plan to unite Germany? Had he really decided to do that? Probably not. It is more likely that Bismarck cleverly turned events to Prussia's advantage. He himself said, 'Man cannot create the current of events. He can only float with it and steer'. So how did Bismarck 'steer'?

Der Berliner Pfau.

Kein Wunder, daß er stolz ist!

Bismarck did not enter politics until 1847. He had been rather a failure as a civil servant and in managing his estates. In 1847 he became a member of the Prussian Diet (Parliament). He disliked the Revolution in 1848 and was opposed to reforms. After he became Prime Minister he ignored Parliament: he collected extra taxes which the Parliament had refused to agree to and used the money to strengthen the army. After he became Chancellor of the new German Empire he kept Parliament (now called the Reichstag) very weak. He was worried by the Social Democratic Party. This was formed to try to put into practice the Communist ideas of Karl Marx (see page 66). Bismarck made the party illegal. But he did introduce a sort of 'welfare state' in the 1880s; Germany had accident, sickness and old age insurance and pensions schemes before any other country.

After 1871 Germany was the strongest country in Europe. But Bismarck was worried that other countries might 'gang up' on Germany, so he made treaties with Russia and Austria. Many believe Germany suffered because Bismarck allowed so little political freedom. The cartoon was drawn in Austria in 1870. The title is 'The Berlin Peacock. No wonder he is so proud!'. It refers to Bismarck's pride in all the Prussian victories in the war against France: the place-names are displayed on his tail.

Wars of unification

If Prussia took control of Germany, two other countries would get very worried: Austria and France. To have a powerful country on your borders *is* worrying and dangerous. Bismarck realized that Prussia and Austria were competing to be the strongest country in central Europe. He decided that it was Prussia who would win, and quickly.

1 War with Denmark (see map). This started because of an argument over who should govern the tiny duchies of Schleswig and Holstein. The British Prime Minister Lord Palmerston said that the problem was so complicated that only three people had understood it: himself, and he had forgotten; the Prince Consort, and he was dead; and a German professor, and he was in a lunatic asylum! Bismarck saw his opportunity. He would make Prussia the champion of the Germans living there by fighting against the Danes. Prussia and Austria fought Denmark and soon defeated that little country. Austria and Prussia then occupied Schleswig and Holstein.

2 War with Austria (see map). Bismarck made friends with Italy and France so that they would not interfere. Austria and Prussia quarrelled, partly over Schleswig-Holstein. Nine other German states sided with Austria. Many thought the two sides were evenly matched and that it would be a long war. In fact it lasted only six weeks. The Prussian army had been re-equipped

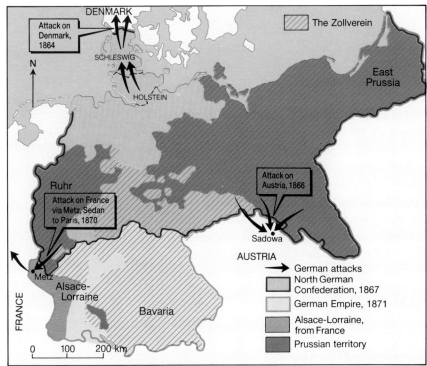

The Wars of Unification.

with modern rifles and field-guns. The Austrian army was beaten at the Battle of Sadowa. As a result of the Six-Week War Prussia took over some north German states. She also set up the North German Confederation. This was a combination of other states which Prussia really controlled. The old German Confederation of 1815 had ended. Austria was excluded from the new Germany.

3 War with France (see map). There were still five states in southern Germany outside Prussian control. Perhaps Bismarck would like these? The Emperor of France, Napoleon III, thought that if Prussia gained these states France might

During the 1860s the Prussian army was improved: made bigger; was re-equipped with up-to-date weapons; and trained to move fast in response to orders. These improvements were the work of the Minister of War, von Roon, and the Chief of the General Staff, von Moltke and were particularly successful at the Battle of Sadowa when the Prussians, shown here advancing, defeated the Austrian army.

get some extra land. But he was old and sick and in any case had never had the skill of his uncle Napoleon Bonaparte. He was no match for Bismarck. A quarrel developed over who should be the King of Spain. One candidate was related to the King of Prussia. Bismarck made Napoleon III look as though he was in the wrong. France declared war in July 1870.

The Franco-Prussian war lasted longer than the war with Austria. However, it was obvious again that the Prussian army was better than the French. It was better equipped and more efficient. Paris suffered a terrible siege, being reduced to chaos and starvation. Eventually, in May 1871, the French signed a peace treaty.

The German Empire

But even before this treaty was signed Bismarck had arranged an important ceremony. On 18 January 1871 in the great Hall of Mirrors in the French Palace of Versailles the King of Prussia was proclaimed Emperor of Germany. The new Empire was made up of the North German Confederation; the southern German states (which had been excluded in 1867); and Alsace and Lorraine (taken from France) (see map, page 107). But Bismarck was personally not happy about taking the French-speaking parts of Lorraine. He said,

'The Emperor has too many foreigners for subjects as it is. We have had more than enough trouble with our Poles ... And we shall have still more with these Lorrainers, who hate us like poison ...'

Bismarck hoped that his new Germany could remain at peace with the rest of Europe. He was Chancellor until 1890 when he was dismissed by the new Emperor, Wilhelm II. In fact Germany was to remain united for only 74 years, until 1945 when it was again divided. And during those years it was largely responsible for two of the most terrible wars in history, the First and Second World Wars. ☐

The Franco-Prussian War started in July 1870. By September the Prussian army had:
1 defeated and captured one French army at Metz;
2 defeated and captured another French army (including the Emperor Napoleon III) at Sedan;
3 besieged Paris. This siege caused many problems.

The people became desperate for food and all kinds of animals were killed to be eaten, even those in the zoo, as shown here. One French writer noticed that: 'soon the animals observed that man was regarding them in a strange manner and that, under the pretext of caressing them, his hand was feeling them like the fingers of a butcher ...'. An American believed that the stories about the eating of rats were exaggerated: only 300 were eaten, compared with 5,000 cats and 1,200 dogs. But how could he have made these calculations? The war lasted longer than Bismarck had expected because a French politician, Gambetta, escaped from Paris in a balloon and organized new armies.

1 You are a member of a student secret society in Prussia in 1819. Write a speech in favour of German unification.
2 Write a short biography of Bismarck. Explain whether you think he was a great man or not.
3 Study the maps on pages 103, 104, and 107 and answer the following questions:
   a) List the six main non-German peoples inside the German Confederation in 1815.
   b) What was the main non-German people in Prussia in the nineteenth century?
   c) In which present-day country is the Ruhr?

108

Japan

Traditional Japan

For well over 2,000 years now Japan has had Emperors. However, the Emperor, as today, has sometimes been no more than a figurehead with no real power. This was true from 1603 to 1868. During those years Japan was in practice ruled by the 'Shogun' (military leader). The Emperor lived in his palace in the capital city of Kyoto. The Shogun governed Japan from the city of Yedo (which was renamed Tokyo, or 'eastern capital' in 1869).

While the Shoguns governed Japan a feudal system was set up rather like the feudal systems of the Middle Ages in Europe (see Book 1). The country was divided into about 250 great estates owned by feudal lords. And the 'samurai' (or knights) kept strict control of the country. A samurai had the right to kill on the spot anyone who was disrespectful to him. No one dared question the laws or the system of government. Permission had to be obtained even to travel – and if anyone wandered from the prescribed route they could be punished by death.

Japan was a strict country to live in, but at least it was peaceful and some people, especially the merchants, became quite wealthy.

Trade with other countries was almost entirely prohibited. Contact with foreigners might be dangerous – Japanese people might get ideas and start to question the dreadful power of the Shogun and samurai. So no Japanese person was allowed to travel abroad; only a few Chinese, Korean and Dutch people were allowed to visit Japan for trade.

How changes came about

By the nineteenth century many Japanese people were starting to criticize this policy of isolation. The Government did not know what to do. Then in July 1853, something happened to change things. American warships, led by Commodore Perry, arrived at the fortified harbour of Uraga at the mouth of the bay where the city of Yedo stood. Perry handed over some letters. There was one from the US President. It asked for 'friendship, commerce, a supply of coal and provisions and protection for our shipwrecked people.' Perry had written his own letter and it wasn't so polite. He called the Japanese policy of isolation 'unwise and impracticable'.

For the next fifteen years there was a

For many centuries soldiers were highly respected in Japan. When the Shoguns controlled Japan the samurai were the most important class in society. They made up about 6 per cent of the population. Their lives revolved round programmes of very strict exercise and military training. In keeping strict control over the rest of the country they could be quite brutal. This Japanese print shows the Shogun Ashikaga Tokakigi presiding over the State Council. The Ashikaga family were Shoguns from 1339 to 1573. Notice all the food and servants bringing even more. Notice also that the Councillors are sitting on the floor, as was the custom in Japan.

lot of confusion inside Japan. Would they allow foreign trade and influence or not? A treaty was signed with the Americans and a US consul (permanent represent-ative) was sent to Yedo. The treaty did not allow the Americans full trading rights as they had hoped – merely 'the exchange of gold and silver coins, and articles of goods, for other articles of goods'. However, it was a start and the Americans in fact soon began trading.

Then other countries forced trading treaties on the Japanese – Britain, France, Holland, and Russia. Several ports were opened to foreign trade. But still some Japanese wanted to keep the foreigners out. They attacked foreigners; shore batteries fired on foreign ships. And so foreign ships fought back and bombarded Japanese ports.

Inside Japan quarrels over this grew more and more bitter. The Emperor quar-relled with the Shogun. The country seemed to be drifting into civil war. Then in 1867 the Emperor died. His successor was a boy of twelve called Mutsuhito. Powerful opponents forced the Shogun to resign, and in 1868 the young Emperor was truly governing Japan. He reigned for forty-five years, until his death in 1912. These years are called the Meiji Era, from a Japanese phrase meaning 'the illuminated reign of the Emperor'.

Adopting western ways

The Emperor and his advisers were determined to modernize Japan. He issued a decree: 'All absurd old usages shall be abandoned. Knowledge shall be sought throughout the world so that the found-ations of the Empire may be strengthened.' He realized that Japan had to be reformed to avoid being divided up into colonies by the Europeans and Americans. The country's slogan became 'National prosperity and military strength'.

As if to make up for lost time the Japanese rushed to copy western ways. Sometimes the effect seemed comical. The following is from a circular issued by a tailor to advertise the opening of his shop in Tokyo in 1871:

'What strange sights we see these days! We see many a man wearing a

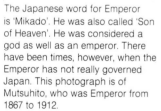

The Japanese word for Emperor is 'Mikado'. He was also called 'Son of Heaven'. He was considered a god as well as an emperor. There have been times, however, when the Emperor has not really governed Japan. This photograph is of Mutsuhito, who was Emperor from 1867 to 1912.

The Emperor of Japan since 1926 has been Hirohito. He claims to be directly descended from Jimmu Tenno, who became Emperor in 660 BC.

Prussian cap and French shoes, with a coat of the British navy and the trousers of the American navy – a mosaic [*pattern*] of different western countries plaited on a Japanese basis.' Sometimes the contact with foreigners was sad. The kind of problems that could occur were presented to western audiences by the famous opera by Puccini, *Madame Butterfly*. Butterfly is deserted by her American husband, the naval officer, Pinkerton, and commits suicide.

A lot of reforms were made, as you can see below. Do you think these changes were for the better?

1 Feudal system was abolished, 1871;

2 Foreign travel was allowed, 1871;

3 A national system of schools was introduced, 1872;

4 The army was reorganized, largely with the help of German advisers, 1873;

5 The tax system was reformed and the Bank of Japan set up, 1873;

6 Samurai privileges were abolished, 1873–77;

7 Western-style laws were introduced, from 1883;

8 Western-style cabinet of ministers appointed, 1885;

9 Western-style constitution introduced with a parliament (though most power remained with the Emperor), 1889.

Foreign policy

By the end of the nineteenth century Japan was a wealthy and powerful country. The Japanese learned western industrial methods quickly. As a result they built up a strong, well-equipped army and navy.

In 1894 Japan and China quarrelled over Korea (see map page 112). War broke out. The Japanese army defeated the Chinese. Japan won the island of Formosa (Taiwan) and the Chinese agreed that Korea should be independent. This success excited the Japanese people. The foreign minister noted, 'The populace seemed to be carried away with patriotic songs and their ambitions for the future knew no bounds'.

The British Government was impressed by the growing strength of Japan. In 1902 the two countries signed a treaty of alliance. This surprised many people. But the Japanese sprang a far greater surprise on the world. Three years later they defeated Russia in war.

The Sino-Japanese War. The word 'Sino' means Chinese. The mountains and trees in this wood-block print are characteristic of Japanese art. The western people behind the Japanese are journalists reporting on the invasion of Korea in 1894. Notice also the flag – symbol of Japan as 'the land of the rising sun'. The Chinese claimed that Korea was part of their empire. But when they sent soldiers there the Japanese became worried. Korea is a peninsula which projects from the mainland of Asia towards Japan. The Japanese also sent soldiers to Korea and so the war started. Many people in the west believed that the Japanese would be beaten: it was a much smaller country than China.

Japanese wars with China, 1894–95; with Russia, 1904–5.

Map legend:
- Japan 1894
- Korea (under Japanese influence, 1905; gained by Japan, 1910)
- Formosa (taken from China, 1895)
- Land taken from Russia, 1905
- Land under Japanese influence after 1905
- ✕ Battles

The two countries had quarrelled over the influence each wanted in Korea and southern Manchuria. The armies of both sides met at Mukden. The Japanese won. Meanwhile the Russians sent their fleet half-way round the world from the Baltic to the Yellow Sea. It met the Japanese in Tsushima Strait. The ships were old and the crew inefficient. (They fired on British fishing-trawlers at Dogger Bank thinking they had already arrived and these boats were Japanese junks!) The Japanese destroyed the Russian fleet.

For the first time in world history a powerful, white European country had been defeated by an Asiatic country using western weapons. The Japanese victory had many effects:

1 A revolution broke out in Russia.
2 Other Asiatic people now began to hope that one day they could throw off the control of their European masters (see page 133). As Lord Curzon, the Viceroy of India, said, the Japanese victories 'reverberated [echoed] through the whispering galleries of the East'. slaughter on Manchurian battlefields.' the west. As one wise Japanese writer commented, 'The average Westerner ... was wont [likely] to regard Japan as barbarous while she indulged in the gentle arts of peace: he calls her civilized since she began to commit wholesale slaughter on Manchurian battlefields.'

☐

1 Imagine you are a member of Commodore Perry's crew. Write a letter to your friend in the USA describing the differences between Japan and the USA at the time.
2 You are a samurai, born in 1840. In 1910 you look back over all the changes you have seen. Compile two lists – of those changes you approve of and those you disapprove of. Explain your reasons.

This Japanese painting shows one part of the Battle of Tsushima. Japanese torpedo boats and destroyers (the smaller ships) are attacking the Russian warships with torpedoes. Here is one Japanese description:

'According to the statement since made by prisoners of war, the severity of the torpedo attack on that night was almost beyond description. Our destroyers and boats advanced in such quick succession to the attack that the enemy had no time to prepare for defence.'

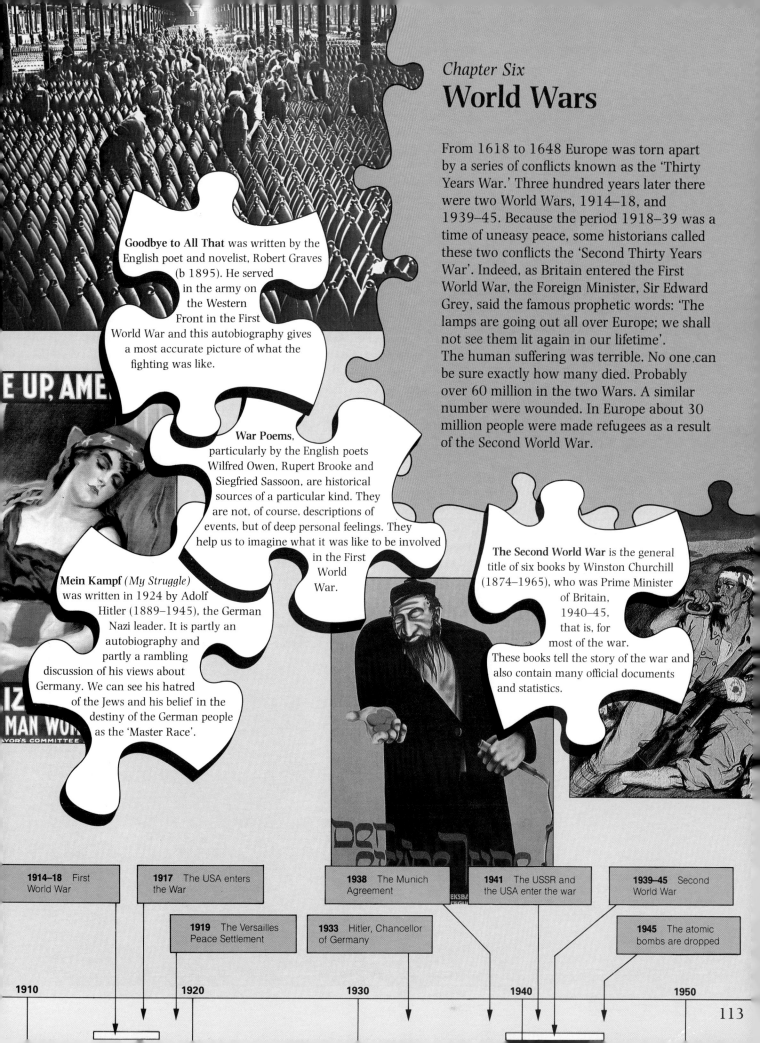

Chapter Six
World Wars

From 1618 to 1648 Europe was torn apart by a series of conflicts known as the 'Thirty Years War.' Three hundred years later there were two World Wars, 1914–18, and 1939–45. Because the period 1918–39 was a time of uneasy peace, some historians called these two conflicts the 'Second Thirty Years War'. Indeed, as Britain entered the First World War, the Foreign Minister, Sir Edward Grey, said the famous prophetic words: 'The lamps are going out all over Europe; we shall not see them lit again in our lifetime'. The human suffering was terrible. No one can be sure exactly how many died. Probably over 60 million in the two Wars. A similar number were wounded. In Europe about 30 million people were made refugees as a result of the Second World War.

Goodbye to All That was written by the English poet and novelist, Robert Graves (b 1895). He served in the army on the Western Front in the First World War and this autobiography gives a most accurate picture of what the fighting was like.

War Poems, particularly by the English poets Wilfred Owen, Rupert Brooke and Siegfried Sassoon, are historical sources of a particular kind. They are not, of course, descriptions of events, but of deep personal feelings. They help us to imagine what it was like to be involved in the First World War.

Mein Kampf (*My Struggle*) was written in 1924 by Adolf Hitler (1889–1945), the German Nazi leader. It is partly an autobiography and partly a rambling discussion of his views about Germany. We can see his hatred of the Jews and his belief in the destiny of the German people as the 'Master Race'.

The Second World War is the general title of six books by Winston Churchill (1874–1965), who was Prime Minister of Britain, 1940–45, that is, for most of the war. These books tell the story of the war and also contain many official documents and statistics.

1914–18 First World War

1917 The USA enters the War

1919 The Versailles Peace Settlement

1938 The Munich Agreement

1933 Hitler, Chancellor of Germany

1941 The USSR and the USA enter the war

1939–45 Second World War

1945 The atomic bombs are dropped

1910   1920   1930   1940   1950

The First World War

Origins

At the beginning of the twentieth century several European countries quarrelled with each other.

1 France versus Germany. Germany had defeated France in 1870–71 (see page 108). So many French people wanted a war of revenge against Germany; in particular to regain Alsace-Lorraine (see map below).

2 Britain versus Germany. Britain also quarrelled with Germany. Britain needed a large and strong navy to defend herself and to defend her widespread Empire. But Germany started to build large battleships. A naval race began between the two countries. The British built a super-battleship named HMS *Dreadnought*, which was finished in 1906. The Germans started building their own versions of such warships. So the British Government planned to build eight of these vessels. But there was some opposition among politicians who wanted to use the money for social reforms. But the people of Britain were afraid of the German challenge. The slogan was chanted; 'We want eight and we won't wait'.

3 Austria versus Serbia. As it turned out, it was the Balkans, the south-east corner of Europe (see map below), that proved to be the most dangerous spot. There, tension was mounting between the sprawling Austrian Empire on the one hand and the tiny country of Serbia on the other. What made this quarrel dangerous was that each side had powerful friends. Serbia was befriended by Russia. And Austria was on Germany's side. In the final crisis Kaiser Wilhelm told the Austrians that Germany was standing behind them 'like a knight in shining armour'.

That final crisis happened in the southern Austrian province of Bosnia. The heir to the Austrian throne, the Archduke Franz Ferdinand, made an official visit to the provincial capital of Sarajevo. As he was leaving the town hall on the morning of Sunday 28 June 1914, a young man stepped from the crowd. The Archduke and his wife were sitting in the back of an open-topped car. The young man, whose name was Gavrilo Princip, fired two shots. The Archduke and Archduchess were killed. Princip was

Origins of the First World War. Before the First World War Germany, Austria, and Italy formed the 'Triple Alliance'. (In fact Italy did not fight on Germany's side in the war.) During the war Germany and her friends were called the 'Central Powers'. France, Russia and Britain, from 1907, were members of the 'Triple Entente' (a French word meaning a getting-together). During the war Britain and her friends were called the 'Allies'.

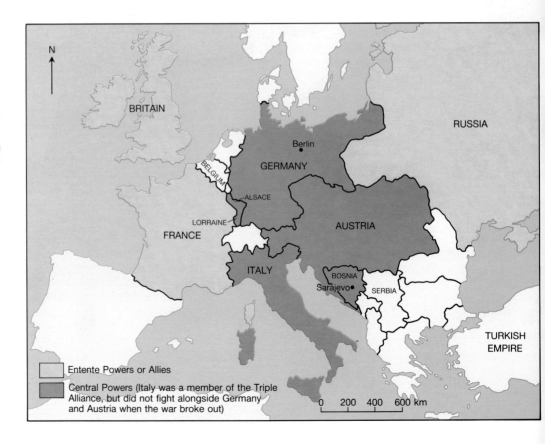

Wilhelm II became Emperor of Germany (Kaiser) in 1888, aged 29. He was born with a withered arm, and had a harsh upbringing. He grew into a strange, unpleasant man. Even his own mother (writing to her mother, Queen Victoria) declared, 'He has not heart!'. He was an arrogant bully, obsessed with warfare and making Germany powerful.

During the War hatred grew in Britain and France against the Germans and the Kaiser in particular. Rumours spread of the horrible tortures they were said to have practised. And when the War ended there was a loud demand of 'Hang the Kaiser' for his responsibility for the suffering caused by the War. But he escaped to Holland, where he lived until 1941.

Some historians have argued that the causes of the First World War were not just the policies of the Kaiser, that the causes were more complicated. On the other hand, recent historical research has shown that the Kaiser definitely wanted war in 1914. Perhaps the Sarajevo crisis might not have led to general war if it had not been for him. This *Punch* cartoon shows the Kaiser as responsible for the killings of the First World War. He had boasted that Germany was civilized.

THE TRIUMPH OF "CULTURE."

only one of several conspirators. They were all Serbians.

As a result, Austria declared war on Serbia. So did Germany. Russia helped Serbia. France helped Russia. Then, on 4 August, German armies invaded Belgium as a way of attacking France. The British Ambassador in Berlin went to see the German Chancellor. Both countries had signed a treaty in 1839 promising that Belgium would always be neutral in any future war. The Ambassador asked the Germans to honour this treaty and withdraw their troops. The Chancellor became angry: would Britain go to war, he asked, over 'a scrap of paper'?. He refused Britain's request. So Britain too joined in the war. The Turkish Empire sided with the Central Powers (Germany and Austria); and Italy sided with the Allies.

The fighting

At the time the war was called 'the Great War'. It is also known as the 'First World War'. But what made it a *World* War? In the first place, a lot of the countries of the world joined in. Also fighting happened in so many parts of the world (see map left). The Germans had colonies in Africa and the Pacific. So there was fighting in these parts to capture the German possessions. Fighting took place in the Middle East with Turkey as well. But even though it was a *World* War, the really big battles happened in Europe.

In Eastern Europe huge Russian armies were mobilized. The Germans and Austrians were afraid of being crushed by

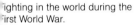
fighting in the world during the First World War.

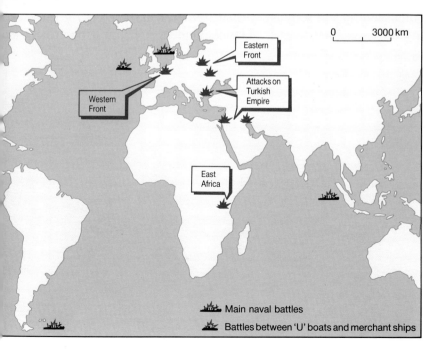
Eastern Front

Western Front

Attacks on Turkish Empire

East Africa

0   3000 km

⚓ Main naval battles

💥 Battles between 'U' boats and merchant ships

The World's Greatest and Foulest Crime.

LUSITANIA TORPEDOED & SUNK IN FIFTEEN MINUTES.

1,502 LIVES LOST AND 658 SAVED.

TERRIBLE TOTAL OF MURDERERS' VICTIMS.

OFFICIAL ACCOUNT.

MANY INJURED IN HOSPITAL.

FEW FIRST-CLASS SURVIVORS.

DOES IT MEAN WAR?

THE ONE QUESTION THAT IS ASKED IN AMERICA.

OFFICIAL ATTITUDE.

STORM OF POPULAR INDIGNATION.

NOTICE!

TRAVELLERS intending to embark on the Atlantic voyage are reminded that a state of war exists between Germany and her allies and Great Britain and her allies; that the zone of war includes the waters adjacent to the British Isles; that in accordance with formal notice given by the Imperial German Government, vessels flying the flag of Great Britain, or of any of her allies, are liable to destruction in those waters and that travellers sailing in the war zone on ships of Great Britain or her allies do so at their own risk.

IMPERIAL GERMAN EMBASSY

WASHINGTON, D.C.

The *Lusitania* was a British passenger liner, which was sunk by a German U-boat as she was crossing the Atlantic bound for Liverpool. You can see from this newspaper how horrified people were at the time. Some of the passengers who died were Americans and so the USA, which was not yet in the War, became angry with Germany.

the 'Russian steamroller'. Within the first few weeks of the War, the Germans stopped the Russian advance into East Prussia in a great battle at Tannenberg. The Russians lost a lot of men. Indeed, in the course of the war Russia suffered more casualties than any of the other Allies. A German officer described a dramatic incident in the Battle of Tannenberg: of 'the mowing down of the cavalry brigade [of] ... 500 mounted men on white horses, all killed and packed so closely together that they remained standing'. The Russians were, in fact, too inefficient to be a serious threat to Germany for long: their troops

ran out of supplies of food and ammunition. The dreadful conditions in the Russian army helped spark off the Revolution in 1917 (see Chapter 3).

At sea there were few important battles. By 1914 both Britain and Germany had large navies, including great battleships like the *Dreadnought*. Yet each fleet was frightened to set sail in case the other one left port and sank too many of its ships! Eventually, in 1916 they did venture out and met off the Danish coast of Jutland. Both sides said they had won: the Germans sank many more British ships than they lost; but the Germans turned around and sailed back to port. So much for the great naval race! More seriously each country tried to starve the other into surrender. The Germans used submarines (U-boats) to sink merchant ships bringing supplies to Britain; and the British navy blockaded German ports to prevent their supplies getting through. By 1918 the British were being more successful than the Germans in causing hunger among the enemy population.

Until 1918 the war was in many ways a 'stalemate' (that is, neither side won). This was particularly obvious on the Western Front in France. There the two sides dug lines of trenches, defended by barbed-wire and machine-guns. Every now and then, hundreds of thousands of soldiers would be ordered to climb out of their trenches, dash across the 'no-man's land' (land not occupied by either side)

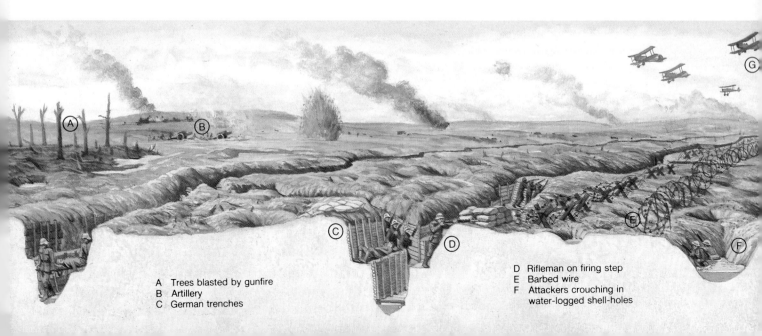

A   Trees blasted by gunfire
B   Artillery
C   German trenches

D   Rifleman on firing step
E   Barbed wire
F   Attackers crouching in water-logged shell-holes

between to try to capture the enemy trenches. And each time thousands were mown down. The generals were stubborn. They could not think up any other strategy so they kept ordering the men to go 'over the top'. Courage, together with fear of what would happen if they deserted, pushed the troops to continue sacrificing themselves in this way.

The stubbornness (or was it determination?) of the generals was summed up by General Pétain. In February 1916 the Germans lauched a heavy attack near Verdun. The French commander, Pétain, said, 'Ils ne passeront pas' ('They shall not pass'). They did not. But 700,000 men died in the battle. About 150,000 corpses were sucked into the foul, churned up mud and sank without trace.

Courage, wounds and death

What was it like for an ordinary soldier? A British infantryman wrote this:

'Each tried to come to terms with the fact that in a few minutes he was likely to be killed or horribly maimed. Every instinct screamed to stay where he was, to hide, to run back … Each man struggled with his intense private fears and nearly all triumphed simply because they would rather be dead than be revealed to their fellows as cowards.'

The Last Call

When the First World War started many countries relied on volunteers for their armies: there was no conscription. So posters were produced to persuade men to join up. This one is Australian. It shows a wounded soldier among dead comrades. He is calling for help with his bugle.

Below: the purpose of digging a trench was for protection from enemy gunfire. The Allied and German lines of trenches stretched from the English Channel to the frontier of Switzerland, a neutral country. Apart from the dangers of 'going over the top' to make an attack on the enemy line, even daily life in the trenches was unpleasant. They were often waterlogged and muddy. Soldiers ate basic food, stood guard and slept in mud. The picture shows how a typical trench system was organized. At first the attackers were always at a disadvantage because of the lethal fire-power of the machine-gun. So neither side could advance. The failure of the leaders of the army to cope with this stalemate is summed up by Lord Kitchener, the British Minister of War, who said, 'I don't know what is to be done; this is not war'. The introduction of the tank (a British invention in 1916) eventually gave protection for attacking troops. The first armoured vehicles were lumbering machines. But their invention was thought to be so important that during their development they were kept a close secret. They were referred to as 'water tanks' because that is what they rather looked like. The name 'tank' stuck!

G Aeroplanes (to spot enemy artillery)
H Tank
J Allies' trenches
K Officer's headquarters

But in any case, deserters were shot. The experience of trench warfare produced a lot of vivid and moving poetry. Here is a verse from *The Chances* by Wilfred Owen (killed in 1918):

'One of us got the knockout, blown to chops.
T'other was 'urt, like, losin' both 'is props.
An' one, to use the word of 'ypercrites,
'Ad the misfortune to be took be Fritz.
Now me, I wasn't scratched, praise God Almighty,
(Though next time please I'll thank 'im for a blighty).
But poor Jim, 'e's livin' an' 'e's not:
'E reckoned 'e'd five chances, an' 'e 'ad;
'E's wounded, killed, and pris'ner, all the lot,
The bloody lot all rolled in one. Jim's mad.'

'Blighty' meant Britain. A 'blighty' was a wound just serious enough for the victim to be sent back to Britain. We saw in Chapter 1 how the British borrowed Indian words. This is another one. It comes from the Indian word 'bilayati', meaning a foreign land (i.e. Britain). Other poems expressed the patriotism rather than the horrors of the war. The following famous lines are from *The Soldier* by Rupert Brooke (killed in 1915):

'If I should die, think only this of me:
That there's some corner of a foreign field
That is forever England. There shall be
In that rich earth a richer dust concealed;
A dust whom England bore, shaped, made aware, . . .'

But one person, at least, boldly declared: 'I realize that patriotism is not enough. I must have no hatred or bitterness towards any one.' These were the last words of the English nurse, Edith Cavell, before she was executed by a German firing squad. Her hospital had been overrun by the Germans. She considered it her duty as a nurse to help her patients. She helped some British wounded soldiers to escape. And that was why she was shot. She

In order to persuade men to join the armed forces the British Government issued a large number of posters. The best known had a portrait of the famous General, Lord Kitchener (who was made Minister of War in 1914). It read, 'Your country needs you'. Others played on the fear of being accused of cowardice. The poster shown here is one of the most famous of this kind.

Daddy, what did *YOU* do in the Great War?

WAKE UP, AMERICA!

CIVILIZATION CALLS
EVERY MAN WOMAN and CHILD!
MAYOR'S COMMITTEE 50 EAST 42ND ST

During the nineteenth century the USA kept out of European wars. This policy was called 'isolationism'. So, when the Great War broke out in 1914, the USA remained neutral. But Germany tried to starve Britain into surrender. This involved U-boats (submarines) sinking ships carrying food from the USA to Britain across the Atlantic. From February to March 1917, U-boats sank eight American ships. In April the USA declared war. The US army was small; so recruiting posters like this one were produced to encourage men to join up.

became one of the greatest heroines of the war: her statue is near the Church of St Martin-in-the-Fields in London.

What had been happening meanwhile on 'the Home Front'?

The Home Front

What was it like to be a civilian in the war? Were ordinary people affected by it? They were. A lot of civilians were killed. Countries which were hit hardest by the war were Russia, Germany, France, Belgium and Britain. In Russia, for example, about 2 million civilians were killed in the war. The war changed people's lives. Let us take Britain as an example.

For the first two years of the war Britain recruited only volunteers to fight. A lot joined but not enough. Voluntary recruitment could not bring in enough men to replace the great numbers who were being killed in trench warfare. And so, in 1916 'conscription' was introduced – that is, it became compulsory to join the armed forces. Altogether over $2\frac{1}{2}$ million British soldiers, sailors and airmen were killed, wounded, reported missing or taken prisoner. That was over 5 per cent of the total population. As a result many more people had family or friends who were fighting; many suffered worry and bereavement. Vera Brittain, (mother of the British politician, Shirley Williams) wrote a famous book about her experiences during the war, in which her fiancé was killed. Here is a short passage:

'I had arrived at the cottage that morning to find his mother and sister, standing in helpless distress in the midst of his returned kit, which was lying, just opened, all over the floor ... I wondered, and I wonder still, why it was thought necessary to return such relics – the tunic torn back and front by the bullet, a khaki vest dark and stiff with blood ...'

Vera Brittain worked as a nurse. Many women did the same. It has a brave, harrowing and vital work. Because so many men were called up to fight there were not many left to do the jobs in Britain. And so they had to be done by women. Women began to work in offices, on the buses, as policewomen, as agricultural labourers (in the Land Army) and as factory workers. The way women did these essential tasks during the war proved that they were the equal of men. This helped them win the right to vote in 1918 (see Chapter 4).

The war also affected how much food could reach Britain from abroad. By 1917 the German U-boats were becoming especially menacing: they were sinking

In west European countries like Britain it has been rare for women actually to fight in the army. In Russia, however, many women fought and died as soldiers in both World Wars. This is a photograph taken during the First World War of the Russian women's 'Battalion of Death'.

A war cannot, of course, be fought without weapons and ammunition. Factories had to be quickly converted to their production. Many women were employed in this work. At the beginning of the War a special Minister of Munitions was appointed in Britain. This was Lloyd George, who later became Prime Minister. The increase in output was huge. For example, when the War started the army had 1,330 machine guns. During the four years of the War 240,506 were made. Millions of bullets were produced each year. This photograph is of a factory where shells are being filled with explosive.

London. Attacks from the air were a new kind of warfare. The Government was taken by surprise and was criticized for not preparing the country to defend itself. Altogether 1,414 people were killed in air raids.

Peace again

By 1918 both sides were exhausted. The new Bolshevik Government of Russia (see page 67) made peace with Germany by the Treaty of Brest-Litovsk. Then, on the Western Front, the Allies were substantially strengthened by the arrival of fresh troops from the USA, which had declared war in 1917. Also, because food was short a lot of people were discontent with the war inside Germany. So the Germans asked for peace. The war came to an end at 11.00 a.m. on the eleventh day of the eleventh month, 1918. It had been a bitter struggle, in which civilians as well as the armed forces had been involved. ☐

The Allied navies were able to stop imports of food into Germany during the First World War. By 1917 many Germans were suffering from hunger because rations were cut so low. By 1918 riots broke out as people in towns desperately demanded more food. As you can see in this photograph, taken in Berlin, soldiers patrolled the streets, especially to protect the food shops.

British merchant ships faster than they could be replaced. Food which had to be imported started to run short. By the end of the war the quality of food was worse and there was not so much of it. Sugar, meat, butter, jam and tea were rationed.

Nor were civilians entirely safe from enemy attack. German warships shelled some eastern coastal towns of Britain. Airships (called 'zeppelins') and aeroplanes bombed various towns, including

1 Imagine you are a nurse serving in France during the First World War. Write a series of letters to your mother describing your work and what you think about the war.
2 It is 1917. A British soldier, who has served in the trenches for two years is walking along a French lane. There is a car which has broken down. Inside is a British general waiting for the return of his driver who is seeking help. Write a dialogue between the general and the soldier about the war and fighting in the trenches.
3 Do you think the First World War was necessary? Give your reasons.
4 Study the posters on pages 117 and 118 (top) and explain what you think the men are thinking.

Between the wars

The Peace Settlement

When the war ended, representatives of the Allied countries met together in Paris, to work out the details of peace treaties. The US President, Woodrow Wilson, drew up a list of Fourteen Points to act as a guideline. The basic idea Wilson wanted to see put into practice was 'national self-determination'. What was that? Really it was the two nineteenth-century ideas of 'democracy' and 'nationalism' (see page 91).

Each nation should form a nation-state and decide its own government. As a result new countries were created, for example, Czechoslovakia, Yugoslavia, Poland were made independent from the Austrian and Russian Empires (see map). The Turkish Empire was divided into a number of new European colonies and independent states (see page 144).

The really difficult problem was what to do with Germany. Eventually, they made four major decisions:

1 Germany lost land. She was made to surrender all her overseas colonies; Alsace-Lorraine was returned to France; and a portion of land in the east was given to the new country of Poland (see map).

2 Austria and Germany were forbidden to unite. Although the people of Austria speak German and might well have thought of themselves as part of the German nation, the two countries were forbidden to join together.

3 German military power was reduced. She was allowed no large warships or submarines, no tanks and no warplanes. Her army was to be no more than 100,000 men. No German soldiers were allowed to be stationed in the Rhineland, on the borders of France and Belgium.

4 Germany was declared responsible for

European peace settlements. Notice particularly:
1 How Germany was punished.
2 How the Austrian Empire was split into three new countries and gave land to four other states.

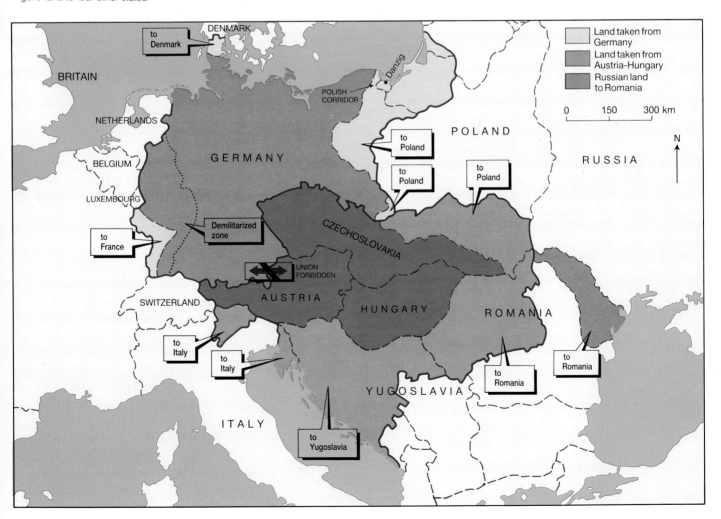

This cartoon appeared in the *Daily Herald* in 1919. It shows the 'Big Four' who in practice made the decisions about the peace settlements after the First World War. The Prime Minister of Italy, Orlando (with black hair and moustache) was the least important of the four.

Most important was Woodrow Wilson, the President of the USA from 1913 to 1921 (the tall man on the right). He was important partly because the USA was so powerful and partly because he provided the framework for the treaties – his 'Fourteen Points'. Wilson believed it the duty of the statesmen to produce a just and lasting settlement. Although he could be relaxed and amusing with friends (he enjoyed making up limericks!), he was cold and aloof with strangers, including fellow peace-makers.

In contrast was Lloyd George, the British Prime Minister, 1916–22, (at the back in the cartoon). He was known alternatively as the 'Welsh wizard' or the 'Welsh goat'. The first nickname referred to his rapid and sharp mind in discussion; the second to his habit of seducing attractive young ladies. He disagreed with Wilson's belief that there could be a perfect settlement.

Clemenceau (at the front of the cartoon, with a walrus moustache) wanted to go even further than Lloyd George against Germany. He was a fierce man, whose nickname was the 'Tiger'. He had been a mayor in Paris during the Franco-Prussian War of 1870–71 and was Prime Minister of France, 1917–20. He experienced the suffering of France in two wars with Germany. He wanted to destroy Germany as a powerful country for ever.

So, inevitably, the peace settlement with Germany was a compromise. A few pessimistic and far-sighted people felt that it was storing up trouble for the future. This cartoon was an amazingly accurate prophecy: a child, representing the generation who will be young adults in 1940, sobs behind the pillar after reading the peace treaty. The Second World War broke out in 1939. The belief that a 'second round' of conflict was inevitable has led some historians to refer to the period 1919–39 as 'The Twenty Years Truce'.

the War. Clause 231 of the Treaty of Versailles read as follows:

'The Allied and Associated Governments affirm and Germany accepts the responsibility of Germany and her allies for causing all the loss and damage to which the Allied and Associated Governments and their nationals have been subjected as a consequence of the war imposed upon them by the aggression of Germany and her allies.'

When the German representatives were given this to sign, they refused. The Allied statesmen threatened to start the war again. The Germans signed. Germany had to pay 'reparations' (compensation) of £6,600 million. That was a very large sum to find at that time, especially for a country exhausted by a war.

Woodrow Wilson hoped that countries in the future would be able to settle their quarrels peacefully. He arranged for the League of Nations to be established. This was an organisation to keep peace in the world. Many people were enthusiastic. But the US Congress refused to agree to this; and so the USA, the most powerful country in the world, was never a member. Also, even those countries which were members were reluctant to make the League work. In 1931 Japan invaded Manchuria (see page 137); in 1935–36 Italy invaded Abyssinia (Ethiopia) in East Africa. The League made feeble protests; Japan and Italy simply ignored them. The world was once again becoming a very dangerous place . . .

Nazism

While Japan and Italy were busy conquering lands in Asia and Africa, Hitler and the Nazi Party were gaining strength in Germany and becoming a threat to Europe. After the First World War many Germans resented the harshness of the Treaty of Versailles. They were keen to find opportunities to reverse some of the decisions. The governments which were in power in Germany from 1919 to 1933 became unpopular because they seemed to be doing so little to make Germany a great country again. Also, by the early 1930s there was a great deal of unemployment. The figures rose sharply: from 1.3 million in 1929, to 3 million in 1930, to nearly 6 million in 1933. Hitler and the Nazi Party became popular because they promised to solve these problems.

Adolf Hitler was born in 1889 in a little town just inside the Austrian border with Germany. His father was an Austrian customs official. At the age of 18 Adolf went to Vienna in the hope of becoming an artist or an architect. He was a failure and seems to have been a strange, lonely sort of person. He showed some courage while serving in the German army during the First World War. But it was not until he joined the Nazi Party, in which he became an hysterical speaker and a keen organizer, that he had any sense of personal direction. And by then he was 30 years old.

Hitler had a magnetic personality and the most frightening temper. He seemed to hypnotize people with his piercing blue eyes. And his rages were like those of a spoilt child. As one historian explained, 'His face became mottled and swollen with fury, he screamed at the top of his voice . . ., drumming on the table or wall with his fists'. It is difficult to know whether he was fully sane. During the Second World War he took military decisions himself, often against the advice of his generals. In 1944 some German officers tried to rid Germany of him by leaving a bomb under a table at a meeting. But Hitler survived. In 1945, as the Russians were advancing into the ruins of Berlin, he committed suicide.

Ein Volk, ein Reich, ein Führer!

A Nazi Rally. Hitler could whip up the emotions of a crowd. Huge open-air rallies were organized, attended by thousands. They would roar 'Heil Hitler!' ('Long live Hitler') and chant 'Ein Volk, ein Reich, ein Führer' (one People, one Empire, one Leader). Hitler promised that the German people would be united under his leadership in an Empire (the Third Reich), which would last for a thousand years. This photograph, taken in 1939, shows a crowd listening to a speech by Hitler in Berlin.

The word 'Nazi' is an abbreviation for National Socialist German Workers' Party. It was formed in 1919 with 7 members and Adolf Hitler soon became its leader. Many loyal members were recruited to the party – 1 million by 1932. Young people were recruited into youth movements and their minds filled with Nazi propaganda. A book for children, called *A Flight Through the Storm*, is an example.

It described how Hitler flew to a rally through a violent storm even though all other aeroplanes were grounded:

'This is no longer flying, this is a whirling dance which today we remember only as a faraway dream. Now we jump across the aerial downdrifts, now we whip our way through tattered clouds, again a whirlpool threatens to drag us down, and then it seems that a giant catapult hurls us into the steep heights.

'And yet, what a feeling of security is in us in the face of this fury of the elements. The *Führer's* absolute serenity transmits itself to all of us.'

Huge, carefully stage-managed rallies were arranged. Party members paraded in uniforms and with banners, often at night so that powerful lights could intensify the mood. The climax of these events was a speech by Hitler. Here is a description by the Berlin correspondent of the *Chicago Daily News*, expelled from Germany in 1933 for being too critical of Hitler:

'Military bands crash a gigantic salute. Then the LEADER rises, stands silent for an impressive moment, and speaks. In a rough but powerful voice. One hour. Two hours. Four hours. The

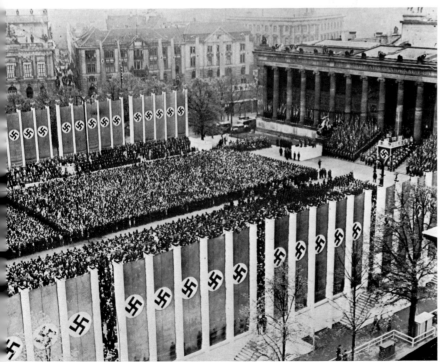

SS – Protection units or 'Black Shirts'. They started as Hitler's bodyguard. The SS grew in the 1930s and 1940s to become the most loyal and fanatical group. They were responsible for the concentration and extermination camps.

SA – Storm-troopers or 'Brown Shirts'. The Nazi private army, which was used to bully opponents in the 1920s and 1930s.

'Master Race', controlling the world. He once said, 'The Jew has never founded any civilization, though he has destroyed hundreds'. And in his long rambling book, *Mein Kampf* ('My Struggle'), he wrote: 'All culture, all the results of art, science and crowd hangs on his words. They have ceased to be beings with minds . . . He states – the most astonishing and totally inaccurate things. He roars, he pleads; if need be, he can weep.'

Anyone who was not convinced, and tried to oppose the Nazis would probably be beaten up or put in a concentration camp. The Nazis built up their own armies and police force – the SA, SS and Gestapo. The Gestapo were used to hunt down and arrest opponents of the Nazis.

But it was not just political opponents who were persecuted. The Nazis believed that Jews had caused German miseries and that if only the Germans (or 'Aryans' as Hitler called them) could be made a 'pure' race, they would become the

For centuries Jews had been envied, feared and persecuted by people in Europe. But the Nazis stirred up hatred (called anti-semitism) in the most sinister and brutal ways.

At first the persecution was just a campaign of hatred, illustrated by this poster, made in 1937. It shows a Jew as a cruel (the whip) moneylender (the coins in his hand) who already owns the Soviet Union (tucked under his left arm). Then laws were passed forbidding Jews to practise various professions in Germany or to marry an 'Aryan' (i.e. a non-Jewish German). These were followed by attacks on Jewish shops and synagogues. Finally, Jews were arrested, just for being Jews, sent to concentration camps, some of which were made extermination camps. Here the prisoners were sent to their deaths in gas chambers and their bodies incinerated. The Nazis called this terrible slaughter 'the Final Solution'; the Jews called it 'the Holocaust.'

technology that we see before us today, are almost exclusively the creative product of the Aryan'.

All this was fiction, of course. But the Nazis became so popular that in 1933 Hitler was made Chancellor (that is, prime minister) of Germany. The following year he became Führer (leader), a dictator with complete control. What did he do with this power? He set about persecuting the Jews. He destroyed many of the terms of the Versailles Treaty. He conquered extra land, which he called 'lebensraum' (living-space) for his 'Master Race'. As a result nearly 6 million Jews were killed and the world was plunged into the Second World War.

Hitler destroys the Versailles Settlement

Immediately Hitler came to power he started to build up the armed forces; slowly at first, then when no one protested loudly, more quickly. In 1936 he sent troops into the Rhineland. This was out of bounds according to the Versailles Treaty. France and Britain did complain rather feebly; they did not want another war. Hitler was encouraged. In March 1938 he sent his army into Austria and declared that country to be united with Germany. Again, he got away with it.

Hitler then started to threaten Czechoslovakia: 3 million Germans lived on the western fringes of Czechoslovakia, called Sudetenland. Hitler used them as an excuse for interfering in Czechoslovak affairs, for example, by helping the local Nazi Party.

Britain and France now started to wonder where Hitler would stop. Would it be war? The British prime minister, Neville Chamberlain flew to Germany three times in September 1938. It was the first time a British prime minister had used an aeroplane to travel for urgent diplomatic discussions. Just before leaving for the first meeting he made a broadcast in which he said:

'How horrible, fantastic, incredible that we should be digging trenches [i.e. air-raid shelters] ... here because of a quarrel in a far away country between people of whom we know nothing.'

The last thing Chamberlain wanted was for Britain to go to war over a 'far away country'. He went to Germany to try to arrange for Hitler to get most of what he wanted: this policy came to be called 'appeasement'.

The third and most famous meeting was at Munich. The French prime minister and the Italian dictator, Mussolini, were also there. They agreed that Germany should have the Sudetenland. The Czechs were not consulted! However, when Chamberlain returned to London he was given a rapturous reception. People were relieved when he declared that the Munich agreement was 'peace with honour' and that 'it is peace for our time'.

Still Hitler was not satisfied. In March 1939 he took over the rest of Czechoslovakia. In August, he signed a treaty with the Soviet Union. He now knew that if war broke out between Germany on the one side and Britain and France on the other, he had no fear of an attack from the east. So he felt strong enough to quarrel with Poland about the city of Danzig (present-day Gdansk, which then had a German population). On 1 September 1939 the Germans invaded Poland. Britain and France demanded the withdrawal of German troops. It was too late. Hitler was too confident and powerful now. Britain and France declared war. The Second World War had begun. □

1 What can you tell about Nazi Germany from studying the photograph at the bottom of page 123?
2 What does 'national self-determination' mean? Why were the Germans denied this in 1919? Would it have been better if all Germans were united in 1919?
3 It is 1936. You make a visit to Germany to stay with a family where the son is in the Hitler Youth and the daughter, in the Union of German Girls. Write a letter home about your experiences and conversations.

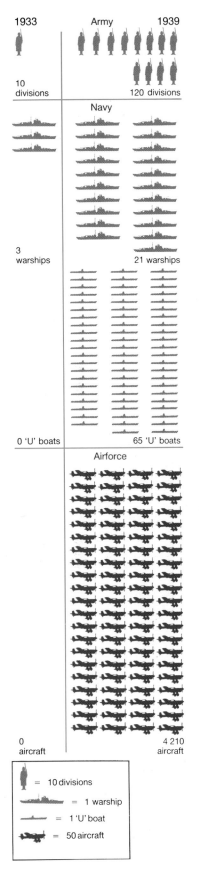

The build up of arms in Germany 1933–1939.

The Second World War

The fighting in Europe

The Polish forces were heroic but out-of-date. They were no match for the Germans, who used 'blitzkrieg' ('lightning war') tactics of rapid movement. And the Polish cavalry was not very effective against the German 'panzers' (tanks)! When the Russians invaded from the east, Poland was partitioned. The Germans took over the western half; the Russians took over the eastern half (see map).

Meanwhile what was going on in western Europe? Nothing seemed to be

happening. People even started to talk about the 'phoney war'. But Hitler was preparing his next move. On 9 April 1940 he struck to the north, invading Denmark and Norway. By 22 June he had defeated and occupied them – and not only those countries but Holland, Belgium, Luxembourg and France as well. The incredible speed with which the Germans overwhelmed the French was a dreadful shock. The British army had been sent to France to fight there (as in the First World War). The Allies had to retreat; but most of the British soldiers managed to escape from the French port of Dunkirk. But the varied collection of ships and little boats which evacuated them could not take their heavy equipment on board.

By the summer of 1940 Britain was the only country still at war with the 'Axis' (i.e. Germany and Italy, who also entered the war in 1940). Yet she had a small army with hardly any tanks or artillery. Hitler ordered plans for invasion, code-name 'Operation Sealion'. But how would he invade Britain – an island? The English Channel is narrow but it is not easy to transport an invading army across it. It has not been done since 1066! In the twentieth century slow-moving ships are vulnerable from air attack. So Hitler turned his attention to the air. He ordered the chief of his air force (or 'Luftwaffe'), Herman Göring, to destroy the Royal Air Force (RAF). This duel in the air came to be called the 'Battle of Britain'. The Luftwaffe failed: partly because British fighter-planes used radar which accurately directed them to incoming German squadrons; and partly because the British were skilled and their aircraft good. But it was also because of the miscalculations made by Göring. Probably his biggest blunder was to stop the attacks on the British command stations. These airfields were vital for directing the British fighters towards the incoming German aircraft. Yet just when damage to these buildings was having an effect, Göring switched his attack to London.

In the midst of this desperate battle, on 20 August 1940, Churchill made one of his famous speeches, in which he praised

The War in Europe, 1939–40.

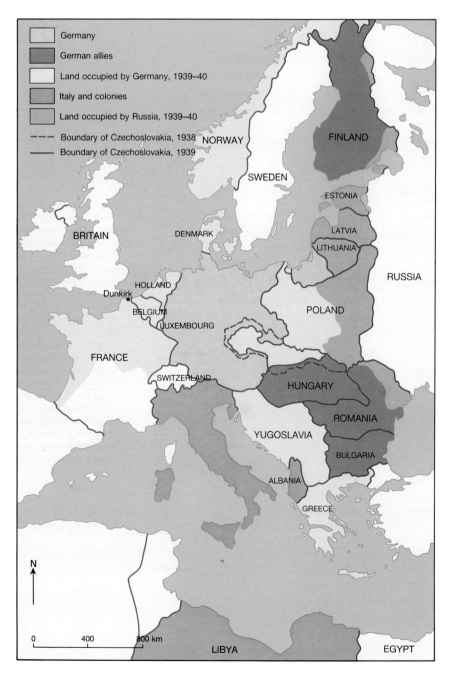

Germany

German allies

Land occupied by Germany, 1939–40

Italy and colonies

Land occupied by Russia, 1939–40

- - - Boundary of Czechoslovakia, 1938
——— Boundary of Czechoslovakia, 1939

NORWAY

SWEDEN

FINLAND

ESTONIA

LATVIA

LITHUANIA

BRITAIN

DENMARK

RUSSIA

HOLLAND

Dunkirk

BELGIUM

LUXEMBOURG

POLAND

FRANCE

SWITZERLAND

HUNGARY

ROMANIA

YUGOSLAVIA

BULGARIA

ALBANIA

GREECE

N

0   400   800 km

LIBYA

EGYPT

RAF aircrews, (both fighters and bombers). He said in the House of Commons:

'The gratitude of every home in our Island, in our Empire, and indeed throughout the world, except in the abodes of the guilty, goes out to the British airmen who, undaunted by odds, unwearied in their constant challenge and mortal danger, are turning the tide of world war by their prowess and by their devotion. Never in the field of human conflict was so much owed by so many to so few.'

Churchill included bomber crews in his praise. But the bombing of Germany at that time was not in fact being effective. However, Bomber Command of the RAF was re-equipped with long-range bombers fitted with radar and, after the USA entered the war, American bombers also operated from Britain. These aircraft destroyed large areas of many German cities. Some people thought these air raids would destroy German industry and terrorize the civilian population. It was hoped that as a result Germany would be forced to surrender. But the raids were not that successful.

What was much more effective in defeating Germany was the Russian Red Army. Having failed to invade Britain, Hitler turned his attention to the East. On 22 June 1941 he launched 'Operation Barbarossa', the invasion of Russia. It was a fatal mistake.

At first, it is true, the German armies succeeded (see map page 128). They sped through the USSR and the poorly led and poorly-equipped Russian troops fell back. But the USSR is a huge country and as the Russians retreated they destroyed sources of food in a 'scorched earth' policy (they would burn crops etc.). There was also the Russian winter. The Germans suffered badly in the intense cold.

By the autumn of 1942 the Germans had advanced deeply into southern Russia. Stalin gave strict orders that the city of Stalingrad should be defended: 'Not a step back', he ordered. Why was Stalingrad so important to keep hold of? This city was a great symbol – 'The city of

During the Second World War the Allies had three very determined leaders: Stalin, Roosevelt, and Churchill.

Joseph Stalin was the dictator of the Soviet Union. He was born in 1879. He became a leading member of the Bolshevik Party which organized the Communist Revolution in Russia in 1917 (see page 66). He assumed the name of Stalin ('man of steel') while he was on the run from the Tsar's police. After the death of Lenin, Stalin was in control of the Soviet Government until he died in 1953. He was a sinister and brutal ruler. He took land from the rich peasants to make collective farms and forced many to move to the towns to expand Russian industry; millions died of starvation. Those suspected of opposing him were sent to labour camps in the Arctic and Siberia; millions died from the strenuous work in the freezing conditions. Members of the Communist Party and senior army officers he distrusted were put on trial; thousands were shot. These atrocities made many in Britain and France in the 1930s think that Stalin was more of a menace than Hitler. But when Hitler launched his invasion of Russia in 1941, the British were very relieved and pleased to welcome the Russians as allies. Stalin was then referred to affectionately as 'Uncle Joe'.

Winston Churchill (Prime Minister of Britain, 1940–45 and 1951–55), however, was suspicious of Stalin; he disliked Communism and Soviet secrecy. In October 1939 he described Russia as 'a riddle wrapped in a mystery inside an enigma'. Churchill came from an aristocratic family and led a very full life. Before entering politics he had been a soldier and a journalist. He was also an historian, a novelist, artist and a qualified pilot. As a politician he was a minister in several governments. In the 1930s he was constantly warning against the threat from Hitler.

Chamberlain was forced to resign in May 1940 because he was such a poor Prime Minister. Churchill was then the obvious man to take over. He was particularly important for inspiring the British people to fight on when the odds seemed hopeless. When he took over he explained that he had 'nothing to offer but blood, toil, tears and sweat'.

Churchill, whose mother was American, became very friendly with Franklin D Roosevelt during the War. Roosevelt is the only man to have been elected President of the USA four times (there is now a law against more than two terms). He was President from 1933 until his death in 1945. Roosevelt was a man of considerable courage and determination. He was crippled by polio in 1921 at the age of 39 yet he continued an active political life from his wheelchair. When he became President, the USA was suffering from the Great Depression: over 12 million were unemployed, many starving and depending on charity. Roosevelt boldly tackled the problem by making the Government responsible in a programme of reforms called the 'New Deal'. During the Second World War, even before the USA entered, Roosevelt arranged to send warships, aeroplanes, lorries and tanks to Britain and then Russia to help them continue fighting. Since these countries could not afford to pay, he devised a scheme called 'Lend-Lease'.

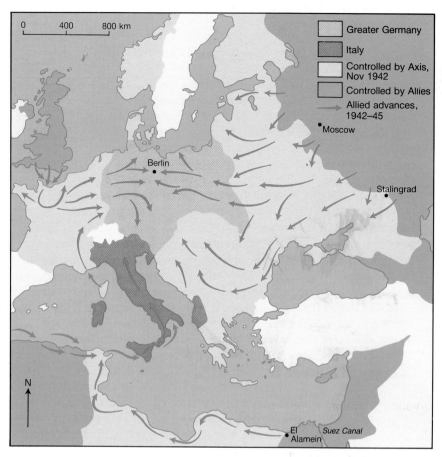

War in Europe and North Africa during the Second World War. The battles of Stalingrad and El Alamein in 1942, stopped the German advances.

Stalin'. It was also a vital position on the River Volga. If the Germans took Stalingrad, the way would be open for them to advance further to the south or east.

The battle raged in a city pounded to rubble. Here is part of a report from a member of the Russian 42nd Regiment:

'Two groups, six in each, went up to the third floor and the garret. Their job was to break down walls, and prepare lumps of stone and beams to throw at the Germans when they came up close. Our garrison consisted of forty men ... The basement was full of wounded; only twelve men were still able to fight. There was no water ... The Germans attacked again. I ran upstairs with my men and could see their thin blackened and strained faces, the bandages on their wounds, dirty and clotted with blood, their guns held firmly in their hands. There was no fear in their eyes. Lyuba Nesterenko, a nurse, was lying, with blood flowing from a wound in her chest. She had a bandage in her hand. Before she died she wanted to help to bind someone's wound, but she failed ...'

Eventually the Russians counter-attacked, surrounded the German army and took 100,000 prisoners. This was in January 1943. It was the turning-point of the war. For the next two years the Russians gradually forced the Germans back into Germany (see map). The Russian army and civilians suffered horribly in what they call 'the Great Patriotic War' – about 20 million died altogether (including one third of the population of Leningrad died during the dreadful eighteen month siege). But they smashed the power of the 'Wehrmacht' (German army).

In order to relieve the intense pressure on Russia Stalin pleaded with Roosevelt and Churchill to invade Europe from the west. From 1940 Britain fought in Egypt and Libya against the Axis to defend the Suez Canal and the Middle East oil supplies (see map). By 1943 the British and Americans had cleared the Germans and Italians from North Africa and had invaded Italy. Then, in 1944 the largest seaborne invasion force ever launched set out from the ports of southern Britain and sailed across the English Channel. They landed on the beaches of Normandy on 6 June, named 'D-Day'. In less than a year Germany was invaded from the west; western and Russian troops met; and Germany was forced to surrender. It was 8 May 1945, 'VE-Day', Victory in Europe.

War with Japan

But VE-Day was not the end of the war. Since December 1941 another part of the war had been raging in Asia and the Pacific. Meanwhile, what had been happening there?

On the morning of Sunday 7 December 1941, without warning, Japanese aircraft took off from aircraft-carriers in the Pacific and bombed and torpedoed American warships in Pearl Harbor in the Hawaiian Islands. On the same day

The USA and Japan were rivals for influence in the Pacific Ocean area and east Asia. The Japanese decided that the best way to win was through war. This photograph was taken on the day that the Japanese attacked Pearl Harbor. In this two-hour attack: 18 American warships were destroyed or damaged; 350 aeroplanes were destroyed or damaged; and over 3,500 Americans were killed or wounded. The USA entered what now became the Second *World* War.

they launched attacks on other American Pacific islands, and against the British in Hong Kong, Malaya and Singapore (see map, below). So Japan had entered the war most dramatically. Very quickly the Japanese captured many of the Pacific Islands and the whole of south-east Asia. By 1942 it seemed likely that they might invade Australia and India.

The Japanese soldiers, airmen and sailors became known as fanatical fighters and brutal captors. They rarely surrendered and they treated their prisoners of war (POWs) atrociously. The most notorious case was the way they used POWs to build the Kwai railway between

War with Japan. The battles of Midway, Coral Sea, and Leyte Gulf were important American naval and air victories.

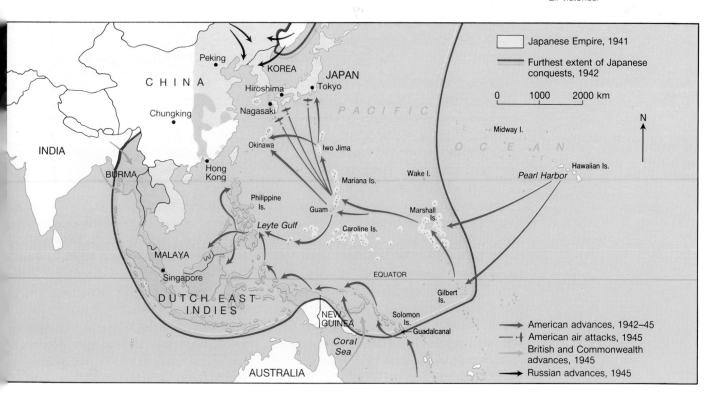

| | Japanese Empire, 1941 |
| | Furthest extent of Japanese conquests, 1942 |

	American advances, 1942–45
	American air attacks, 1945
	British and Commonwealth advances, 1945
	Russian advances, 1945

Hiroshima after the nuclear bomb was dropped. When a nuclear weapon is exploded, many are killed immediately. Many survive but with radiation sickness, and this can kill them years later. Since the bombs were dropped on Hiroshima and Nagasaki about 300,000 people have died as a result; about the same number as the total number of American servicemen killed in the whole of the Second World War. The destruction of buildings and the death and suffering of people were horrific. Here are two extracts from the diary of a Hiroshima doctor:

'Hiroshima was no longer a city, but a burnt-over prairie. To the east and to the west everything was flattened. The distant mountains seemed nearer than I could ever remember.'

' "It was a horrible sight," said Dr Tabuchi. "Hundreds of injured people who were trying to escape to the hills passed our house. The sight of them was almost unbearable. Their faces and hands were burnt and swollen; and great sheets of skin had peeled away from their tissues to hang down like rags on a scarecrow." '

Thailand and Burma. Out of about 40,000 men used, one third died. Here is a description by one of the lucky survivors:

'The medical attention provided by the Japanese was negligible [*almost none*] ... Men died of starvation, from the climate, exhaustion, accident, disease, and despair, and occasionally from personal assault ... The experience has left its mark on nearly every ex-prisoner. Some will never regain full mental or physical health.'

In June 1942 the Japanese went too far. A powerful naval force attacked the American Pacific islands of Midway. There was a fierce battle which the Americans won. This was the turning-point in the war with Japan. US forces now started to recapture Japanese-held islands across the Pacific. Each side suffered casualties.

One of the most famous novels about the Second World War is *The Naked and the Dead* by Norman Mailer. It is based on these operations. Here is a short extract:

'There were about fifty men in the column, and they moved very slowly down a narrow trail through the jungle ... Their feet sank into the deep mud ... The men on the guns would lunge forward for a few feet and then halt. Every ten yards a gun would bog down ... Huge roots continually tripped the men, and their faces and hands became scratched and bleeding from the branches and thorns ... Some Japanese might easily have been waiting in ambush, but it was impossible to keep silent ... the men swore helplessly, panted with deep sobbing sounds like wrestlers at the end of a long bout.'

By 1945 plans were being made to invade Japan itself. Such an operation would have caused huge casualties on both sides. Then, in July of that year an experiment took place in the desert of New Mexico, USA: the first atomic bomb was test exploded. The new American President after Roosevelt died was Harry S Truman. He decided that this new devastating nuclear weapon should be used against Japan. It would force her to surrender quickly. In August two bombs were dropped: one on Hiroshima; the other on Nagasaki. A week later Japan surrendered.

The Home Front

In 1932 the British minister, Baldwin speaking in the House of Commons, said 'the bomber will always get through'. And that was how most people felt. How could they really defend themselves against air raids? People made exaggerated estimates of what would happen if there was a German raid once the War started. For example, it was believed that 2 million Londoners would be killed or injured in a few months. (During the German air attack on Britain from 1940 to 1945 in fact there were about 100,000 casualties.) Plans were made to evacuate children from areas which might be attacked. They were sent from cities and towns into the safety of rural villages. Here is what one of the evacuees remembers of what happened to him, at the age of six:

'We went down by train and found ourselves in a little village on Bodmin moor. Our residence was a large house and about 20 mothers and children were crammed in there ... One of the things which worried me most was my new school ... It's funny but the only thing I can remember at that school was that first day and the village bullies who beat you up in the playground every day and lay in wait for you as you went home from school.'

Altogether 1½ million people were moved by the Government in 1939–40; another 2 million moved by private arrangements; and another 1½ million in 1944.

There were two main phases of the aerial bombardment of Britain. Many cities, including London, Plymouth and Coventry, suffered in what was known as 'the Blitz', 1940–41. Attacks began again in 1944 – this time by pilotless-bombs (V-1s) and rockets (V-2s). Altogether about 60,000 people were killed in air raids. An expanded National Fire Service, civilian air-raid wardens, ambulance and rescue services struggled to save as many lives and as much property as possible.

As in the First World War many people, including women, were drafted into 'war work', particularly into factories. Also important was the work of the female Land Army.

Many civilians were killed in air raids. The most terrible were made by the Allies – on Berlin, Hamburg, Dresden and Tokyo. People living in cities under attack had to sleep in air-raid shelters (most of the raids were at night). Many air-force leaders on both sides thought that morale would crack under these conditions. In fact, the raids tended to stiffen the determination of the people to continue the War. This photograph shows the effect of one explosion. It was taken in London in November 1944 and was caused by a V-2 rocket. Notice the rescue service clearing the rubble to try to reach people trapped in the destroyed houses.

Who'll help Mrs. Harrison?

Mrs. Harrison has had Molly with her for six months now. Molly arrived in those troubled September days, and she came pinched and peeked and feeling very strange. Molly doesn't feel strange any more. Neither is she pinched or peeked. It's been hard work for Mrs. Harrison; but she hasn't grudged it. First she did it for her country's sake; and now she'd like to do it for the girl's as well.

should be shared. Will you be neighbourly and take Molly for a while?

All you need do is enrol your name with your local Authority. You may be asked to take a child now, or your name may be kept against the time when raids make a second evacuation necessary. When you enrol, you will be doing a splendid service for the nation. You may be saving a child's life. The child, the parents and the

This is a poster produced during the Second World War to encourage people to volunteer to look after evacuees. Notice the shadows of bombers over the town on the right, contrasting with the peaceful rural scene on the left.

The amount of imported food coming into Britain (as well as other vital supplies like oil) was in fact put at risk by the great success of German U-boats in sinking British merchant ships. This came to be called the 'Battle of the Atlantic.' Over 30,000 merchant seamen died.

We have described the effects the war had on the British civilian population. But civilians in other countries suffered much more severely. The Second World War was in the true sense a 'total' war: civilians were just as likely to be killed as soldiers, sailors and airmen. In fact about twice as many civilians died in the war as members of the armed forces. Also millions were recruited as slave-labour in the countries occupied by Germany.

By 1945 the nature of warfare had changed dramatically: from the colonial conflicts of the eighteenth century, fought by small armies, (see Chapter 1), to 'total' war, involving armies of millions of men and civilians as well.

It was vital to increase food production so that the country would not have to rely too much on imports. A Minister of Food was appointed – Lord Woolton. He introduced rationing and a publicity campaign against waste. Here is one slogan of the time:

'Those who have the will to win
Cook potatoes in their skin,
For they know the sight of peelings
Deeply hurts Lord Woolton's feelings.'

1 It is 1940. You live in south London during the Battle of Britain and the Blitz. You are then evacuated to Norfolk. Compile a diary of your experiences.
2 If you had been President Truman would you have ordered the dropping of the atomic bombs? Give your reasons.
3 Of all the famous people mentioned in this Chapter, which one would you have most liked to be? Explain your reasons.
4 Compare the two World Wars and draw up lists of similarities and differences.

Rationing. Each person had a ration-book containing 'coupons' for basic foods. This picture shows what each person was allowed each week (except the tin of salmon). In addition, 'points' were allocated for luxuries. For example, a person needed to save about six weeks' worth of points for a tin of salmon. Although these amounts may appear small, the British people enjoyed a balanced diet during the War; and in fact some poor people were better fed than before.

8 oz (230g) cheese

8 oz (230g) fats (of which only 2 oz (60g) could be butter)

Tinned salmon (32 points)

4 oz (110g) ba

2 pints milk

1 lb (450g) meat

2½ oz (75g) tea

8 oz (230g) sugar

4 oz (110g

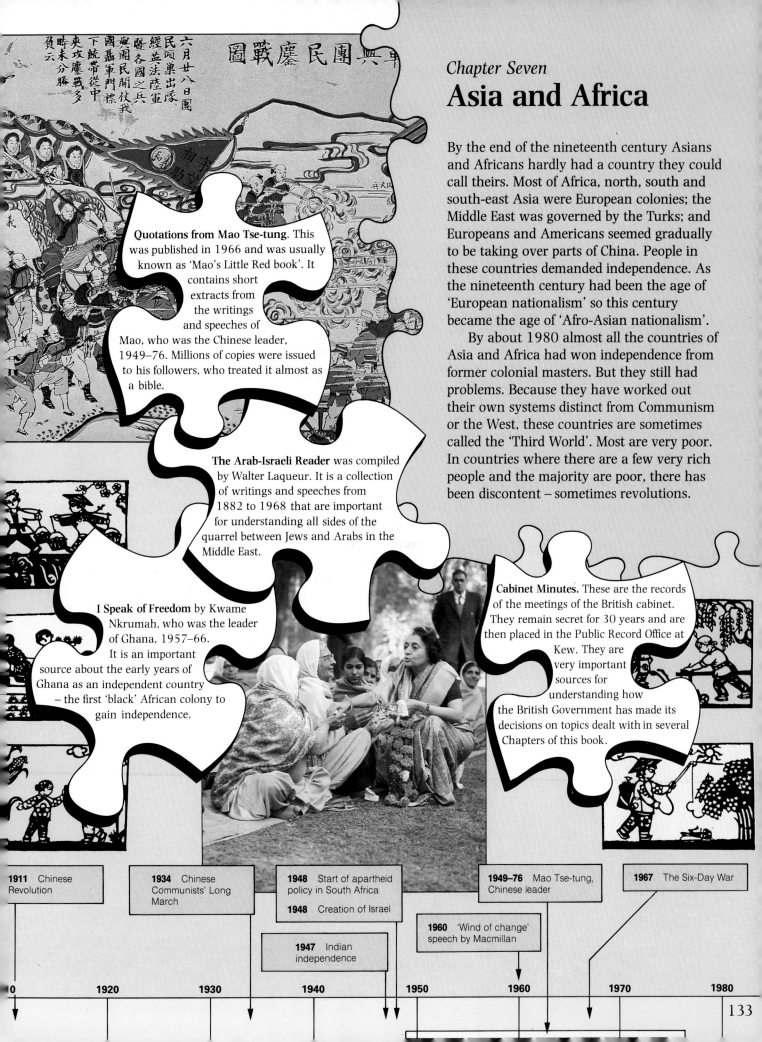

Chapter Seven
Asia and Africa

By the end of the nineteenth century Asians and Africans hardly had a country they could call theirs. Most of Africa, north, south and south-east Asia were European colonies; the Middle East was governed by the Turks; and Europeans and Americans seemed gradually to be taking over parts of China. People in these countries demanded independence. As the nineteenth century had been the age of 'European nationalism' so this century became the age of 'Afro-Asian nationalism'.

By about 1980 almost all the countries of Asia and Africa had won independence from former colonial masters. But they still had problems. Because they have worked out their own systems distinct from Communism or the West, these countries are sometimes called the 'Third World'. Most are very poor. In countries where there are a few very rich people and the majority are poor, there has been discontent – sometimes revolutions.

Quotations from Mao Tse-tung. This was published in 1966 and was usually known as 'Mao's Little Red book'. It contains short extracts from the writings and speeches of Mao, who was the Chinese leader, 1949–76. Millions of copies were issued to his followers, who treated it almost as a bible.

The Arab-Israeli Reader was compiled by Walter Laqueur. It is a collection of writings and speeches from 1882 to 1968 that are important for understanding all sides of the quarrel between Jews and Arabs in the Middle East.

I Speak of Freedom by Kwame Nkrumah, who was the leader of Ghana, 1957–66. It is an important source about the early years of Ghana as an independent country – the first 'black' African colony to gain independence.

Cabinet Minutes. These are the records of the meetings of the British cabinet. They remain secret for 30 years and are then placed in the Public Record Office at Kew. They are very important sources for understanding how the British Government has made its decisions on topics dealt with in several Chapters of this book.

1911 Chinese Revolution

1934 Chinese Communists' Long March

1948 Start of apartheid policy in South Africa

1948 Creation of Israel

1947 Indian independence

1949–76 Mao Tse-tung, Chinese leader

1960 'Wind of change' speech by Macmillan

1967 The Six-Day War

| 0 | 1920 | 1930 | 1940 | 1950 | 1960 | 1970 | 1980 |

China

Fall of the Manchus

There are more Chinese in the world today than any other race. About one fifth of all human beings are Chinese! At the beginning of this century the population of China was between 300 and 400 million. (We cannot tell exactly how many people there were because no full census was taken at the time). Today it is about one billion. Imagine what it must be like to try to rule that many people – it is not an easy task! Also China has one of the oldest civilizations in the world and the people were wary of any new western ideas.

From the middle of the seventeenth century China was ruled by a family of Emperors called the Manchus. In fact, for nearly half a century (1860–1908) China was governed (or rather misgoverned) by the Empress Dowager, Tzu-hsi. She was so formidable that she terrorized all the other members of the imperial family. And she was so incompetent that rumours spread that she was deliberately destroying the Manchu dynasty. But why should she want to? Because her family came from a rival tribe from that of the first Manchu Emperor!

The Chinese people became more and more discontented with the Government during the nineteenth century. Added to this they resented foreigners interfering in Chinese affairs, as they had ever since the Opium War (see pages 25–26). A secret organization grew up called the 'I Ho Chuan'. This means 'Righteous Harmony Fists' – so foreigners called them 'Boxers'!. Their slogan was 'Protect the country, destroy the foreigner'. They rose in rebellion in 1899–1900 and slaughtered foreigners and Chinese who had taken up the foreigners' religion and become Christians. So several foreign countries sent armies and killed Chinese in revenge.

It was clear to many Chinese that the old system of government with an emperor had to be replaced. From 1899 to 1911 ten uprisings were organized to bring about a revolution. At last, on 10 October 1911 (the 'Double Tenth') the revolutionaries were successful. The leader of this movement was a doctor called Sun Yat-sen, who had created a 'Revive China Society' in 1894. Members took an oath to 'expel the Manchus, restore the Chinese rule, and establish a federal republic'. The revolutionaries soon had

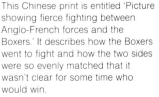

This Chinese print is entitled 'Picture showing fierce fighting between Anglo-French forces and the Boxers.' It describes how the Boxers went to fight and how the two sides were so evenly matched that it wasn't clear for some time who would win.

control of China. The young Emperor, Pu I, abdicated. He was later to become Emperor of Manchukuo under the Japanese (see page 137) and by the 1960s was working as a gardener in Peking. It was a humble end for the last of a line of grand Emperors who had ruled China for thousands of years.

The Kuomintang

In 1912 Sun created the Kuomintang (KMT or National People's Party. The word is pronounced 'kwo min dahng'). But there were problems:

1 People disagreed about the kind of Government China should have and what kind of reforms should be introduced.

2 Local war-lords had their own armies and they refused to obey the Government.

3 Also the war-lords and other bandits looted what they could from the poor peasants.

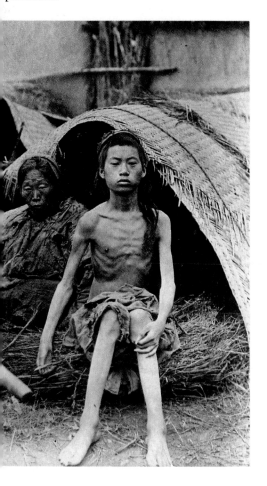

The condition of the peasants, who were the majority of the population, was vividly described by a British economist in 1932 after a visit to China:

'The rural population ... is taxed by one ruffian who calls himself a general, by another, by a third, and when it has bought them off, still owes taxes to the Government; in some places actually more than twenty years taxation has been paid in advance ... It must cut its crops at the point of a bayonet, and hand them over without payment to the local garrison, though it will starve without them ...'

When Sun established the KMT he declared its policy to be the Three People's Principles: 'People's Nationalism, People's Democracy, People's Livelihood'. It is clear from what the British economist wrote that Sun had little success in achieving the third principle – improving the 'People's Livelihood'. To try to achieve the 'People's Democracy', Sun allowed Communists to become members and received advice from the Communist government of Russia. What about the first principle – 'People's Nationalism'? Sun tried to restore Chinese pride. For example, he had European signs removed, like the ones in Shanghai's parks which read 'Chinamen and dogs not admitted'. He also tried to resist Japanese interference in China.

Sun died in 1925. The new leader of the KMT was a 38-year-old army officer, Chiang Kai-shek. Chiang tried to govern China for nearly a quarter of a century. But, although he defeated the war-lords, Chiang was beaten by three of the problems which Sun failed to solve:

1 The condition of the peasantry remained wretched – millions in fact died of starvation.

2 The Communists became very restless allies of the KMT.

3 The Japanese made war on China.

In modern times there has been too little fertile land to feed the huge population of China. Civil War, inefficient agricultural methods, floods, and droughts have all caused dreadful famines. This photograph was taken in the 1940s.

Sun Yat-sen lived 1867–1925. His father sent him to an American school in Hawaii. He became a Christian and qualified as a doctor. When young he decided that China was very backward. For example, he wrote on the voyage to Hawaii on the great American ship: 'I immediately realized that something was wrong with China for we could not do the things that the foreigners do. If the foreigners could make and raise into place those massive girders of solid metal, was it not an indication that they were superior to us?' As a young man he tried to organize a revolution – but from *outside* China. For if the Chinese Government agents had captured him (as they nearly did once in London), he would have been tortured to death. When the revolution occurred in October 1911 he returned to China. He then founded the political party called the Kuomintang (KMT). **Chiang Kai-Shek** was the leader of the KMT after Dr Sun. He was defeated by the Communists in 1949 and fled to the island of Taiwan, which he governed until his death in 1975.

The Long March

The Chinese Communist Party was founded in 1921. In the summer of that year a Congress of twelve delegates held their first meeting in secret in a girl's school in Shanghai. Shanghai remained the headquarters of the party during the 1920s when they were close allies of the KMT. But in 1927 Chiang decided that the Communists were becoming too powerful for his liking. In March Chiang struck. His police, secret agents and army rounded up known Communists and members of trade unions in Shanghai. The Communist headquarters were attacked. Most of the survivors were taken prisoner and massacred. This is how the French novelist, André Malraux, imagined the siege of the HQ:

> 'Their last dawn ... Almost no ammunition left. No rising of the people had occurred to bring them succour [help]. Shooting in the Chapei direction: their comrades besieged like themselves ... at any moment Chiang Kai Shek's men would bring up a small calibre field-gun ... [then their] walls and mattress bulwarks would collapse like an Aunt Sally [a sort of doll knocked down for prizes at fairgrounds].

The Communists who survived decided to move to the country-side. They could not rely on the town-workers to support them. Their new leader was Mao Tse-tung. He believed that the ordinary people of China could enjoy a decent life only if there was a Communist revolution, and that this would be brought about by the mass power of the peasants. After the Shanghai Massacre he wrote: 'The force of the peasantry is like that of raging winds and driving rain.' On the borders of the provinces of Hunan and Kiangsi he organized a 'soviet' (a government run by the people themselves). The land was taken from the landlords and given to the peasants. Food, clothes and medical care were made available to all.

In 1934 Chiang surrounded the Communist-held area. He was ready to launch an attack to destroy the Soviet. The Communists decided to break

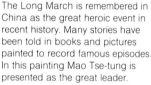

The Long March is remembered in China as the great heroic event in recent history. Many stories have been told in books and pictures painted to record famous episodes. In this painting Mao Tse-tung is presented as the great leader.

through the surrounding government army. They then marched to the mountainous parts of northern China where they could more easily defend themselves. Led by their party Chairman, Mao, the 'Long March' started in October. It was to be one of the most remarkable adventures in the whole of History. Those who took part have become legendary heroes.

100,000 set off, most of them soldiers. They marched 6,000 miles! That is the 20,000 who survived marched that distance. They braved every hazard you could imagine. There was Chiang's attacking army; the hostile local people; the rushing torrents of wide rivers; the squelching, sucking bogland; the freezing, icy mountains; the fever and starvation. Mao wrote poems describing all this. Here are a few lines from two of them:

'Keen is the west wind;
In the endless void the wild geese cry at
    the frosty morning moon,
The frosty morning moon.
The clatter of horses' hoofs rings
    sharp,
And the bugle's note is muted.
They say the strong pass is iron hard,
And yet this very day with a mighty
    step we shall cross its summit,
We shall cross its summit!'

'If we reach not the Great Wall, we are
    no true men!
Already we have come two thousand
    leagues.'

A new soviet was set up in the province of Yenan. Homes, schools, hospitals and workshops were set up in primitive huts and in caves hewn out of the sandstone cliffs.

War with Japan

Japan had become a powerful country at the turn of the century (see Chapter 5) and started to gain influence on the mainland of Asia, including China. In 1931 the Japanese arranged an 'incident' at Mukden in southern Manchuria, a great province of China. The Japanese invaded and

Mao Tse-tung. It is very difficult to represent Chinese sounds with western letters. Mao's name is now sometimes spelt 'Mao Zedong'. It is pronounced 'mow tzuh doong'. He was born in 1893 in the southern province of Hunan. His father was a peasant. He was quite clever at school and went on to college to train as a teacher. He read a lot and also became physically tough by living rough. By about 1920 he started to become interested in Communism, and was one of the first to join the Chinese Communist Party when it was formed. During the Long March he became recognized as the leader and for much of the rest of his life he became known as Chairman Mao. He was also in later life referred to as 'the Great Helmsman' – steering the Chinese ship of state. Mao died in 1976.

During the last ten years or so of his life he enjoyed being praised to the skies, being treated almost like a god – or a Chinese emperor! In 1966 millions of copies of a book were published containing quotations from his writings. *The Thoughts of Chairman Mao*, or Mao's *Little Red Book*, as it was also called. Young people particularly were encouraged to read it and gain inspiration from it. The keenest supporters of Mao were called the 'Red Guards'. They bullied people who were not so enthusiastic about the changes Mao made during the Cultural Revolution. This photograph shows a group of Red Guards hard at study beneath a banner-picture of Mao.

deep ploughing

irrigation projects

close planting

tools reform

captured it. They renamed it 'Manchukuo', and made Pu I Emperor in name, but in actual fact governed it themselves.

From Manchukuo the Japanese tried to interfere in parts of northern China. Yet rather than use his army against the Japanese, Chiang preferred to fight against the Communist Red Army in Yenan. But in 1936 Chiang himself was taken prisoner by one of his own generals. He was forced to make an agreement with the Communists: they would combine forces against the Japanese. It was none too soon: in July 1937 the Japanese army struck and captured Peking, the Chinese capital. In was a bitter war and lasted until 1945. After the Japanese attack on Pearl Harbor in 1941 (see Chapter 6) the war between Japan and China became part of the Second World War.

Mao's Red Army became very popular with the people of China during this war for the following reasons:

1   The KMT Government was very inefficient. An American general who tried to help Chiang reported in 1944: 'Greed, corruption, favouritism, more taxes, a ruined currency, terrible waste of life, callous disregard of all the rights of man.'

2   The Red Army treated the people well and were successful in fighting the Japanese. They used the guerrilla tactics taught them by Mao:

'The enemy attacks, we retreat;
The enemy camps, we harrass;
The enemy tires, we attack;
The enemy retreats, we pursue.'

Because of the support of the civilian population, as Mao explained, 'The Red Army lives among the people as a fish dwells in water'.

The Communist Revolution

What everyone wanted to know once the Second World War ended in 1945 was: would the Communists be able to live in harmony with Chiang and the KMT? The answer was no. A full-scale civil war broke out in 1947. The Red Army won quickly. By 1949 the KMT were retreating and eventually Chiang and the remnants of his army escaped to the island of Taiwan. On 1 October Mao formally proclaimed the establishment of the People's Republic of China.

The most urgent task was land reform, that is, taking most of the land from the rich landowners so that the peasants could enjoy more of its produce. Members of the Communist Party and officers of the People's Liberation Army (PLA, as the army was now called) visited the villages and talked to the peasants. They persuaded them to talk about the injustices of the landlords. Meetings were held, primitive 'courts', in which the landlords were accused and sentenced. Their land and livestock were confiscated; the lucky ones were allowed to work on their former fields as peasants; the unlucky ones were executed for their past cruelty.

But the fertile parts of China are densely-populated, and even when the landlords' land had been divided among

adequate manuring

plant protection

good seed

field management

Above: for many years after the Communists took control of China, the Government had the problem of how to communicate with the people. There were no televisions and few radios and newspapers. In any case many millions were illiterate. These pictures show the traditional art of 'paper-cuts' being used to teach the peasants better agricultural methods. During the Cultural Revolution the lack of newspapers was met in towns, especially Peking, by fixing posters and sheets of information on walls for those increasing numbers of people who could read. *Right*: the disappointing results of of the 'Great Leap Forward': poor quality metal goods; Russian technical advisers left in 1960; drought; flood.

138

the peasants, there was still not very much to be shared. The next move by the Government was to persuade the peasants to farm the land 'co-operatively', that is, to pool (or share) their land, animals and work. This was not just for efficiency (in fact in many ways the scheme proved inefficient); but it was also felt to be the proper Communist way of arranging matters. A great effort was made in 1955 as a result of which, as Mao wrote in the following year:

'... more than 60 million peasant households in various parts of the country have already joined cooperatives. It is as if a raging tidal wave has swept away all the demons and ghosts.'

But, quite understandably, there were many peasants who were extremely reluctant to give up their land. And so they had to be persuaded, as Mao explained, by:

'... the assault of argument, discussion, sleepless self-examination and public self-criticism. Some were convinced. Some ... [gave way] through sheer physical and mental exhaustion. Others again were changed by the usual mixture of promises, persuasion and coercion [force].'

There was a lot to be done to make China a better and more modern country. And many of the party leaders were impatient to bring about changes quickly. Naturally mistakes were made. In 1956 Mao had thought discussion would be valuable. He urged, 'Let a hundred flowers blossom. Let a hundred schools of thought contend'. There was a great torrent of criticism about arrogant and bullying Communist officials. Some complaints were quite detailed. For example, housewives complained that wives of army officers 'put on airs' and wore expensive leather shoes; mothers protested that they had to work too hard in factories while they were pregnant. So Mao decided that most of the 'plants' that had blossomed were 'poisonous weeds' which had to be rooted out! From now on critics were arrested and imprisoned in labour camps for many years. The Government did not like to be criticized!

The next big task was to expand and modernize Chinese industry. A Five-Year Plan had been introduced in 1952. A lot was achieved: for example, oil production was trebled and steel production quadrupled. But Mao was still not satisfied. He announced in 1958 that China would make a 'Great Leap Forward'. However, the results were disappointing as you can see from the picture.

The Cultural Revolution

Mao was impatient to make China a real Communist country. So in 1966 he launched the 'Great Proletarian Cultural Revolution'. It was to last for ten remarkable and chaotic years.

Mao believed that progress was being held back by the middle-aged and the middle-class. Millions of young Red Guards were recruited to make deep, swift changes that could not be reversed. Red was the colour of revolution. Red became

the symbol of progress. Even a red traffic-light was reinterpreted to mean 'go' instead of 'stop'! Physical work was thought to be good, mental work, useless. Schools and universities were closed. Teachers and students were forced to work tilling the land. Anyone who appeared unenthusiastic about such changes was humiliated, even assaulted by the Red Guards who rampaged through the cities. Many old party officials were dismissed from their posts.

By 1968 the most fanatic phase was over. But the general policy of keeping up the pace of change continued until Mao's death in 1976. Mao was aided and supported in the Cultural Revolution by a group which became known as the 'Gang of Four'. It was led by his wife, Chiang Ching. Chiang Ching was Mao's fourth wife, and he married her in 1939. After Mao's death she was put on trial. It then became clear that the former sexy actress had become a hard, vicious woman, who had been responsible for the deaths and imprisonment of many people during the Cultural Revolution. But her death sentence was commuted (reduced) to life imprisonment by the new Government under Deng Xiaoping, who set about repairing some of the damage brought about by the Cultural Revolution.

In thirty years what had the Chinese Communists achieved?
1 Most were better fed and clothed.
2 Most enjoyed the benefits of education and health services.
3 Industry had been expanded and modernized dramatically and was starting to provide some consumer goods like bicycles and televisions for millions of people.
4 The whole country was reorganized into communes so that people could live and work with a sense of community.

But what was the cost in human suffering? China has always been a secretive country and it is still extremely difficult to obtain accurate information. It is likely that millions of people were executed – mostly landlords and Mao's political opponents. Also stories are now being collected about the huge mistake

Mao made by insisting on collectivization in the late 1950s. The peasants were not allowed to benefit from any increase in the amount of food they produced: it was taken by the Government for the workers in the towns. So the peasants did not bother to produce even enough for the country as a whole. As a result it is estimated that nearly 20 million people died of starvation in a catastrophic famine from 1959 to 1961. ☐

Many changes have taken place in China since Mao died in 1976. There is very much more freedom and both peasants and owners of businesses are allowed to make profits for themselves. These changes are sometimes called the Chinese third revolution. (The first was in 1911 and the second started in 1949.) This photograph was taken in Peking. Notice the western-style clothes and advertisements. The scene would have been very different in Mao's time.

1 Collect all the evidence from pages 134–140 about the problems of agriculture and food supplies in China in recent history. Explain how far the problems have been caused by nature and how far by people.
2 Imagine you are a Communist Party official on the Long March. Make a list of arguments to persuade an exhausted comrade why the March was started and why he should press on.
3 What does the word 'indoctrination' mean? Do you think that the Chinese Red Guards were indoctrinated? Give reasons.

India

Struggle for independence

After China, India has the second largest population in the world. Both countries have had similar problems of:

1 how to get rid of foreign influence;
2 how to cope with the backwardness and poverty of millions of peasants;
3 how to develop modern industries.

China used the methods of force and Communism; India used the gentler methods of the western kind of democracy. Many people have been interested to compare the achievements of the two systems.

We left the story of India in Chapter 1 with Victoria becoming Empress. Just under nine years later, in 1885, the first meeting of the Indian National Congress took place. It was held in Bombay. Its purpose was 'the eradication ... of [*doing away with*] all possible race, creed or provincial prejudices amongst all lovers of their country' and to 'form the germ of a Native Parliament'. In other words the people were to be united and allowed to choose their own Government. Demonstrations against British rule started in 1905. The most famous demonstration happened in 1919, at Amritsar in the northern state of Punjab. It is famous because of its dreadful outcome. The British commander, General Dyer, ordered his men to shoot into an unarmed crowd. Nearly 400 were killed and over 1,000 wounded in the massacre. The reason he did this was not to disperse the crowd, but to frighten the people of the Punjab to stop their demonstrations. But the effect was that the British were even more hated.

The next year Congress officially adopted Gandhi's policy of 'satyagraha'. Gandhi organized three waves of demonstrations: 1920–22, 1930–34, 1942–47. One of the most famous events was the 'salt march' in 1930. The march was a protest against the tax on salt. Salt is a vital preservative in such a hot country – it prevents food going bad The sixty-one-year-old Gandhi walked at the head of a gathering crowd of protesters for 24 days until they reached the sea-shore where they obtained salt for nothing! During his campaigns Gandhi was arrested and imprisoned several times. But what saddened him most was the fact that those who followed him did not demonstrate as he wanted. They did not turn the other cheek when struck by police clubs! There was considerable violence. To restore peace Gandhi fasted. Such was his influence that the demonstrators stopped their violence,

Mahatma Gandhi was born in 1869 in western India. At nineteen he went to England to study, and qualified as a lawyer. At 24 he went to South Africa where he stayed for 21 years, suffering humiliations of racial persecution by white people.

He studied both the Christian and Hindu religions and came to believe in the importance of leading a simple, non-violent life. He was particularly affected by the Sermon on the Mount. He wrote that the words, ' "But I say unto you, that ye resist not evil: but whosoever shall smite thee on thy right cheek, turn to him the other also" ... delighted me beyond measure.' He tried most sincerely to live his own life according to these ideals. While he was in South Africa he developed his ideas about how an oppressed people can best resist a powerful government. He put these ideas into dramatic effect after he returned to India in 1915. He called his method 'satyagraha'. A rough translation is 'the force of truth'. Gandhi explained, 'Truth (*satya*) implies love, and firmness (*agraha*) engenders and therefore serves as a synonym for force ... 'Satyagraha' ... is ... the force which is born of Truth and Love or non-violence.' Gandhi's campaigns of non-violent demonstrations were so effective that he was invited to London to discuss ways in which Britain could give India some independence. Notice the simplicity of Gandhi's clothes shown in this photograph, taken in London, 1931.

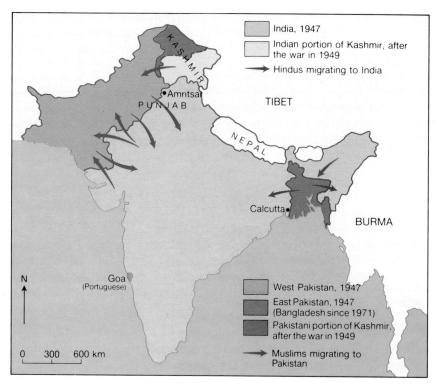

The Indian partition.

The Hindu versus Muslim riots in Delhi, 1947.

as Hindus and Muslims massacred each other, especially in cities like Calcutta which had mixed populations. Gandhi was appalled and tried everything in his power to stop the slaughter. But on 30 January 1948, while at a prayer meeting in New Delhi, he was shot dead by an assassin.

Modern India

It is, of course, impossible to partition a country exactly. In India it was impossible to draw frontiers so that all Hindus were in India and all Muslims in Pakistan. Those who found themselves in the 'wrong' country were terrified. And so families collected their possessions and started to trek – Hindus to India, Muslims to Pakistan. Vast convoys of people – one 57 miles long – journeyed from West Punjab (now in Pakistan) to India. Gandhi spoke about this four months before his death: 'It makes my brain reel to think that can be. Such a thing is unparalleled in the history of the world, and it makes me ... hang my head in shame'.

Perhaps 10, perhaps even 15, million people journeyed in this way. The journeys were dangerous. The convoys and trains were attacked. Some say as many as a million died. Here is one story, told by Colonel Sher Khan. He tells of murders carried out by Sikhs (equally horrific stories could be told about Muslims and Hindus):

'The following morning I went to the station, where the train had been pulled in during the night ... I talked to some of the survivors ... [They told me that] ... hundreds of Sikhs rushed the train. They first started collecting valuables off the women ... Having done all the looting etc. they started killing ...

'It is impossible to estimate the number of dead, as they were piled up on top of each other in the compartments; between 1,200–1,500 ... The police said they were going to dump the bodies in the Beas river.'

afraid that the Mahatma would die.

In 1947 the British Government agreed to give India its independence. But in the meantime, quarrels had developed inside India between the two main religious groups, the Muslims and the Hindus. The Muslims were a minority of the population and they feared that the Hindus would completely control India once the British had left. So the British agreed that the country should be partitioned to allow for a separate Muslim country, Pakistan. The two new countries came into existence in August 1947. But riots broke out

India's first Prime Minister, from 1947 until his death in 1964, was Jawaharlal Nehru. He was born, in 1889, into a rich family of the highest (Brahmin) caste. He was educated in England, at Harrow and Cambridge and in later years described himself as 'a queer mixture of East and West, out of place everywhere, at home nowhere'. In 1929 he became President of Congress. He had a first-rate mind and enjoyed extremely good health. But, especially after the death of his delicate wife in 1936, he was a lonely man.

While Prime Minister he pursued four main policies:
1 To establish a parliamentary system of government like Britain's.
2 To nationalize industry and plan industrial development as had been done in the USSR.
3 To introduce social reforms such as education and to reduce discrimination against women and untouchables.
4 To avoid becoming involved in the Cold War (see Chapter 8). This policy came to be called 'non-alignment', that is, not lining up with either the USA or the USSR.
The photograph shows Nehru wearing a western-style suit and an Indian 'Gandhi cap'.

Yet India settled down to its tasks. A democratic form of government was set up, the Congress being the most important political party. And many reforms have been attempted. For centuries India has had a 'caste system' – that is, a rigid division into social classes. The lowest are the 'untouchables'. Laws have been passed to prevent discrimination against them. Great efforts have also been made to develop industry. Important progress has been made, though the pace has been slow. The great majority of the population are poor peasants who are reluctant to have smaller families or to change their ways of farming. And the Government has been reluctant to use force to make changes, as has happened in China. □

Two years after Nehru's death his daughter, Mrs Indira Gandhi, became Prime Minister. (Her husband was not, in fact, any relation of Mahatma Gandhi.) She was Prime Minister, 1966–77 and again 1980–84. Mrs Gandhi was a formidable person and no other politician since the death of her father had so much influence in India. However, she was seriously criticized for the way she governed India. She often seemed callous and arrogant. For example, in an interview on 1 April 1976 she said, 'The Indian people have a terrific capacity to bear their hardships' and 'We are going to run this country as we think best'. Demonstrations against her were so serious in 1975 that she declared a State of Emergency: opponents were arrested and newspapers were censored. Many Indians feared that she was preparing to become a dictator: hence her defeat in the elections of 1977. Yet three years later she became Prime Minister again. One of the fears in the minds of her opponents in the 1970s was that she would be able to make her son, Sanjay, succeed her as Prime Minister. But he was killed in an air accident in 1980. In 1984 she was shot dead by Sikhs who were concerned about the way she was treating their province, the Punjab.

1 Write character-sketches of Mao Tse-tung and Mahatma Gandhi. Explain the differences between them.
2 Compare the photographs of Gandi (page 141) and Nehru (above). What do they tell you about the differences between them?

The Middle East

Between the two World Wars

During the First World War (Chapter 6) Turkey fought on the side of Germany. Much of western Asia was then part of the Turkish Empire (see map). So the British encouraged the Arabs living there to rebel against the Turks. Naturally, when the war came to an end and the Turkish Empire was broken up, the Arabs expected to be given their independence. In fact, Britain and France took control of some of this land instead – to the great disappointment of many Arab people.

But that was not the only problem. In the land of Palestine, which the British took over, there was another complication. In Biblical times this was the home of the Jewish people. But, over the centuries, they had become scattered into many other countries. (This scattering is called the 'Diaspora' or dispersal.) Then, during the nineteenth century, a movement grew up called 'Zionism'. Its aim was to get the Jewish people back to the land of Zion (Palestine) where they could have their own nation-state (see page 91).

In 1917 the leader of the Jewish community in Britain persuaded the Government that it was a just cause. This declaration was issued (called the 'Balfour Declaration' because A J Balfour was the Foreign Secretary, who wrote it):

'His Majesty's Government view with favour the establishment in Palestine of a National Home for the Jewish people, ... it being clearly understood that nothing shall be done which may prejudice the civil and religious rights of existing non-Jewish communities in Palestine.'

It is easy to understand why people should have been so sympathetic to the Jewish cause:

1 It seemed only right that the Jewish people should have their own country. After all, the British people lived in Britain, the French people lived in France.

2 It seemed right that it should be the one they had had in the past.

3 Many Jews had suffered persecution in several European countries, especially Russia.

Then, in the 1930s, the brutal Nazi campaign was started against the Jews in Germany (see Chapter 6). Refugees started to pour into Palestine.

The trouble was, what was going to happen about the existing non-Jewish

The Middle East after 1918.

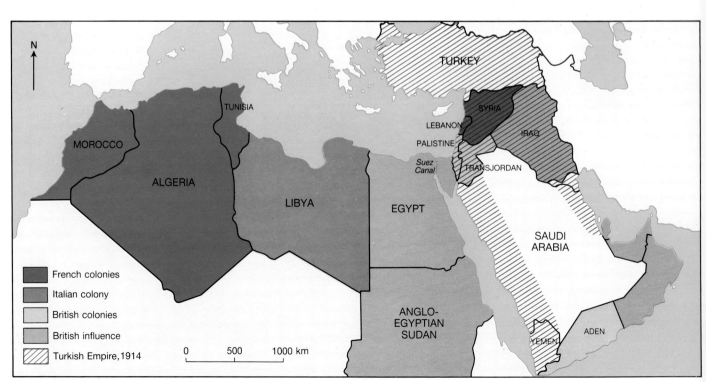

communities (that is, the Arab people of Palestine)? It was bad enough that the British were in their country, let alone these other foreigners. Fighting broke out between the Jews and Arabs – with the British police and soldiers trying to keep order in the middle!

The creation of Israel

By 1945 one of the most frightening horror stories of all time was emerging. It was about the Nazi extermination camps; how 6 million Jews were starved, tortured and murdered. Many of the survivors begged to be allowed to settle in Palestine. When the British Government hesitated, Jewish terrorist groups in desperation attacked British people in Palestine. The most daring and heartless was the attack on the King David Hotel in Jerusalem. One wing of this building was taken over as the British headquarters. A Jewish terrorist unit managed to install some explosive packed in milk-churns. At 12.37 p.m. on 22 July 1946 they were detonated. The leader of the unit, Menachem Begin (later Prime Minister of Israel), described what happened:

'Suddenly the whole town seemed to shudder ... The milk-cans "reached" the whole height of the building, from basement to roof, six storeys of stone, concrete and steel. As the BBC put it – the entire wing of a huge building was cut as with a knife.'

Over 80 people died in the explosion – including 15 Jews who were working in the offices.

The British, exhausted by six years of World War, could not cope with such an extraordinarily difficult problem. The next year, 1947, they asked the new United Nations Organisation to take over. The UN produced a plan which partitioned Palestine (see map right). But the scheme satisfied neither side. The Arabs thought that it gave the Jews too much; and the Jews thought that it gave them too little – they were especially sad not to get Jerusalem, which they felt should be their capital.

The King David Hotel, Jerusalem, after the bombing July 1946. This was the most dramatic act of terrorism by the Jews in their struggle for their own independent state.

Israel, 1947–49, and 1967.

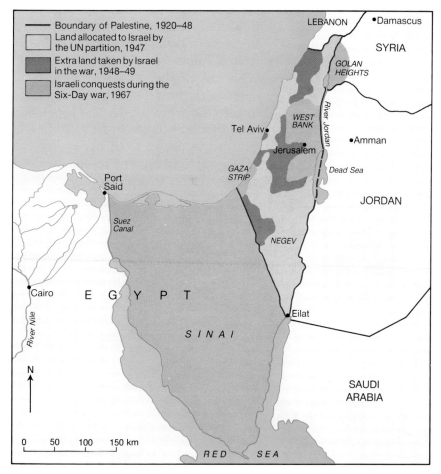

- ── Boundary of Palestine, 1920–48
- Land allocated to Israel by the UN partition, 1947
- Extra land taken by Israel in the war, 1948–49
- Israeli conquests during the Six-Day war, 1967

An Israeli kibbutz. The word comes from the Hebrew, meaning 'a gathering'. This system of living and working together has been very successful and famous.

were made in the desert. The most interesting were 'kibbutzim'. These were agricultural communities, owned and administered by all the members together. But the land has so few natural resources and so much money was spent on the armed forces that Israel depended heavily on large sums of money from the USA.

Arab-Israeli wars

Since Israel came into existence she has fought five wars with her Arab neighbours:

1. War of Independence, 1948–49
2. Suez War, 1956
3. Six-Day War, 1967
4. Yom Kippur War, 1973
5. Lebanon War, 1982

(The 'Yom Kippur War' is given that name because it started on the Jewish holy day – 'Yom Yippur'.) The most important of these wars for the Middle East was the Six-Day War, so we shall look at this closely (see map page 145).

After the war of 1948–49 the Arab people of (what used to be) Palestine were in a wretched condition. Some were refugees living in primitive camps in land between Israel and Egypt, called the Gaza Strip; some were living in foreign countries; others were being governed by the Jews. As a result these Palestinians started to hate Israel bitterly. Many young men organized themselves into commando units in the countries around Israel and

Jerusalem was their holy city.

Despite these complaints, the UN went ahead. The new Jewish state of Israel was proclaimed on 14 May 1948. The next day armies from five neighbouring countries invaded. Israel was surrounded; but her army fought so desperately that when the war came to an end, Israel had more land than had been given to her by the UN. She ended up with 77 per cent of Palestine instead of 57 per cent, including the western half of Jerusalem.

Israel now started to organize herself. What she needed most was people – to cultivate the land, build up industries and to keep the army strong. The population in 1948 was 800,000. In 1950 the Law of Return was passed to encourage Jews to immigrate to Israel. The result? By 1964 the population trebled. Now settlements

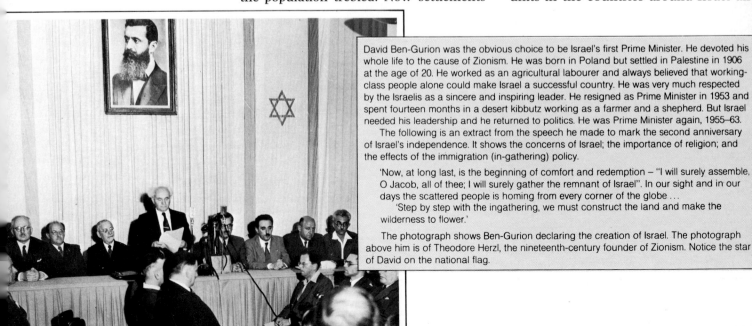

David Ben-Gurion was the obvious choice to be Israel's first Prime Minister. He devoted his whole life to the cause of Zionism. He was born in Poland but settled in Palestine in 1906 at the age of 20. He worked as an agricultural labourer and always believed that working-class people alone could make Israel a successful country. He was very much respected by the Israelis as a sincere and inspiring leader. He resigned as Prime Minister in 1953 and spent fourteen months in a desert kibbutz working as a farmer and a shepherd. But Israel needed his leadership and he returned to politics. He was Prime Minister again, 1955–63.

The following is an extract from the speech he made to mark the second anniversary of Israel's independence. It shows the concerns of Israel; the importance of religion; and the effects of the immigration (in-gathering) policy.

'Now, at long last, is the beginning of comfort and redemption – "I will surely assemble, O Jacob, all of thee; I will surely gather the remnant of Israel". In our sight and in our days the scattered people is homing from every corner of the globe . . .

'Step by step with the ingathering, we must construct the land and make the wilderness to flower.'

The photograph shows Ben-Gurion declaring the creation of Israel. The photograph above him is of Theodore Herzl, the nineteenth-century founder of Zionism. Notice the star of David on the national flag.

Tanks were important in the desert fighting between Israel and her Arab neighbours. Fierce tank battles were fought especially in the Yom Kippur War: in one battle alone 250 Egyptian tanks were 'knocked out' (that is, so damaged they could not move).

airfields. It was brilliantly successful. The attacks were timed for 8.45 a.m., just as the Egyptian dawn fighter patrols had landed and the commanders of the army were having breakfast or driving to their offices. The Israelis destroyed 416 aircraft. Then they launched their land attacks. These were equally brilliant. Within six days Israel had defeated the Egyptian, Syrian, and Jordanian armies; killed 20,000 of their soldiers for only 679 of its own; and captured three-and-a-half times the area of Israel itself.

Ten years later Begin, by then Prime Minister of Israel, agreed to return Egypt's land (Sinai). But he refused to help the Palestinians whose plight was more desperate: it seemed as if they would never have a country of their own again. ☐

made attacks on Israel's border villages. Israel also had separate quarrels with Egypt and with Syria. War looked very likely.

On Saturday 3 June 1967 many Israeli troops were sent home on leave. It was a trick. They wanted to make the Egyptians believe Israel was not preparing for war. On the Monday the Israelis launched surprise attacks, mainly against Egyptian

1 Hold a class discussion on the following statement: 'Since the Second World War there has been continual fighting between Israel and her neighbours. This has been Britain's fault because she failed to solve the problem of Palestine.'

2 What does the photograph below tell you about Colonel Nasser?

Gamal Abdel Nasser was the most popular of Arab leaders in modern times. When he died, in 1970, worn out by excessive work in governing Egypt, countless throngs of people jammed the streets of Cairo to mourn his passing at his funeral.

He was born in 1918 and made the army his career. In 1952 a group of army officers forced the incompetent Egyptian King Farouk to abdicate. Colonel Nasser was one of their leaders. Two years later he became Prime Minister, then President. At the time there was much talk of Arab nationalism; of ousting foreigners from influential positions in Arab countries and modernizing them. Nasser became the most important leader in this movement. While he governed Egypt he fought two wars with Israel. In the first, the Suez War of 1956, Britain and France also fought against Egypt. These two European countries quarrelled with Nasser when he took over control of the Suez Canal, previously operated by a European-controlled international company. But when the British and French plotted with the Israelis and attacked Egypt many other countries were shocked. The attackers had to withdraw and Nasser became a great hero throughout the Arab world. He was also popular inside Egypt because he introduced land reforms for the benefit of the poor peasants. The photograph shows the enthusiastic support he received when he announced the nationalization of the Suez Canal.

Africa

The 'Scramble for Africa'

Towards the end of the fifteenth century the Portuguese started to build forts and trading stations in various places on the coast of Africa in order to protect their trade routes to India and the East Indies. But it was not until five hundred years later that European countries decided to take over the *interior* of the continent as colonies (see Chapter 1). The late nineteenth century was the 'age of imperialism' – the main European countries and the USA occupied other lands for economic and military benefit. There was another reason for occupying other lands. Some Europeans also believed that they had a moral duty to bring Christianity and civilization to 'backward' and 'heathen' peoples. The English writer, Rudyard Kipling, summed up this attitude of mind most famously in his poem, *The White Man's Burden*, published in 1898. Here are some of the lines:

'Take up the White Man's burden –
Send forth the best ye breed –
Go bind your sons to exile
To serve your captive's need.
To wait in heavy harness
On fluttered folk and wild –
Your new-caught, sullen peoples
Half devil and half child.'

Although Africa is a whole continent, some Europeans became incredibly greedy for land. This is what the British Cecil Rhodes wrote (he was talking about 'red' because maps used to show the British Empire in red):

'I believe it to be my duty to God, my Queen and my country to paint the whole of Africa red, red from the Cape to Cairo. That is my creed, my dream and my mission.'

In practice what the imperial countries came to be interested in was obtaining cheap raw materials and food from the colonies – copper from central Africa, cocoa from west Africa, for example. Such greed might have led to war. So in 1884–85 a conference was summoned in Berlin at which the countries agreed on the frontiers to be drawn on the maps. Then they set about occupying the actual lands (see map, left).

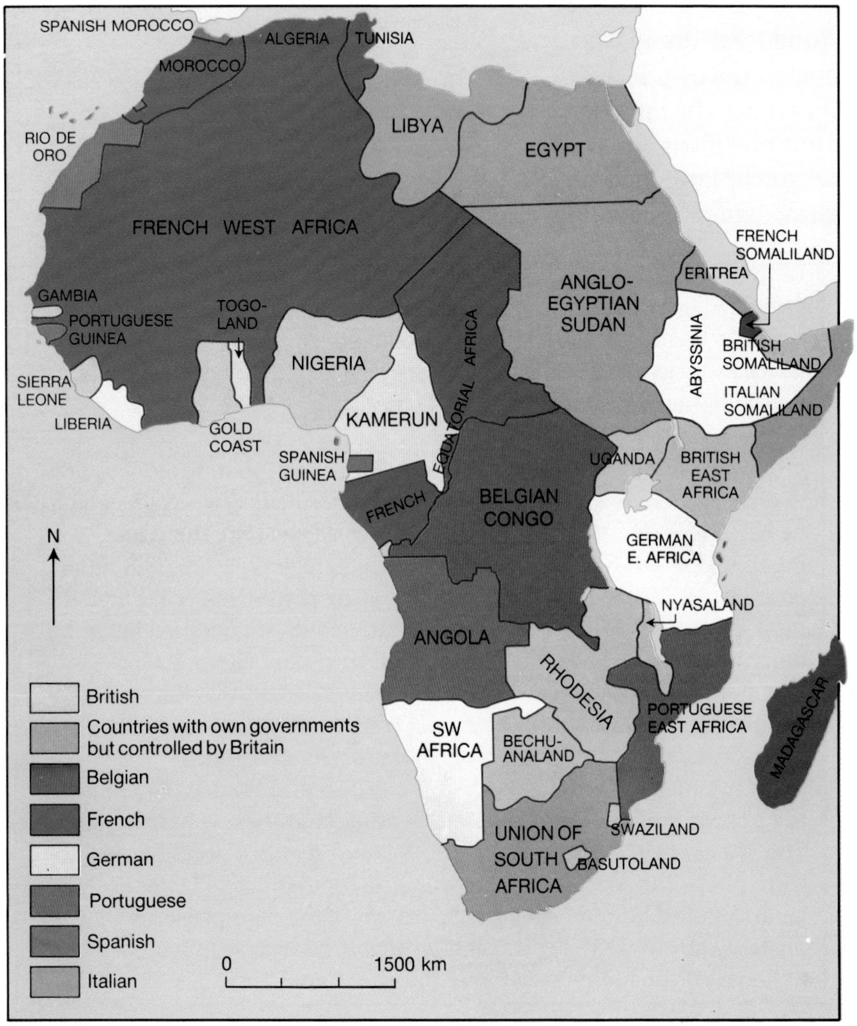

African nationalism

In 1947, Britain gave India independence (see page 142). African people who wanted independence for their own countries were encouraged by this news. If Britain was willing to give independence to India, she might also treat other colonies in the same way. But, in comparison with India, African colonies were poor and their people were uneducated in modern, European ways. In 1947 it was only the most optimistic who dared hope for independence in their own lifetimes. Yet just over 30 years later almost the whole continent was governed by the African people.

One of the earliest African colonies to

Africa, 1914. Notice that Abyssinia and Liberia were the only countries not controlled by Europeans.

SPANISH MOROCCO
ALGERIA
TUNISIA
MOROCCO
RIO DE ORO
LIBYA
EGYPT
FRENCH WEST AFRICA
FRENCH SOMALILAND
GAMBIA
PORTUGUESE GUINEA
TOGO-LAND
ERITREA
ANGLO-EGYPTIAN SUDAN
ABYSSINIA
BRITISH SOMALILAND
ITALIAN SOMALILAND
SIERRA LEONE
LIBERIA
GOLD COAST
NIGERIA
KAMERUN
SPANISH GUINEA
EQUATORIAL AFRICA
UGANDA
BRITISH EAST AFRICA
FRENCH
BELGIAN CONGO
GERMAN E. AFRICA
NYASALAND
ANGOLA
RHODESIA
PORTUGUESE EAST AFRICA
MADAGASCAR
SW AFRICA
BECHU-ANALAND
UNION OF SOUTH AFRICA
SWAZILAND
BASUTOLAND

N

British
Countries with own governments but controlled by Britain
Belgian
French
German
Portuguese
Spanish
Italian

0   1500 km

Africa today. The poor countries tend to be those without any modern industries. They are therefore sometimes called Least Developed Countries.

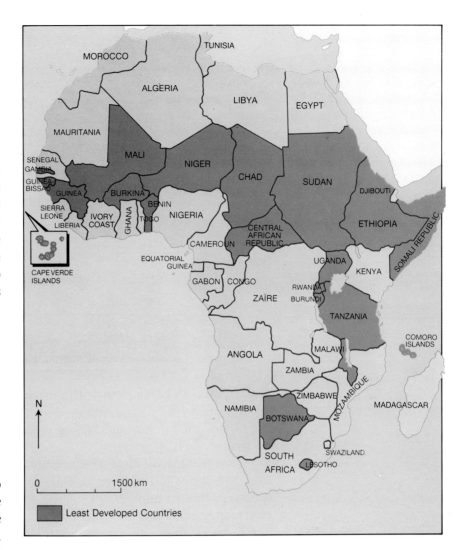

Least Developed Countries

be given independence was Ghana. Until 1957 this was the British West African colony of the Gold Coast. It gained independence through the work of people like its first prime minister, Kwame Nkrumah. After the Second World War he became convinced that his country should become independent. He made speeches which drew large crowds. The British could not ignore the fact that so many people wanted their freedom. In his autobiography Nkrumah wrote:

'We had succeeded because we had talked with the people and by so doing knew their feelings and grievances. And we had excluded no one. For, if a national movement is to succeed, every man and woman of goodwill must be allowed to play a part.'

The strength of nationalist feeling was too powerful for the imperial countries to resist. At first only a few colonies were made independent. But, by 1960, as the British prime minister, Harold Macmillan, said, 'a wind of change' was blowing through the continent.

But winning independence brought its difficulties. The new African countries have had serious problems to cope with:
1 Poverty. The United Nations has a list of the world's 31 poorest countries called the Least Developed Countries; 21 are in Africa (see map above).
2 Drought. Most of these 21 countries stretch across the north-central part of Africa. Much of this area is the Sahara desert and the Sahel wilderness, where there have been two dreadful droughts in

Countries most affected by famine in the mid-1980s were Ethiopia and the Sudan. Here the effects of the drought were worsened by civil wars, which prevented farmers from planting crops. People walked miles to food-supply camps, as shown in this photograph taken in Ethiopia. Many in the rich countries gave money to help. The most famous scheme was a great pop concert called Live Aid, arranged by Bob Geldof of the Boomtown Rats in 1985. This was shown on television throughout the world and raised £50 million.

Julius Nyerere has been one of the most pleasant personalities in African politics since 1945. And he remained in power for a long time. He studied at Edinburgh University and became a teacher. In 1955 he decided to devote himself to politics. He became Prime Minister of Tanganyika (now Tanzania) in 1961 and was President from 1962 to 1985. In 1967 he made a statement called the Arusha Declaration. The key word was 'Ujamaa', which he translated as 'Familyhood'. He wrote, 'The foundation, and the objective, of African socialism is the extended family'. The idea was to create a kind of co-operative society based on African traditions. Yet Tanzania remained very poor and Nyerere was criticized for being unrealistic.

recent years; 1974 and 1984. Hundreds of thousands of people and animals died of starvation, though no one knows even approximately how many.

3 Trade problems. Most African countries (like others in the Third World) rely on a very limited number of products to earn money from other countries by trade. If the prices they can obtain for their products fall, then so do their earnings. In 1980 a famous book was published about these kinds of problems. It was called the 'Brandt Report'. One example it gave was Zambia, 94 per cent of whose export earnings came from copper:

'There was a boom in copper prices from 1972 with the price peaking in April 1974 at $3,034 per ton; then it suddenly fell to $1,290 before the end of that year. But the price of imports continued to rise so that the volume of imports Zambia could buy fell by 45% between 1974 and 1975 ...'

4 Urbanization. The population of most African countries has increased (despite death from starvation in the Sahel region). Many have drifted to towns and cities in search of work, often in vain. In four African countries the urban population increased by 400 per cent between 1950 and 1975. In some cities, such as Dakar in Senegal and Lagos in Nigeria, squalid shanty-town suburbs have sprung up, breeding disease and crime.

5 Tribal divisions. The frontiers which the imperial countries drew in 1884–85 bore no relation to the distribution of the people in Africa. As a result, some colonies contained many different tribes and some tribes were spread over several different colonies. When the colonies became independent their leaders agreed not to quarrel with each other over these frontiers. Although there have been a few wars between neighbours, the more serious problem has been tribal quarrels *within* countries. The most terrible civil wars happened in the Congo (Zaïre) in 1960, Nigeria in 1967–70 and Burundi in 1971.

6 Government. When the colonies were given independence very few people had ever been in government before – the white people had been firmly in control. It is not surprising that there has been much quarrelling and corruption. And so, in several countries, the army has taken over the Government, sometimes temporarily, sometimes permanently.

South Africa

In most African countries, because of the hot climate, very few white families settled to live there as their permanent home. But South Africa was different. It has a pleasant climate and is a rich, fertile and pleasant land. First the Dutch settled in the Cape of Good Hope in the seventeenth century; then the British arrived in the nineteenth century. Wars were fought with the Zulu inhabitants, but the superior weapons of the Whites soon subdued them. At the turn of the century the Dutch (called 'Boers' or 'Afrikaners') and the British even fought a war with *each other* (the Boer War), 1899–1902.

Since 1948 the Afrikaner National Party has formed the Government. It has put into effect its policy of 'apartheid'. This is an Afrikaans word meaning separateness; the belief that white people should live apart from the black people ('Bantus' as they are called) (see below). The South African Government has claimed that the purpose of apartheid is: 'the advancement of the nations presently under its care ... encouragement ... to them to preserve in accordance with their own wishes their separate identities, culture and heritage'.

In theory it might sound splendid. In practice, there have been problems and injustices:

1   The black people of South Africa outnumber the white people but they have only a small fraction of the land. Although Blacks are 69 per cent of the population,

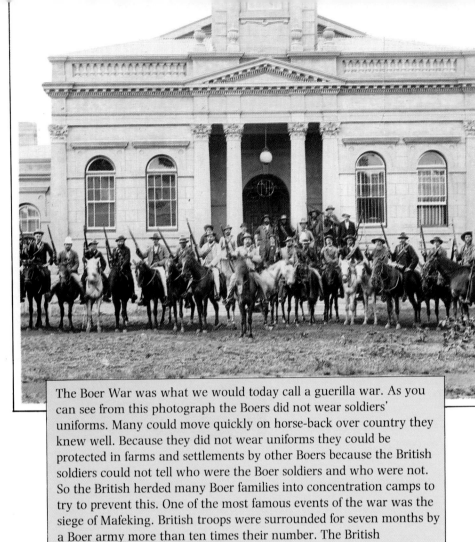

The Boer War was what we would today call a guerilla war. As you can see from this photograph the Boers did not wear soldiers' uniforms. Many could move quickly on horse-back over country they knew well. Because they did not wear uniforms they could be protected in farms and settlements by other Boers because the British soldiers could not tell who were the Boer soldiers and who were not. So the British herded many Boer families into concentration camps to try to prevent this. One of the most famous events of the war was the siege of Mafeking. British troops were surrounded for seven months by a Boer army more than ten times their number. The British Commander was General Baden-Powell, who later founded the Boy Scout movement.

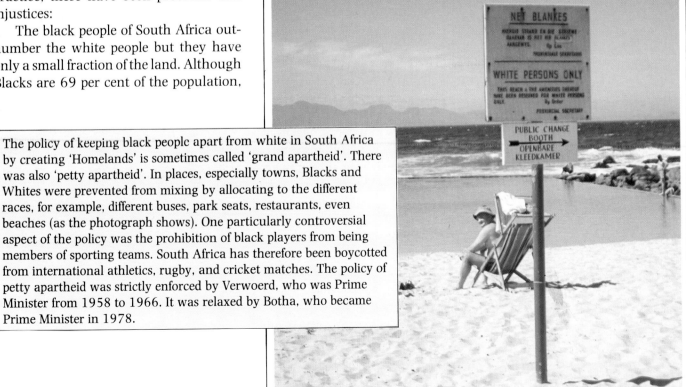

The policy of keeping black people apart from white in South Africa by creating 'Homelands' is sometimes called 'grand apartheid'. There was also 'petty apartheid'. In places, especially towns, Blacks and Whites were prevented from mixing by allocating to the different races, for example, different buses, park seats, restaurants, even beaches (as the photograph shows). One particularly controversial aspect of the policy was the prohibition of black players from being members of sporting teams. South Africa has therefore been boycotted from international athletics, rugby, and cricket matches. The policy of petty apartheid was strictly enforced by Verwoerd, who was Prime Minister from 1958 to 1966. It was relaxed by Botha, who became Prime Minister in 1978.

By 1984 black protests were becoming very common. The police killed many in their attempts to disperse the gatherings. Then the funerals were used as opportunities for further demonstrations.

Notice the armoured police lorry in the background of this photograph, taken in October 1984.

they have been given 'Bantustans' (tribal homelands) to live in which are only 13 per cent of the land area.

2   Black people in fact are needed to work in 'white' areas; in factories and mines for example. Indeed, very few white people do heavy, unpleasant work. The Blacks' wages are low and living conditions poor.

3   Black people have been forced to carry passes. Any attempts at protest about their conditions have been suppressed. People who have written and made long speeches have been given very long prison sentences. There have been demonstrations; but these have been dispersed by the police. In 1960, at Sharpeville, 69 people were killed; in 1976, at Soweto, 176 were killed plus 60 others in different places at the same time. In demonstrations which took place in the year from the anniversary of Sharpeville in September 1984, 1,000 people were killed. Many countries have become increasingly opposed to apartheid over the years. One British representative at the United Nations called it 'morally abominable, intellectually grotesque, spiritually indefensible'.   □

1   Read the quotations on page 148. How useful do you think they are in helping us understand what British people thought about colonies at the time?
2   In 1958 a West African leader said, 'We prefer poverty in freedom, to riches in slavery.' What do you think he meant?
3   Imagine you are a British athlete. Draw up lists of arguments for and against competing in games in South Africa.
4   Make a list of all the people mentioned in this Chapter who were educated outside their own countries. What effect do you think the experience had on them as political leaders?
5   Compile a list of the religions mentioned in this Chapter and explain how each has had an influence on the history and politics of the countries where they are practised.
6   Study the maps on pages 148 and 149 and make lists of all the present-day countries which were in 1914:
a) British colonies.
b) French colonies.

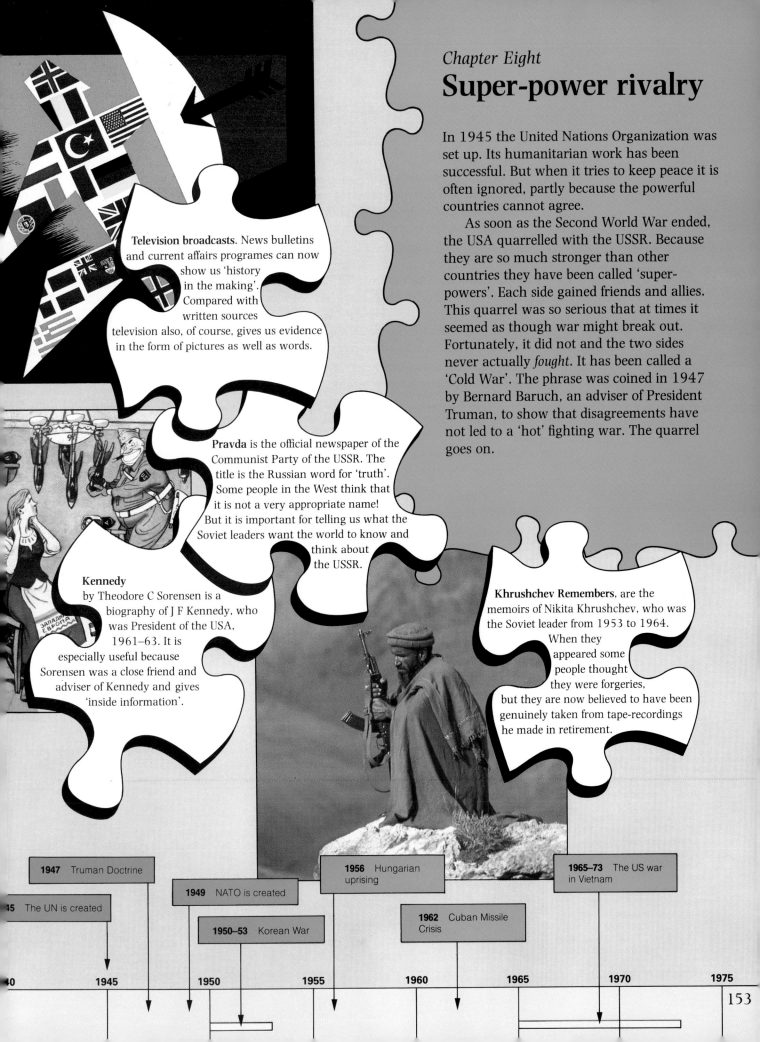

Chapter Eight

Super-power rivalry

In 1945 the United Nations Organization was set up. Its humanitarian work has been successful. But when it tries to keep peace it is often ignored, partly because the powerful countries cannot agree.

As soon as the Second World War ended, the USA quarrelled with the USSR. Because they are so much stronger than other countries they have been called 'super-powers'. Each side gained friends and allies. This quarrel was so serious that at times it seemed as though war might break out. Fortunately, it did not and the two sides never actually *fought*. It has been called a 'Cold War'. The phrase was coined in 1947 by Bernard Baruch, an adviser of President Truman, to show that disagreements have not led to a 'hot' fighting war. The quarrel goes on.

Television broadcasts. News bulletins and current affairs programes can now show us 'history in the making'. Compared with written sources television also, of course, gives us evidence in the form of pictures as well as words.

Pravda is the official newspaper of the Communist Party of the USSR. The title is the Russian word for 'truth'. Some people in the West think that it is not a very appropriate name! But it is important for telling us what the Soviet leaders want the world to know and think about the USSR.

Kennedy by Theodore C Sorensen is a biography of J F Kennedy, who was President of the USA, 1961–63. It is especially useful because Sorensen was a close friend and adviser of Kennedy and gives 'inside information'.

Khrushchev Remembers, are the memoirs of Nikita Khrushchev, who was the Soviet leader from 1953 to 1964. When they appeared some people thought they were forgeries, but they are now believed to have been genuinely taken from tape-recordings he made in retirement.

1947 Truman Doctrine

1949 NATO is created

45 The UN is created

1950–53 Korean War

1956 Hungarian uprising

1962 Cuban Missile Crisis

1965–73 The US war in Vietnam

40   1945   1950   1955   1960   1965   1970   1975

Cold War

The two sides in the Cold War are opposites in many ways:

1   In economics. The Russians are Communists and believe the Government should control all production. The Americans are Capitalists and believe production should depend on what is profitable to produce and the Government should interfere as little as possible.

2   In politics. The Communist Party is in control in the USSR. Anyone who criticizes the Government is likely to be arrested and badly treated. In the USA people can say and write what they want about the Government, and regularly there are free elections.

3   In religion. In the USA people are free to worship; in the USSR some churches are illegal. Indeed, many Americans are Christians; many Russians are atheists.

Each side fears that it will be destroyed by the other, given the opportunity. Each tends to believe that the other is bad: the Americans pity the Russian political prisoners; the Russians pity those kept poor by wealthy Americans. The leaders do not hide their views: Khrushchev (Russian leader 1953–64) once said,

'we will bury our enemies'; more recently President Reagan has described the USSR as an 'evil empire'.

Many of the most dramatic events of the world (some involving Britain) have been caused by this Cold War quarrel.

Soviet satellites

By 1944 it was clear that Germany would be defeated. But it was also clear that Britain and the USA might quarrel with the USSR about what should happen to the eastern European countries once they had been freed from the Germans. Churchill, the British prime minister, went to Moscow to discuss the matter with Stalin. Churchill suggested that Russia and the two western allies (Britain and the USA) should share their influence over countries: Russia would have more influence in some countries; Britain and America in others. He wrote the suggestions on half a sheet of paper:

'I pushed this across to Stalin, who had by then heard the translation. There was a slight pause. Then he took his blue pencil and made a large tick upon it, and passed it back to us. It was all settled in no more time than it takes to set down.'

Four months later, in February 1945, Churchill (UK), Stalin (USSR) and Roosevelt (USA) met at the Russian seaside resort of Yalta. Here they made more detailed agreements, especially about Poland. Then, in July 1945, the leaders of the three victorious countries met at

It is only in Europe that the two sides in the Cold War have a common frontier. The countries of Western Europe have never felt strong enough to defend themselves against the Soviet Union. They have therefore relied on American support. The first of these cartoons (*right*) is from the Russian magazine, *Krokodil* in 1958, and shows Europe (the girl) looking worried about all the nuclear weapons which the American soldier is placing round her room. The second is from the West German paper, *Die Zeit* in 1960, and shows a plump Europe nevertheless still relying on America, through NATO, for her defence.

КРОКОДИЛ

Lech Walesa

Alexander Dubcěck

Wladislav Gomulka

Imre Nagy

Gdansk 1980
Stettin
EAST
Berlin 1958
POLAND
Warsaw 1956
GERMANY
Prague 1968
CZECHOSLOVAKIA
Budapest 1956
AUSTRIA
HUNGARY
ROMANIA
USSR
Trieste
YUGOSLAVIA
BULGARIA
ALBANIA

N

0   200   400 km

Communist gains in Eastern Europe, 1939–48

—— The Iron Curtain as defined by Winston Churchill

USSR

Territory gained by USSR, 1939–45

'Satellites' of the USSR

Independent Communist countries

Uprisings in Eastern Europe, 1953–80

⚔ Main uprisings against USSR

Soviet influence in Eastern Europe after 1945, and opposition to it.

Potsdam near Berlin to decide what should be done about Germany.

Russia and the western allies were in fact soon quarrelling. On their side, the Russians feared another attack from Europe. Well over 20 million Russians had been killed in the two World Wars with Germany. After 1945 the Russian Army occupied the countries of eastern Europe and set about arranging friendly, Communist Governments in them (see map). Because these countries became so closely involved with Russia they came to be called Russian 'satellites'. The western countries objected to this: they wanted these countries to be able to choose their own governments. They were particularly worried about Poland. After all, the Second World War had started when Hitler attacked Poland – and Britain and France tried to help. What is more, the Russians refused to allow anyone from the west to visit eastern Europe.

In March 1946 Churchill made a speech in the USA describing the situation. He said:

'From Stettin in the Baltic to Trieste in the Adriatic, an Iron Curtain has descended across the continent. Behind that line lie all the capitals of the ancient states of central and eastern Europe ... all these famous cities and the populations around them ... are subject ... to a very high and increasing measure of control from Moscow.'

A year later the American President Truman spoke to Congress about what he considered to be the danger of Communist control of Greece and Turkey. He declared:

'I believe that it must be the policy of the United States to support free peoples who are resisting attempted subjugation [*loss of freedom*] by armed minorities or by outside pressures.'

This speech came to be called the 'Truman Doctrine'. It marks the real start of the Cold War: from now on it would be difficult for the two sides to patch up their disagreements.

Berlin blockade

At the Potsdam conference the three leaders (Stalin, Truman and Attlee) agreed that Germany should be temporarily divided into four zones of occupation (see map), to be run by the USSR, USA, Britain and France. Berlin, which was inside the Soviet zone, should be divided into four occupation sectors.

In 1948 the western allies had a dispute with the Russians about Germany. So the Russians tried to force the western allies out of their sectors of Berlin by

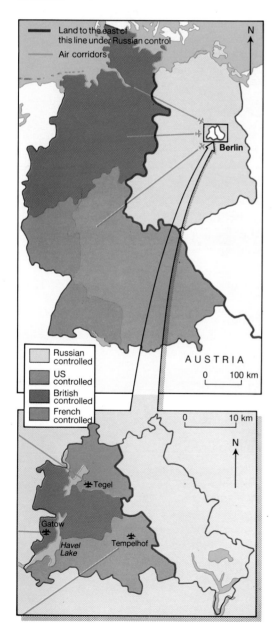

Germany and Berlin: the four areas of control.

Land to the east of this line under Russian control
Air corridors

Berlin

AUSTRIA

0   100 km

Russian controlled
US controlled
British controlled
French controlled

0   10 km

N

Tegel

Gatow

Havel Lake

Tempelhof

closing all the road, rail and canal routes through their own zone. The western part of Berlin relied entirely on the west for all its supplies of food, fuel and clothing. What was to be done? Should the western governments surrender their sectors to the Russians? Or should they try to use force to convoy supplies through the Soviet zone? In the event a remarkable third solution was found to the Berlin crisis.

The blockade lasted eleven months. During that time the western portion of Berlin, containing 2 million people, was supplied from the air. Altogether 277,728 flights were made. When the airlift was at its busiest, aircraft were arriving every 45 seconds – day and night! Every possible transport plane was used. One American pilot, not recognizing a particularly ungainly British aeroplane, called up the control-tower: 'What's this coming in now, fella?' he asked. 'A *Wayfarer*' was the reply. 'Did you say the *Mayflower?*' queried the astonished pilot. 'You guys sure are throwing in everything!' (The *Mayflower* was the ship which carried the original English settlers to America in the seventeenth century!) Faced with this skill and determination the Russians admitted defeat and reopened the land and water routes.

The Berlin Airlift. The western allies had been trying to reach agreement with the Russians ever since 1945 for a permanent arrangement for Germany. The Russians were very reluctant. They were frightened of the possibility of a reunited and rearmed Germany, which might be a danger to Russia yet again. In 1948 the three western allies introduced a new currency for their zones. The Russians objected. It was this that sparked off the blockade of Berlin. In fact, in 1949 the three western zones were joined together to form the Federal German Republic (West Germany). The Soviet zone then became the German Democratic Republic (East Germany). The painting is of a Douglas DC-4 and is entitled 'Return for a Reload'. Many of these aircraft were used in the airlift.

NATO

If the Berlin crisis had led to war, the Russians would have had a great advantage. They had more soldiers in eastern and central Europe than the USA and her allies had in western Europe. So in 1949 the countries of western Europe and North America decided to improve their defences. A treaty was signed. The most important part stated:

> 'The Parties agree that an armed attack against one or more of them in Europe or North America shall be considered an attack against them all.'

In this way NATO (North Atlantic Treaty Organization) was formed (see map). At first twelve countries belonged. In 1955 the Russians created a similar organization by an agreement made between European states behind the Iron Curtain called the Warsaw Pact. ☐

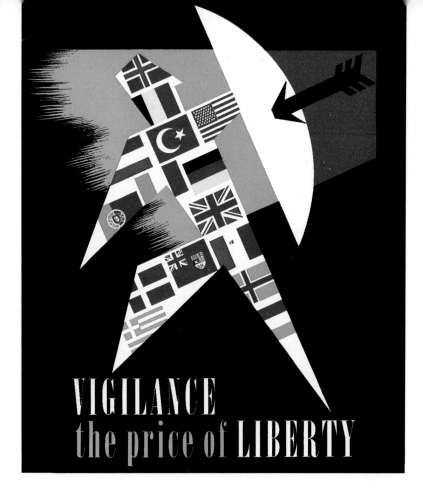

VIGILANCE the price of LIBERTY

1   Hold a class discussion on the statement that 'Stalin should not have been allowed to take control of Eastern Europe after the Second World War'.

2   The map below shows the world as seen from the North Pole. Why do you think it is useful to have this view rather than the usual one?

This picture represents NATO. From the flags you can tell who were the members when the cartoon was made. Notice the shield: this emphasizes that NATO is a defensive alliance, that it was not created to attack anyone. Notice too the caption about defending liberty.

NATO countries
1 USA, 1949
2 Canada, 1949
3 Iceland, 1949
4 Norway, 1949
5 Great Britain, 1949
6 Denmark, 1949
7 Netherlands, 1949
8 Belgium, 1949
9 France, 1949
10 Portugal, 1949
11 Italy, 1949
12 Greece, 1952
13 Turkey, 1952
14 West Germany, 1958
15 Spain, 1983

Warsaw Pact countries
1 USSR, 1955
2 Poland, 1955
3 East Germany, 1955
4 Czechoslovakia, 1955
5 Hungary, 1955
6 Romania, 1955
7 Bulgaria, 1955

NATO and the Warsaw Pact. The dates show when the countries joined.

From Korea to Cuba

The Korean war

Since the late 1940s many Americans have been convinced that the Soviet Government plans to make the whole world Communist. This belief was especially strong in about 1950. In 1949 Communists took over control of China (see Chapter 7). This was a great shock to the USA, who had been quite friendly with the government of the now defeated Chiang Kai-shek. Then, in the following year, the army of Communist North Korea invaded South Korea, which was friendly with the USA. We saw in Chapter 6 how Japan obtained Korea in the early years of this century. After Japan's defeat in 1945 Korea was partitioned. Like Germany, it was a temporary arrangement which became permanent. Although the Government of South Korea was an unpleasant one, the Americans believed it had to be defended. The Americans appealed to the UN. The UN condemned the North Koreans and called upon member-countries to expel them from South Korea. North Korea's strongest friends were China and Russia. But they could not support her in the UN. China was not a member; and at this time the Russians were not attending meetings as a way of making a protest against the Americans.

Several countries did send forces, though the Americans supplied by far the largest numbers. The Korean war lasted three years. It lasted that long because the Chinese sent a large number of soldiers to help the North Koreans. Although the fighting was confined to Korea, it was very intense and moved back and forth over almost the whole peninsula.

Casualties were high (see pie-chart). Villages and towns were destroyed; Koreans were made homeless refugees; and they suffered intensely during the almost arctic Korean winters.

The Chinese and North Koreans fought furiously: they suffered three times as many casualties as the UN forces. What is more, they treated their prisoners of war very badly: they tortured and brainwashed them. 'Brain-washing' is a

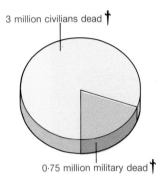

3 million civilians dead †

0·75 million military dead †

Numbers killed during or as a result of the Korean War

A scene from MASH. This was a very popular American television series about treating the wounded in the Korean War. This picture is from the film version.

technique of making a person's mind blank, and then re-filling it with new ideas. In this way, for example, a person can be made to accept the opposite of what he or she previously believed: loyal patriots were made to hate America. Faced with the problems of fighting such an enemy, and because of the especially large numbers of Chinese, the American commander wanted to use atomic bombs against China. President Truman sacked him.

McCarthyism

From 1950–54 a frightening campaign took place in America. It was like a seventeenth century 'witch-hunt' – except that the victims were now men. It was led by one man – Joseph McCarthy – a Senator from Wisconsin. Many Americans supported him. The campaign and the hatred it stirred up has become known as 'McCarthyism'.

The Korean war had increased the hatred and fear of Communism in the USA. Joseph McCarthy played on this mood in a campaign against important people. He falsely accused them of being Communist spies or sympathisers. In February 1950 he made a speech. He waved a piece of paper which, he said, contained a list of 205 known Communists in the State Department (the US Foreign Ministry). During his campaign he ruined the careers and reputations of many loyal Americans.

The atmosphere of 'McCarthyism' is revealed in this newspaper description of his office in the Senate:

'A visit to the McCarthy lair on Capitol Hill is rather like being transported to the set of one of Hollywood's minor thrillers. The ante-room is generally full of furtive-looking characters . . . A visitor is likely to find [McCarthy] with his heavy shoulders hunched forward, a telephone in his huge hands . . . "Yeah, yeah, I can listen, but I can't talk. Get me? You really got the goods on the guy?"'

Eventually the Senate forced him to

YEAH — SO HELP ME GOD !

LOYALTY OATH

withdraw from public life altogether. But it had been a nasty episode, revealing how easily feelings of hatred could be stirred up and sustained.

This is an American cartoon showing what McCarthy believed; that American Communists were falsely swearing to be loyal to their country when all the time they were working for the Soviet Union.

Hungary

By the late 1940s almost all the countries near Russia in eastern Europe had come under Soviet control. The exceptions were Finland, Greece and Turkey; Yugoslavia became Communist but quarrelled with Russia. There have been uprisings or protests in several of these countries against the Communist governments – for example, East Germany in 1953, Czechoslovakia in 1968, Poland in 1980. In each case the Russians have seen to it that Communists friendly to them remained in power and the countries remained members of the Warsaw Pact. The most serious challenge to Soviet control came in 1956 in Hungary.

At the end of October young people started demonstrating in the streets of the Hungarian capital, Budapest. They wanted a change of government and

159

withdrawal of Russian soldiers from their country. A huge metal statue of Stalin was pulled down as the crowd cheered and jeered. Workers from the factories and even soldiers of the Hungarian army joined in. Demonstrations also took place in other parts of the country. The Prime Minister resigned and was replaced by the popular Imre Nagy (pronounced 'imray nodge').

The Soviet Government did not know what to do. Eventually it decided to use force. On 4 November the Russians brought in 6,000 tanks against the main centres of rebellion. Budapest was bombarded. The people of Budapest gathered what weapons they could. Nagy made a frantic broadcast to the world for help:

'Soviet troops have launched an attack against our capital city with the obvious intention of overthrowing the lawful democratic Hungarian Government. Our troops are fighting. The Government is in its place. I hereby inform the people of Hungary and world opinion of the situation.'

However, trying to resist such forces was hopeless. And the Americans dared not help the Hungarians because if they did, they would risk war with the Soviet

Union. The Russians occupied Hungary; 100,000 refugees fled, rather than stay in their own, conquered country; and Nagy was taken secretly to Moscow and later executed. Many people throughout the world were horrified at the Russian brutality. In Britain, over 20 per cent of the members of the British Communist Party resigned their membership.

When the Russians invaded Hungary to crush the rebellion, many people decided to leave the country as refugees. Most fled across the border into Austria.

Russian tanks destroyed by a 'Molotov cocktail' in Budapest, 1956. The most effective, easily-made weapon for use against a tank is the 'Molotov cocktail'. This was named after the Russian Communist who was Foreign Minister of the Soviet Union, 1939–49 and 1953–56. It consists of a bottle filled with petrol and plugged with a petrol-soaked rag.

The Berlin Wall

The numbers of people who fled from Hungary were in fact small compared with the number of people who, over the years, escaped to the West from East Germany. In the 16 years after the end of the Second World War it is estimated that well over 3 million East Germans fled to the West. To try to prevent this loss of people formidable barriers were constructed on the border between the two Germanies: barbed-wire, minefields, watch-towers, guard-dogs. But there was still an escape route through Berlin.

In August 1961 the East German Government decided to close the border between East and West Berlin. A wall and barbed-wire entanglements were put up, thus physically cutting the city of Berlin in two. Anyone who dared try to cross this barrier would be shot. In the following year about 50 people were killed trying to escape. The most dramatic attempt was on 17 August 1962. An eighteen-year-old brick-layer was shot while trying to clamber over the wall. He fell on the Communist side, where he lay mortally wounded. The East German guards left him to bleed to death, watched by horrified West Berliners powerless to help.

The Berlin Wall became a symbol in the 1960s of the imprisonment of the peoples of eastern Europe in their own countries.

One of the best fiction books about the Cold War is John Le Carré's *The Spy Who Came in from the Cold*. This picture is a still from the film made of the book. The British spy, Leamas, is led to believe that he and a friend, Liz, will be allowed to climb over the Berlin Wall to the safety of the West. They are tricked. A searchlight shines on them as they are climbing and Liz is shot dead. The notice, for East German guards, reads: 'Soldier – you too are forbidden to leave!'.

One of the reasons so many people wanted to emigrate from East to West Germany after 1945 was that the standard of living in West Germany was very much higher than in the East. And the contrast was particularly vivid in Berlin, of course, because the East Berliners could actually see the goods in the West Berlin shops. By about 1980 the standard of living in East Germany had so improved that there was much less discontent.

The Cuban Missile Crisis

The building of the Berlin Wall was part of a campaign by the Soviet leader Khrushchev, to force the American President, Kennedy, to surrender West Berlin to East Germany. It was a battle of nerves which Kennedy won. In the autumn of 1962 these two men engaged in another battle of nerves – this time the most serious crisis in the whole history of the Cold War, when the world was brought to the brink of nuclear war. Let us look at the story of this crisis in some detail.

The scene is set in the Caribbean island of Cuba in 1959 (see map page 162). A handful of discontented but determined men succeeded in overthrowing the hated Government of Cuba. The new Government was headed by the revolutionary leader, Fidel Castro. He quickly introduced many reforms, some of which affected American businesses. Many Americans believed that Castro was a Communist, though he himself denied it at the time.

The north-western coast of Cuba is only 90 miles from the tip of Florida, and obviously the USA is very interested in what happens there. And so the US secret service, the Central Intelligence Agency

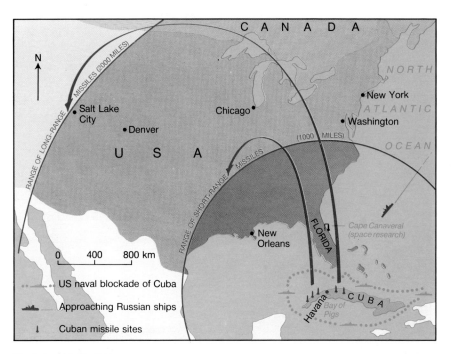

The Cuban Missile Crisis.

aerial photographs. On those taken on 14 October 1962, the missile site was spotted. The only possible targets for these missiles were cities of the USA. For a week the American President, Kennedy, kept his knowledge of these missiles a closely-guarded secret among a small circle of advisers. During that time more photographs were taken revealing that more missiles were being assembled. At the same time Kennedy and his advisers agonized over what should be done.

They decided that they must make the USSR remove them. But how? Violent action, like an air strike or invasion, was dismissed. It was too dangerous: it might have provoked a response from the Russians in support of Cuba and so trigger off a third world war. The plan adopted was to put US nuclear forces on the alert and to send a powerful naval force to blockade Cuba. This would then show that the USA was determined to take action and it would also prevent further missiles and supplies, already in ships steaming across the Atlantic, from being landed.

On Monday 22 October Kennedy made a dramatic broadcast on television. He explained what had been discovered and the orders he had issued for placing

(CIA), backed a hare-brained scheme by some opponents of Castro's in exile in the USA to invade Cuba. They were pathetic-ally ill-equipped and quickly defeated by Castro's army. Castro now felt threatened. He appealed to the USSR for help. Help was sent in the form of nuclear missiles.

The rumours that rockets were being installed in Cuba started to leak into the USA. Aircraft were sent over Cuba to take

John F Kennedy became President of the USA in 1961. He seemed a glamorous person who would provide vigorous and honest leadership for America: he came from a rich family; he served heroically in the navy during the Second World War; he was married to an attractive wife; and, above all, he was young. He was born in 1917; his predecessor, Eisenhower, was 27 years older.

Kennedy set the tone of his government in his Inaugural Address as President, in which he declared, 'Let every nation know, whether it wishes us well or ill, that we shall pay any price, bear any burden, meet any hardship, support any friend, oppose any foe to assure the survival and the success of liberty'.

Some historians now see this policy as disastrous: it led Kennedy to send troops to Vietnam and to the involvement of the USA in that long and terrible war. However, during his Presidency and immediately after, the glamour remained; partly because of publicity and partly because of his success in the tense drama of the Cuban Crisis. But partly too because of the manner of his death. In November 1963 he visited Dallas in Texas. While being driven in an open car he was shot in the head. Moreover, mystery surrounds the man arrested as his assassin, for he was himself shot dead before he could stand trial.

When Stalin died in 1953 a group of men governed the Soviet Union. However, by 1956 one of these had become the leading politician. This was Nikita Khrushchev (pronounced hrooshchoff). He was a colourful personality, with both a sense of humour and a fearful temper. He once took off a shoe to pound his desk when making a speech at the United Nations! He found John Foster Dulles a difficult and dangerous person to deal with. Dulles was US Secretary of State (Foreign Minister) from 1953 to 1959. Dulles threatened to 'liberate' Eastern Europe from Russian control and to take the world 'to the brink' of nuclear war in challenging the Soviet Union. However, Khrushchev had hopes of more friendly relations with Eisenhower (President of the USA, 1953–61), whom he met on several occasions.

But at a meeting in Paris in 1960 Khrushchev felt deceived by Eisenhower. An American spy aeroplane had flown over Russia taking photographs. It was shot down. Eisenhower told Khrushchev that no such flight had taken place. Khrushchev was furious and broke up the meeting. Khrushchev frequently used analogies from daily life in his speeches. On this occasion he said, 'When our cat stole the cream, my mother would seize him by the scruff of his neck, give him a shaking, and poke his nose in the cream. ... Wouldn't it be better to take the American imperialists by the scruff of their necks, give them a good shaking, and make them realize that they cannot commit acts of aggression because it means violating international law and may lead to a military catastrophe?'

This cartoon shows the bald Khrushchev and Dulles writing angry letters to each other.

Cuba in 'strict quarantine' as he called it. He ended with an appeal:

'I call upon Chairman Khrushchev to halt and eliminate this clandestine [secret], reckless, and provocative threat to world peace and to stable relations between our two nations.'

The world knew of the crisis and now waited with bated breath. How would Khrushchev respond? Later, Kennedy revealed that he thought at the time that the odds on war were 'somewhere between one out of three and even.'

But the skill of the American action was that it provided time – time for thinking and negotiation while the hundred US ships of the quarantine fleet manoeuvred into position and the Russian supply ships sailed on. On 24 October some Russian ships altered course in order to avoid the American warships. But there was no message from Khrushchev. There seemed to be considerable confusion in Moscow: Khrushchev was unprepared for this kind of action from Kennedy.

On 26 October Kennedy received a letter from Khrushchev. It warned that nuclear war must be avoided and suggested that Russia remove missiles from Cuba in return for America promising not to invade the island. This was encouraging. But the next morning the situation was confused by a broadcast over Moscow Radio: this was the text of a different letter by Khrushchev demanding the removal of US missiles from Turkey in return for the removal of Soviet missiles from Cuba. Kennedy ignored this and sent a letter accepting Khrushchev's first offer. On 28 October Khrushchev replied:

'In order to liquidate [end] with greater speed the dangerous conflict, to serve the cause of peace and to give confidence to all peoples longing for peace, and to calm the people of America ... the Soviet Government ... has issued a new order, for the dismantling of the weapons you describe as "offensive", their crating, and return to the Soviet Union.'

The crisis was over. ☐

1 Compile a list of reasons why you think the Americans helped the South Koreans in 1950 but did not help the Hungarians in 1956. Do you think they made the correct decisions on each occasion?

2 The picture on page 161 is a scene from a film of a novel. How useful do you think fiction writing and fictional films are for understanding the past? Give reasons for your answer.

From test-ban to Vietnam

Hot-line and test-ban

The Cuban Missile Crisis made many people realize just how dangerous the rivalry between the two super-powers had become. In an age of rockets a nuclear attack can be launched in a matter of minutes; so speed is essential in negotiations. But during the Cuban Missile Crisis, negotatiations took days because the two 'Ks' (as they were sometimes called) could communicate only by letter. So, in 1963, a 'hot-line' was installed. Now the American and Soviet leaders could make immediate contact with each other in the event of another similar crisis. The 'hot-line' is a permanently-manned teletype system.

Now although no nuclear weapon has (thankfully) been exploded in anger since 1945, even controlled *tests* (of nuclear weapons) can be dangerous. Radioactive material from an explosion can be sucked up into the atmosphere, blown from the testing site and deposited far away, to contaminate sources of food and even directly poison people. A partial test-ban treaty was signed also in 1963 by many countries (including the USA and the USSR) who promised to conduct tests only underground.

The problem of Vietnam

Many parts of Asia and Africa came under European control during the nineteenth century (see Chapter 7) and then, in our own century, gained their independence.

In the nineteenth century the French made the area of south-east Asia called Indochina into colonies. Then, during the Second World War, Indochina was occupied by the Japanese who reorganized the country into three parts: Laos, Cambodia and Vietnam (see map).

Meanwhile, in Vietnam, in 1941, a nationalist movement was created to work for independence. It was called 'Vietminh'; and it was led by a Communist called Ho Chi Minh.

When Japan surrendered, having lost the war in 1945, the French returned to Indochina. But the Vietminh fought for their independence. The French lost many men. Then, in 1954 a big battle took place in north-west Vietnam, at Dien Bien Phu (see map). Tough French paratroops were surrounded there: over 13,000 were killed, wounded or captured; only 73 escaped. One commentator has described it as 'the most humiliating colonial defeat on France since General Montcalm was defeated and killed at Quebec by the British in 1759' (see page 16).

Because other countries were worried by what was happening, a conference was arranged in Geneva. The following countries were represented: Britain, China, France, the USA, the USSR and representatives from both the Communists and

Indochina in the twentieth century.

Ho Chi Minh, who was born in 1890, devoted almost the whole of his life to seeking the freedom of Vietnam. He even claimed that he was expelled from school at the age of thirteen for anti-French activities. 'Ho Chi Minh' was a name he adopted to escape from the French. It means 'The Seeker of Enlightenment'.

Ho was a remarkable man. He travelled widely and learned to speak several languages. He wrote a great deal, not just political documents, but poetry as well. And he inspired great loyalty in his followers because of his honesty and the simplicity of his life. He was sometimes referred to affectionately as 'Uncle Ho'. When opposition to American fighting in Vietnam grew in the USA, demonstrators would chant rhythmically 'Ho, Ho, Ho Chi Minh'. He was President of his country from 1945 until his death in 1969. The photograph shows Ho (on the right) talking to his brilliant commander, General Giap.

non-Communists in Vietnam. They decided to divide Vietnam. The Vietminh took over North Vietnam, with its capital at Hanoi (see map). The Government in Saigon, the capital of South Vietnam, was very corrupt and unpopular. By the late 1950s a civil war was raging in South Vietnam between the Government and a revolutionary organization called the 'Vietcong', who wanted a Communist Government.

The Americans were interested in Indochina. The Vietminh and Vietcong contained many Communists. If the Vietminh and Vietcong won, then the whole of Vietnam might become Communist. If that happened, many Americans feared that other countries would follow. President Eisenhower talked of the 'domino theory': 'The loss of Indochina', he said 'will cause the fall of South-East Asia like a set of dominoes'. So the Americans supplied South Vietnam with money and equipment to help them defeat North Vietnam. North Vietnam trained the Vietcong in guerrilla warfare and supplied them with military equipment along a jungle route called the 'Ho Chi Minh Trail' (see map).

In October 1961 President Diem of South Vietnam asked President Kennedy for much more help. Kennedy sent troops. The USA became more and more involved in an horrific war which lasted until 1973.

The domino theory. Once one 'domino' 'fell to Communism' it would knock down a neighbouring domino, which would in turn knock down its neighbour ...

The Vietnam war

At first the American soldiers who were sent to Vietnam were 'advisers' – they did not actually fight. But the South Vietnamese army suffered more and more defeats and the Vietcong (VC as the Americans called them) took control of more and more villages. So the USA sent more troops, then aircraft, until a full-scale war was being fought by the Americans. The build-up started in 1964. By the end of that year there were over a hundred thousand Americans in Vietnam. Four years later there were over half a million.

When the Americans first became involved in Vietnam they thought they could win the war by creating 'strategic hamlets'; that is, by defending the scattered villages against the Vietcong. But they seriously under-estimated the skill and ruthlessness of their enemy:

1   The Vietcong had an advantage because many villages actually *welcomed* the Communists; and if they did not, the Vietcong tortured and killed them.

2   When the Americans attacked a Communist-held village (that is, one held by the Vietcong), the Vietcong often disappeared. They either hid their weapons and

Number of troops

The build-up of Americans in Vietnam 1961–68.

This photograph was taken in 1962. It shows an American colonel supervising the escape of South Vietnamese troops from the advancing Vietcong. American pilots flew the helicopters. This was a typical way in which American advisers helped the South Vietnamese government in the early 1960s.

pretended they were ordinary villagers; or they hid themselves in their complex and highly-organized underground tunnels. And the Americans at first had no idea these tunnels existed.

As time went on the Americans became more and more frustrated. How could they defeat the Vietcong? They tried air power. Maybe *that* way they could win:

1   Helicopters were fitted with machine-guns. These 'gun-ships' roamed over the fields and villages shooting at anything the crew thought might be a target. The casual brutality of some crews is illustrated by one pilot who described the fight as: 'Wash out. Got me two VC water buffalo and a pregnant woman'.

2   Light-bombers and fighter-bombers were equipped with napalm bombs. Napalm is a jelly which sticks and ignites. Enormous numbers of Vietnamese suffered horrific burns when these bombs were dropped on villages.

3   Long-range B-52 bombers dropped high-explosive bombs. From 1964 the Americans included North Vietnam in the war. The bombers were used against towns and bridges and railways there.

During the war the Americans dropped more bombs on Vietnam than were used in the *whole* of the Second World War!

The American Government insisted that they were in the right. President Johnson made a speech in April 1965 in which he said:

'The rulers of Hanoi are urged on by Peking ... The contest in Vietnam is part of a wider pattern of aggressive purpose ... over many years we have made a national pledge to help South Vietnam defend its independence. I intend to keep our promise.'

He also described the Vietcong campaign as a 'war of unparalleled brutality. Simple farmers are the targets of assassination and kidnapping. Women and children are strangled in the night because their men are loyal to the Government.'

By the late 1960s the American atrocities seemed to be worse than those of the Vietminh and Vietcong. People were asking questions. Why was the USA killing and maiming so many Vietnamese people? (About 3 million died of various causes during the war.) Why were American men being killed and maimed to defend a corrupt government in Saigon? (56,000 were killed in the war.) And why

Cutaway reconstruction of the Vietcong tunnels. If a group of Vietcong soldiers were in danger of being defeated by the Americans, they could disappear in some places into underground tunnels like these. There they could eat, sleep, and have their wounds tended until it was safe to emerge again.

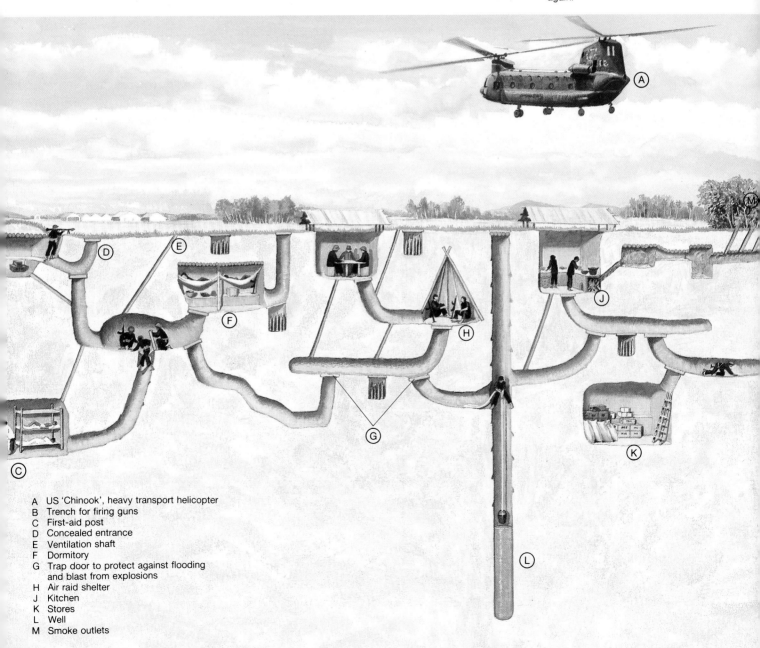

A US 'Chinook', heavy transport helicopter
B Trench for firing guns
C First-aid post
D Concealed entrance
E Ventilation shaft
F Dormitory
G Trap door to protect against flooding and blast from explosions
H Air raid shelter
J Kitchen
K Stores
L Well
M Smoke outlets

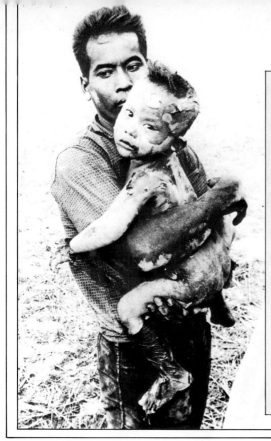

A napalm victim. One of the reasons that opposition to the US war in Vietnam was so intense was that newsreels were constantly shown on television. No war has ever been so fully reported. People knew. And distressing pictures of maimed innocent civilians were quite common. This photograph is typical.

Here is an extract from the report of the American journalist, Martha Gellhorn (a village had been warned by the Americans that it would be attacked):

'That night, the boy and his grandfather, his mother and older brother got away from the hamlet with two of their four buffaloes. The buffaloes were their only capital, their future, without buffaloes they could not cultivate their fields. At first light many of the peasants crept back to the hamlet to rescue more of their livestock and household goods. The old man, too blind to go alone, took the child with him to try to find the remaining buffaloes. But the jet fighter-bombers came at once. The two buffaloes were killed by napalm, the old man said, and so were many of the people, and many were burned.'

The boy too was burned; he was a minute seven-year old: 'the napalmed skin on the little body looks like bloody hardened meat in a butcher's shop' a week after the attack.

Many of the American soldiers who fought in Vietnam were not volunteers but were 'drafted' (that is, conscripted) This system was very unpopular. This was partly because many thought that the war was cruel and unjust; and partly because the system was unfair – many of the American men who were drafted were poor and black. The photograph (taken in 1968) shows one of the many demonstrations in which files containing names of men who could be drafted were burned.

was the USA spending such vast sums of money on the war when so many Americans were living in poverty? ($2 billion per week was spent in 1968!) Demonstrations broke out in the USA (and in other countries too, including Britain). Rather unfairly President LB Johnson was personally accused of continuing the war. Demonstrators cruelly chanted, 'Hey, hey, LBJ! How many kids did you kill today?'

Dispirited by the problem, Johnson did not stand for re-election in 1968. The new President was Nixon. He tried to win the war by making massive bombing attacks on Cambodia to destroy the Ho Chi Minh Trail. Apart from the horrific damage and casualties caused, this achieved nothing. So he sought peace. An important key was China. She had been helping the Vietnamese Communists a great deal. Nixon visited China in 1972 and established friendly relations with Mao Tse-tung. The number of American troops in South Vietnam was gradually reduced and the last soldiers finally left in 1973. The two Vietnams (North and South) were united. All three countries of Indochina became Communist. The USA was humiliated. □

1 Imagine you are Nikita Khrushchev's secretary. Compile a diary of the main events (with your own commentary) in the Cold War from the time he took control of the Soviet Government until his resignation in 1964.

2 On 27 October 1968 a large demonstration was held in London against the American war in Vietnam. If you had been a student living in London at the time, would you have joined in? Give your reasons.

3 Why do you think the USA lost the war in Vietnam?

The New Cold War

Nuclear arms race

President Nixon wanted to make a name for himself as a peace-maker. Not only did he make friends with China and bring the Vietnam war to an end, but he relaxed the tension in relations with the Soviet Union. Unhappily this did not last long and the two countries were quarrelling again by the late 1970s. This renewed quarrelling is sometimes called the 'New Cold War'.

The most frightening part of the quarrelling between the two superpowers is the way they have built up huge 'stockpiles' (that is, stores) of nuclear weapons (see below). In August 1945, after the attacks on Hiroshima and Nagasaki, there were no nuclear bombs in the world. By 1950 it is estimated that the USA had over 70 and the USSR had 15. Several other countries developed a few nuclear weapons. Since 1945 different kinds of nuclear weapons have been developed – warheads for rockets and shells for artillery as well as bombs. By the early 1980s it was estimated that the world contained over 50,000 nuclear weapons! That is the

power equivalent to over three tons of ordinary explosive for every human being on earth!

Since 1969 long discussions have taken place between the USA and the USSR to try to reach agreements to limit the

The nuclear balance. Numbers of long-range bombers and missiles, USA and USSR, 1955–85.

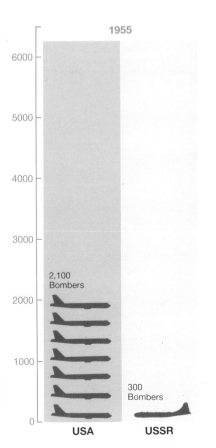

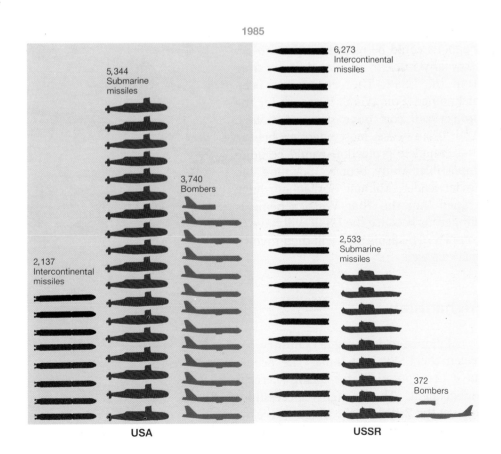

number of 'strategic' (that is, long-range) weapons. Little was achieved. A treaty was signed in 1972, called SALT-1 (first Strategic Arms Limitation Talks). But even then, more and increasingly accurate weapons were still invented and 'deployed' (that is, set up in various places ready to be fired). Some people have argued that because nuclear weapons are so frightening, no one would ever dare use them. These people believe that the two sides in the Cold War would have had a 'hot' war before now if they had not been 'deterred' (that is, frightened) by the effects nuclear weapons would have. Other people, especially in the USA, Britain and western Europe, have protested that such a policy was insane: that having more weapons made nuclear war much *more* likely. And nuclear war could obliterate civilization, even the whole of human life on the planet.

'Star Wars'

In 1983 the President of the USA, Ronald Reagan, made a speech in which he said that he had a scheme for making nuclear weapons useless. The theory is that weapons could be placed in space to destroy any nuclear missiles that are fired from the USSR. The scheme has been nicknamed 'Star Wars'. Research for the project will cost huge sums of money. And, in any case, most scientists believe that complete protection would be quite impossible. Many people, including the Soviet leader, Mikhail Gorbachev, have argued that the 'Star Wars' scheme is dangerous because the USSR will have to compete. The arms race will then involve space as well.

Afghanistan

Afghanistan is a rugged country between the USSR and India. The people have a reputation for being fiercely independent. They fought successfully against the British in the nineteenth century when the British in India had tried to

take control of their country.

In December 1979 Soviet troops invaded Afghanistan. The US Government argued that this was an example of the USSR trying to impose Communism on

The Campaign for Nuclear Disarmament (CND) was formed in Britain in 1957. It was very active in protesting against nuclear weapons for a few years. Its membership suddenly increased again from 1980 as people became frightened that a nuclear war might break out, perhaps even by accident. Demonstrations were held to try to persuade politicians to reduce or even abolish nuclear weapons. Its symbol is made up of the semaphore letters N and D.

The USA made loud complaints about Russian interference in Afghanistan. The protests included calling for a boycott of the Olympic Games, held in Moscow in 1980. Many western countries followed the US lead and did not send teams. Yet, as this US cartoon shows, the American complaints were perhaps rather hypocritical in the light of US interference in central American countries such as El Salvador and Nicaragua.

The Afghan guerrillas are mainly fighting in defence of the Muslim religion against the Communist Government. They have not been able to take control of any towns from the Russian and Afghan armies. Russian interest in Afghanistan is not new – see the *Punch* cartoon on page 24.

another country, against the will of the people. The Russians argued that the Government in Afghanistan had appealed to them for help against rebels.

The war in Afghanistan is still being fought. The Russians have become involved in a difficult war. In many ways it is similar to the American war in Vietnam. Civilians have been killed and maimed by the Russian air-strikes. Millions have fled as refugees to neighbouring Pakistan, where the people, like the Afghans, are Muslims.

The Afghan men are hardy and skilful guerrilla fighters. Here is a description of a typical campaign by a French journalist:

'In 1982, after villages in Panjshir had been systematically bombed and crops destroyed, 10,000 Soviet troops were flown in by helicopter to a dozen or so points within a few hours. The bands of guerrillas ... kept fighting for three weeks and eventually repulsed [*forced back*] the Russians, who took refuge in two small bases surrounded by extensive minefields. The aftermath was the usual pathetic procession of war-wounded and amputees hobbling along the roads to Pakistan.'

The fate of KAL 007

The history of the Cold War between the USA and the USSR has been a story of constant fear and suspicion. The kind of tragedy that can occur when relations are particularly tense is dramatically illustrated by the fate of the South Korean jumbo-jet airliner, a Boeing 747, on Flight KAL 007 on the night of 31 August 1983.

The airliner, with 269 passengers on board, veered from its course on its flight from the USA. Between the Russian island of Sakhalin and the Japanese island of Hokkaido it was shot down by a Soviet fighter-plane. There were no survivors. What caused this terrible tragedy? It

Afghanistan.

seems that this unarmed civilian airliner was destroyed without being warned that it had strayed over Soviet waters. Commenting on this incident, US President Reagan said:

'It means that the words that are spoken about peace are devoid [*empty*] of sense and every elementary respect for human life is lacking.'

On the face of it the Soviet defence systems seem to be manned and commanded by trigger-happy barbarians.

But, as is so often the case in history, there was another side to the story. That area of eastern Siberia contains many highly secret Soviet bases. The Russians believed that the Americans were sending spy-planes to the area to discover the Russian secrets. The Russian Marshal Ogarkov said:

'Can there be any mistake or delusion [*misunderstanding*]? It is quite obvious

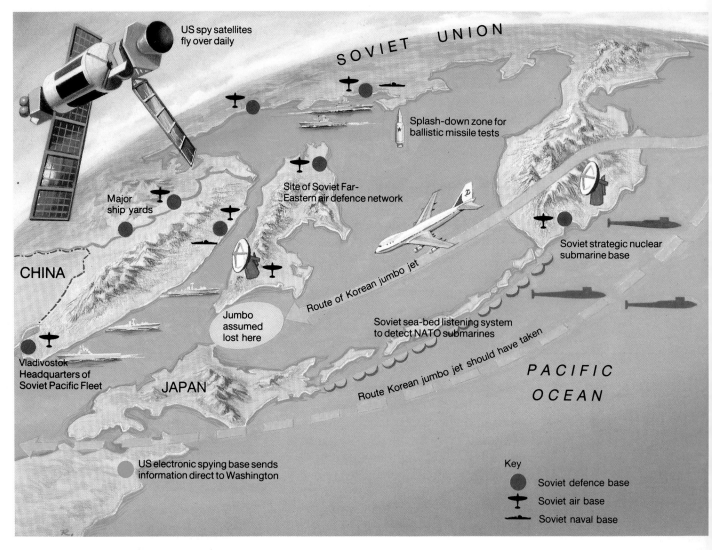

US spy satellites
fly over daily

SOVIET UNION

Splash-down zone for
ballistic missile tests

Site of Soviet Far-
Eastern air defence network

Major
ship yards

Route of Korean jumbo jet

Soviet strategic nuclear
submarine base

CHINA

Jumbo
assumed
lost here

Soviet sea-bed listening system
to detect NATO submarines

Route Korean jumbo jet should have taken

PACIFIC
OCEAN

Vladivostok
Headquarters of
Soviet Pacific Fleet

JAPAN

US electronic spying base sends
information direct to Washington

Key

Soviet defence base

Soviet air base

Soviet naval base

The shooting down of the Korean airliner, 1983.

that the flight of this aircraft was directed, premeditatedly [*intentionally*] directed.'

Perhaps KAL 007 contained electronic or photographic equipment and its change off course was deliberate? Perhaps the Soviet defences mistook KAL 007 for an American spy-plane? (Such an aircraft was indeed not very far away from KAL 007.)

Both sides had been playing the 'game' of secrets and spying far too dangerously. Nearly 300 people lost their lives as a result. Some commentators were quick to point out that perhaps some future, similar mistake might lead to a nuclear war – and the end of all history. ☐

1 What evidence is there in the world today that the USA and the USSR are still quarrelling?

2 There are several quotations in this Chapter. Which one helps you to understand the history of the time best? Explain your reasons.

3 Make a list of the occasions mentioned in this Chapter where nuclear weapons have been important. In what ways do you think the rivalry between the USA and the USSR would have been different if nuclear weapons had not been invented?

4 President Truman, Eisenhower, Kennedy and Johnson are now dead. Imagine that they are still alive; write a conversation in which each defends his own record in the Cold War.

Index

Note: There are no entries for the following countries in the index because there are so many references throughout the book: France, Great Britain (England), Russia (the USSR), the USA.

Historians and their sources

How the historian works

Sources

We can find out about what happened in the past or what life was like in the past by reading books written by historians. But how do they obtain *their* information? The answer is from 'sources'.

We have already listed at the start of each Chapter a few of the sources historians can use for the topics in this book. You may have noticed that there are many different kinds of sources. This is a great advantage as we shall see below.

Detective work

Being an historian involves much more than just copying out information from a source and having it printed in a book. Historians must be detectives in two ways:

1 They must hunt down all the evidence possible for piecing together their word-pictures of the past. After all, if they neglect some sources their descriptions may have important parts missing.

2 They must be suspicious of their sources. For example, if a politician writes his memoirs or keeps a diary, we would expect him to write in such a way as to show himself in a favourable light. The historian would want to know what *other* people thought about him – thoughts that might not have been very flattering! So historians must compare different sources before deciding what really happened.

History changing

As a result, History is always changing as historians find new sources. Take just one example from this book. On page 12 there is a brief description of life in the navy. When I started to write the book I wrote, 'Sailors were punished by merciless flogging'. But I had to change this because an historian has recently shown that discipline in the British navy was not as severe as we used to think.

How you can be an historian

Becoming an historian

It takes a long time to become a professional historian – to learn where all your sources might be and how to interpret them. On the other hand, we can all start in simple ways. Here are a few hints about the kind of History you could research into in the period covered in this book.

Life two generations ago

An easy way to start is with your family. How did your grandparents live? If you see them you can talk to them, or you could ask them questions by letter. How were their lives different from yours?

Can they tell you anything about *their* parents? What can you learn from their photograph albums or scrapbooks? Try to understand how and why their lives were different, before, during and after the Second World War.

Your town or village

Next you could investigate the history of your own town or village. What was it like 200 or 100 years ago? A visit to your museum will help with this. And learn to recognize how old different buildings are: which buildings in your town or which parts of the town were there 200 or 100 years ago?

Your local library may well have back numbers of the local newspaper. You will need to know exactly what dates to ask for and what you are looking for. You can waste a librarian's time very annoyingly if you are vague. Your teacher can help you decide. Your teacher may also be able to arrange a visit to your local record office: each county has one. You might be able to find old maps there, for example.

World events

Much of this book deals with the history of other countries. It is much more difficult for the amateur historian to work in this kind of historical research. But what you can do is to use your skills to study the news and current events.

When an important event is reported in the news, ask yourself the following questions. What do I know from my study of recent History about the background? How are the reports on the television and in my parents' newspaper different? If two politicians, for example, speak on television about the same matter, why do they give different views?

Next steps

This book has given you an introduction to just a few topics in modern History. What you choose to study in more detail will depend on your particular interest. But you will find that whatever you choose, the deeper you delve into the past the more fascinating it becomes.